FARM GIRL
FRESH®

EATING
PURE
IN A
PROCESSED
FOODS
WORLD®

GROW IT   PRESERVE IT   PREPARE IT

Second Edition 2018

Published by:
Farm Girl Fresh, LLC
P.O. Box 331
Litchfield, MN 55355

ISBN# 978-0-9861854-1-0

Co-Authors:	Joyce Kaping, Colleen Anderson
Book Design:	Beth Airhart-Aquilino — Airhart & Company, Inc.
Cover Photos:	Front Cover: Thoen & Associates
	Back Cover: Sarah Pollio Photography

With much love, we dedicate this book to our children and grandchildren. May you and future generations be blessed with an abundant life— one that is healthy spiritually, emotionally and physically.

Joyce and Colleen

What began as a simple tool to use when mentoring young moms in the kitchen has morphed into something way beyond our imagination. A wonderful team surrounded us, using their talents and input to create this resource.

We would like to thank our husbands, Ross and Scott, for their never-ending patience, encouragement and funding during this project. Thanks for being our honorary taste testers; we love you.

Our families have also been incredibly supportive, giving input and feedback from their generation. Thanks for graciously testing new recipes at every family gathering. Phrases like, "Grandma, you make the best food ever!" have made us smile numerous times.

This book would not have been written if not for our pilot test group of young moms whom we mentored from April – November on growing, preserving and preparing fresh produce. Thank you for your enthusiasm and input.

Thank you to Nick and Joan Olson from Prairie Drifter Farm who edited the growing pages and provided us with delicious organic vegetables.

A picture's worth a thousand words and we would like to thank Bill Zobel, Greg Thoen and Sarah Pollio for communicating through your beautiful photos.

Thank you to the many other people who tested our recipes by preparing them for your families. We appreciate your comments. Your requests for recipes were wonderful confirmation.

We would also like to thank Candace Boerema for making time in her schedule to proofread.

Last, but not least, Beth Aquilino, we cannot thank you enough. We went around the mountain more times than we can count and you patiently waited while we processed through everything. You are one of the most creative people we know and we feel blessed to be able to work with you.

Soli Deo Gloria!

Joyce is a true farm girl at heart. She enjoys growing her own food and creating recipes around the fruits and vegetables harvested from her organic garden. Joyce's passion is to teach people how to grow, preserve and prepare healthy food for family and friends, along with sharing insight on healthy living. Her favorite times are spent with her husband, Ross, and their family, which includes 12 grandchildren.

Colleen grew up on a farm, learning the basics of gardening, cooking, canning and freezing from her mother. She came to realize the value of that teaching over the years as her family encountered health challenges. Colleen is passionate to share with others and to help promote healthy lifestyle choices through nutritious eating. She is married to Scott, an organic crop farmer. They have three married children and six grandchildren.

TABLE OF CONTENTS

WHY FARM GIRL FRESH?

For both of us, our story begins by growing up on a small farm in the Midwest. Our memories include swinging in tree swings, making forts and playhouses in the woods, chasing cows and pigs with our dogs, searching for newborn kitties in the haymow and working together as a family. Having watched our parents care for the land and enjoy the simple things in life, we both followed suit, married farmers and raised our children in small town USA.

Fast forward several years when our paths crossed as we were employed at the same workplace. We began sharing notes and stories about our lives and discovered we were on a similar journey, a journey that included some family health concerns— food sensitivities, allergies, irritable bowel syndrome, diverticulitis, fatigue, headaches, chronic sinusitis, etc. We had visited many specialists and tried numerous approaches to eliminate these health concerns, but still did not have optimal health.

We both attended health conferences and started reading several books and articles related to the increasing numbers of people dealing with health issues such as allergies, obesity, diabetes and dementia. After learning more about the rise of these illnesses, we knew the sooner we addressed our health concerns, the better chance we had for optimal health. We wanted this not only for ourselves, but for our children and grandchildren who were just beginning to experience some of these challenges. We quickly realized we needed to begin shifting some of our dollars to purchase good, wholesome food and to try to cook like our grandmas. This meant reading labels and eating real whole foods that didn't contain artificial additives and chemical preservatives.

With this new awareness, we discovered there were other things we had to do to make this lifestyle change. We became more diligent in our menu planning; we began purchasing food in bulk for cost effectiveness; we planted gardens and spent time preserving food for the winter months when fruits and vegetables were not as accessible. Thus began our journey of eating pure in a processed foods world.

As time went on, we slowly (realizing this was a marathon, not a sprint) began to notice changes, not only in us, but in family members as well. Fewer headaches, less joint pain, increased energy, better complexion, improved digestion, no more dry, itchy skin—all of these improvements were enough to keep us on this journey. We were excited! Now the question was, how could we share this with others?

Meanwhile, we experienced a "nudging." We were doing a study on Nehemiah, a leader who set out to help others restore what was broken. As we studied, we talked about our concern for the health of the next generation. We both realized our passion was to share with others what we were learning about healthy living along with teaching them how to cook the way our mothers and grandmothers taught us. We wanted to encourage people to get back to eating real whole food before they experienced a health crisis (a broken situation).

We were now on a mission. We started teaching a class, "Back to the Basics," to a group of young moms every other week, from April to November. We shared with them how to make healthy meals and snacks using real foods, showed them how to grow herbs in pots, taught them how to cut up a whole chicken, shared with them how to preserve different fruits and vegetables; and, we encouraged them to take steps to grow in their faith. During those months, we all learned from each other and formed lasting friendships. But something was still missing.

How could we get the "Back to the Basics" information out to more than just this group of young moms? After many surveys, prayer and much encouragement, we found ourselves becoming the founders of Farm Girl Fresh, LLC. Our company is focused on helping people realize the importance of eating nutrient rich food for better health. Which led us to writing this 3-in-1, garden-to-table resource guide.

We don't believe in coincidences. We believe people and resources were placed in our lives through this entire project. And it is our passion to share with you and upcoming generations how to live an abundant life; growing together in truth through faith, family, food, and friendships.

Colleen & Joyce

FRESH
IS BEST

You are about to embark on a gratifying adventure as you begin your gardening experience. From the fragrant earthy aromas of early spring soil, the delectable flavors of summer produce, to the dazzling colors of pumpkins and apples in late fall, there's nothing like cooking with fresh fruits and vegetables picked from your very own garden.

Let's begin with your garden options. Did you know you can grow plants indoors by placing pots in a sunny location? Or, grow them in containers on your balcony, rooftop, front porch, back deck or even tucked into your landscaping? Consider starting with a small garden plot, a raised bed for space and convenience, or renting a plot at your local community garden.

In our "How Does Your Garden Grow" sections, we have set out to help you discover how easy it is to grow your own food. It includes information on how to plant your seeds or transplants, the desired temperature for each plant, how much water your plant will need, if your plant needs extra fertilizer, when to harvest your crop, and lastly, how to store the fruits and vegetables you have grown.

Try planting a tomato in a pot; or containers of lettuce, kale or herbs to add to your favorite dish. As you develop your gardening skills, you may experience a learning curve; however, don't give up! The accomplishment of growing your own succulent fruits and vegetables is a joy like no other. We hope the overwhelming satisfaction of eating that first ripe tomato bursting with vitamins and minerals will eventually lead you to preserving your bountiful harvest.

Visiting your local Farmers Market is a great place to purchase fresh, locally-grown fruits and vegetables. This market is a group of farmers who purchase a space or booth to sell their goods to the community. When shopping for your fresh produce, remember to ask the farmer if it is free of harmful sprays, fertilizers or chemicals. As you leave, thank the farmer for producing your clean, pure food.

Community Supported Agriculture (CSA) is another popular way to buy fresh seasonal food directly from a local farmer. To participate in a CSA, you purchase a "share." This share consists of several boxes of fresh produce for you to enjoy throughout the growing season. By participating in a local CSA, you also reap the benefit of building a relationship with the farmer that is growing your food. These farmers work hard and are proud of their gardening practices that pursue sustainability by preserving and protecting our resources.

GARDEN TOOLS

When you first begin your gardening experience, you will need a few tools. Think of these tools as your partners in the garden. The amount of tools needed will be determined by the type of gardening you set out to do. To save money, we recommend checking out garage sales or purchasing tools out-of-season. You might also consider sharing some tools with a neighboring garden friend. Here is a list of tools to give you an idea of what you may need.

CONTAINER GARDEN

Containers/ Planters

Garden Scissors

Organic Fertilizer

Potting Soil

Spray Bottles

Trowel

Watering Can

RAISED BED GARDEN

Container garden supplies plus:

Garden Sprinkler

Hoe

Produce Tote

Pruners

Rake

Stakes

Tape Measure

3-Prong Hand Cultivator

Twine

Vegetable Cages

BACKYARD PLOT GARDEN

Raised bed garden supplies plus:

Black & Clear Plastic

Compost Bin

Compost/Mulch/ Straw

Drip Hose

Garden Fork

Garden Hose

Netting

Roto Tiller

Shovel

Soil Test Kit

Soil Thermometer

Spade

Trellis

Trimming Shears

Wheelbarrow or Garden Cart

STARTING SEEDS INDOORS

Grow Light

Heat Mat

Seed Starting Containers

Starter Mix

GARDEN TERMS

Knowing the definition of common garden terms will be beneficial as you begin gardening. Become familiar with these terms before spring, so when the itch hits, you'll be ready to dig in the moist soil and plant seeds.

ANNUALS: Plants whose life cycle lasts only one year.

BARE ROOT: Plants which have had all of the soil removed from their roots.

BEDDING PLANT: Nursery grown plants suitable for growing in beds.

BUD: Early stages of development of a flower.

BULB: A thickened underground fleshy storage structure.

COMPANION PLANTING: Any plant that is intentionally planted next to another plant to enhance growth or flavor and to protect each other from pests.

COMPOST: The decomposition of organic matter added to soil.

CONTAINER GARDENING: The practice of growing plants in containers instead of planting them in the ground.

CROP ROTATION: The practice of growing different crops in succession on the same land.

CULTIVATE: The breaking up of soil to prepare for planting or control weeds during growing season.

DS-DIRECT SEED: To plant seeds directly into garden soil.

DTM-DAYS TO MATURITY: The time it takes a seed directly sown to grow until the crop is mature.

EVAPORATION: Process by which water returns to the air.

FERTILIZER: Liquid or granular organic plant food used to amend soil to improve quality of plant.

FLAT: A shallow tray used to start seedlings.

FROST: The condensation and freezing of moisture in the air.

GERMINATE: The transforming process of turning the seed into a seedling.

GROUND COVER: A group of plants closely sown together to cover bare earth.

GROWING SEASON: The number of days between the last killing frost in spring and the first killing frost in fall.

HARDEN OFF: The process of gradually acclimating indoor grown plants to outdoor growing conditions.

HUMUS: The partial decay of leaves and other matter in soil.

LATHE: Slats of wood used to mark garden rows.

MANURE: Organic matter excreted by animals used as a soil amendment.

MULCH: Loose material placed over soil to control weeds and conserve moisture.

GARDEN TERMS

ORGANIC GARDENING: The method of gardening using materials from living things.

ORGANIC MATERIAL: Any material which originated from a living organism.

PEAT MOSS: Partially decomposed remains of mosses.

PERENNIAL: Plants whose life cycle is more than two years.

PEST: An insect which is detrimental to the wellbeing of a plant.

PINCHING BACK: Nipping back the tip of a branch or stem by using your thumb and forefinger.

POLLINATION: The transfer of pollen from the male part of the flower to the female part of the flower resulting in the formation of a seed.

POTTING SOIL: A soil mixture designed to use in container gardens and potted plants.

PRUNING: The trimming of plants to direct new growth.

RAISED BED GARDENING: A form of gardening in which soil is placed in wide beds of any length or shape.

RHIZOME: A modified plant stem which grows horizontally under the surface of the soil.

ROOT BALL: The group of roots with attached soil of any plant.

ROOT BOUND: When the roots of a plant have outgrown its container.

SEEDLING: A young plant already grown from a seed, ready to place directly into pots or garden beds.

SOIL PH: The measurement of the amount of lime (calcium) contained in soil.

SPROUT: To begin to grow.

STAKING: A method using stakes to support a plant.

SUCKER: A growth from the root stock of a plant.

TP–TRANSPLANT: The process of taking a started plant and planting it in a new location.

TENDRIL: The twisting, clinging growth of a plant allowing them to attach to a trellis.

THINNING: Removing excess seedlings to allow room for remaining plants to grow.

TOP SOIL: The top layer of native soil.

TRANSPLANTING: The process of digging up a plant and moving it to another location.

KEEPING IT PURE

To us, traditional pure food is food prepared and eaten in its most natural state, like it was when our grandmas were growing up. This was before numerous artificial additives and chemical preservatives were added to our food. The fruits and vegetables were picked fresh and purchased locally when in season, eggs were picked daily from the chicken coop in the backyard, and milk came from grass-fed cows with a thick layer of cream on top.

Processed foods are created to impersonate real food and contain lengthy lists of artificial ingredients and additives. The ingredients in these replicas can be addictive and not as healthy as real pure food. By reading the product labels of items you regularly purchase, you will familiarize yourself with what is in your food. If you are like us, you will find yourself making some different choices the next time you are grocery shopping. Try to buy the freshest ingredients available to prepare yummy, nourishing food, using vibrant colored fruits and vegetables, savory spices, and rich, pure oils. With this new, wholesome way of eating, you will experience a rewarding sense of accomplishment and satisfaction knowing you created a pure, nutritious dish to share with family and friends.

Eating Pure in a Processed Foods World® is a fresh approach to home-style cooking by planning your meals around fruits and vegetables. From Apples to Zucchini, we guide you through the basics of growing, preserving and preparing better foods for a better you. Each section contains simple steaming and roasting recipes, healthy juices and smoothies, salads, main dishes and sweet treats, with all ages in mind. Also included are some gluten-free, dairy-free and nut-free recipes for people with special dietary restrictions. With a few substitutions of ingredients, many recipes can be adapted to meet your needs.

Some recipes have ingredient listings which refer you to other recipes within this book—shown as *(page__)*. We encourage you to make as many recipes from scratch as possible. However, we recognize this may not always be possible. If time does not allow, purchase the necessary ingredients and don't feel guilty.

Better food choices today can provide huge health benefits for you tomorrow. Start by taking small, baby steps to gradually make this lifetime investment for better health.

STOCKING UP

Eating Pure in a Processed Foods World® starts with using the right ingredients. We've replaced several items in our pantry with healthier products and homemade staples (broth, yogurt, ketchup, mayonnaise, etc.). Throughout this book, you will find the "whys" behind these changes. Replacing one item per month will ease your family into this lifestyle change. You may want to start with sugar and replace it with raw honey or pure maple syrup. The next month you might buy free-range organic eggs. The third month switch to sea salt or Himalayan salt. The fourth month begin replacing your spices with organic spices, and so on.

We have put together a list of items we try to keep on hand in our pantry, spice cabinet, refrigerator and freezer.

PANTRY ITEMS

Almond Butter
Almond Extract
Almond Flour
Almonds, Raw
Applesauce
Avocado Oil

Black Beans, Dried
Cacao Powder, Raw
Cashews, Raw
Chocolate Chips, Dark, Dairy Free/ Soy Free
Coconut Flakes, Unsweetened
Coconut Flour
Coconut Oil
Coconut Sugar
Date Sugar
Garlic Bulbs
Gelatin, Beef Unflavored
Ghee/Butter, Unsalted

Honey, Raw
Kidney Beans, Dried
Lentils, Dried
Lima Beans, Dried
Maple Syrup
Navy Beans, Dried
Olive Oil
Onions
Pamona's Universal Pectin
Peanut Butter
Pecans, Raw
Pumpkin Seeds, Raw
Pure Bicarbonate Baking Soda
Quinoa
Quinoa Flour

Rice, Brown
Rice, White
Rolled Oats, Gluten Free
Salsa
Sesame Oil
Sunflower Seeds, Raw
Toasted Sesame Oil
Tomato Paste
Tomato Sauce
Tuna
Vanilla
Walnuts, Raw
Whole Wheat Flour
Yogourmet Starter

STOCKING UP

REFRIGERATOR ITEMS

Apple Cider Vinegar
Barbecue Sauce
Beef Broth
Cheddar Cheese, Raw
Chicken Broth
Coconut Aminos
Coconut Milk
Cranberries, Dried Unsweetened
Dijon Mustard
Eggs, Large Free Range
Heavy Cream
Ketchup
Lemon Juice
Lime Juice
Mayonnaise
Medjool Dates
Olives
Parmesan Cheese
Raisins
Red Wine Vinegar
Salad Dressing
Sour Cream
Whole Milk
Yellow Mustard
Yogurt

FREEZER ITEMS

Apples
Bacon
Beef Broth
Beets
Blueberries
Broccoli
Butter
Carrots
Chicken Broth
Cooked Lentils
Cooked Lima Beans
Cooked Navy Beans
Cooked Shredded Beef
Cooked Shredded Chicken
Cookies
Green Beans
Ground Beef
Ground Pork
Jam
Jelly
Muffins
Peas
Pumpkin
Raspberries
Rhubarb
Shredded Raw Cheddar Cheese
Squash
Strawberries
Whole Chicken
Zucchini

HERBS & SPICES

Bay Leaf
Cardamom
Cayenne
Celery Seed
Chili Powder
Crushed Red Pepper
Dill Seed
Dried Basil
Dried Chives
Dried Dill
Dried Marjoram
Dried Mustard
Dried Oregano
Dried Parsley
Dried Rosemary
Dried Sage
Dried Thyme
Garlic Granules
Garlic Powder
Ground Cinnamon
Ground Cumin
Ground Cloves
Ground Coriander
Ground Ginger
Ground Nutmeg
Himalayan Salt
Onion Powder
Paprika
Peppercorns
Sea Salt
Spice Mixes
(page 125)
Turmeric

KITCHEN TOOLS

This lifestyle change will be easier if your kitchen is equipped with the proper tools and utensils. At first glance, this list might appear overwhelming, but don't let it discourage you. Review these kitchen tools and utensils and see what items you need to put on your "wish list." A well equipped kitchen can save time, allowing you to enjoy more free time with your family. Our grandmothers used a wooden spoon and a good, sharp knife to accomplish most tasks; but today, the immersion blender and food processor perform these same tasks more quickly, saving you time in the kitchen. These kitchen tools and utensils are well worth your investment to help you cook better foods for a better you.

- Apron
- Baking Sheets
- Blender
- Canning Funnel
- Cheesecloth
- Colander
- Covered Glass Casserole—large
- Cutting Boards— flexible and bamboo
- Dehydrator
- Dish Towels
- Food Processor
- Garlic Press
- Glass Baking Pans 8x8, 9x9, 9x13
- Glass Jars and Lids—all sizes
- Glass Loaf Pan
- Glass Mixing Bowls
- Glass Pie Pans

- Glass Storage Containers
- Griddle—large
- Hot Pads
- Ice Cream Maker
- Immersion Blender
- Instant Pot
- Juicer
- Knives— assortment
- Ladle
- Measuring Cups
- Measuring Spoons
- Microplane Grater
- Mixer—hand or standing
- Muffin Tin
- Natural Baking Liners—large
- Pastry Brush
- Parchment Paper

- Rimmed Baking Sheets
- Rolling Pin
- Rubber Scraper
- Salad Spinner
- Salt and Pepper Grinders
- Sieve
- Skillets— small and large
- Slotted Spoon
- Slow Cooker
- Small Funnel
- Spatulas— cooking and serving
- Spiralizer
- Springform Pan
- Stainless Steel Pots and Pans
- Steamer Basket
- Stock Pot

- Storage and Freezer Bags— all sizes
- Strainers— small and large
- Thermometer
- Tongs
- Vegetable Peeler
- Waffle Maker
- Water Bath Canner
- Wooden Spoons

COOKING TERMS

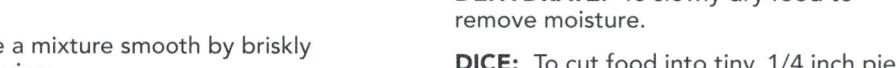

When reading recipes, we hope you find it easy, not puzzling or confusing. If you find yourself reading a recipe and wondering, "What does this mean?", check the following list for cooking terms.

BAKE: To cook food using the direct, dry heat of an oven.

BASTE: To moisten foods, during cooking or grilling, with fats or seasoned liquids to add flavor.

BEAT: To make a mixture smooth by briskly whipping or stirring.

BLANCH: To partially cook vegetables in boiling water or steam to set color and flavor.

BOIL: To cook food in liquid at a temperature that causes bubbles to form.

BRINE: Heavily salted water used to cure vegetables and meat.

BROIL: To cook or brown food a close distance from the heat source.

BROWN: To cook a food in a skillet, broiler or oven to add color and flavor, keeping it moist on the inside.

CANNING: To preserve by quickly heating jars of food to high temperatures to kill microorganisms.

CARAMELIZE: To heat food at temperatures over 350° F turning them golden brown.

CHOP: To cut foods into smaller pieces.

CHEESECLOTH: A thin cotton cloth with a fine weave.

CUBE: To cut food into 1/2 inch cubes.

DEHYDRATE: To slowly dry food to remove moisture.

DICE: To cut food into tiny, 1/4 inch pieces.

DUST: To lightly coat with a dry ingredient.

DRIZZLE: To randomly pour a liquid in a thin stream over food.

FOLD: To mix ingredients gently together.

FREEZE: To preserve food by lowering the temperature to its freezing point.

GLAZE: A thin, glossy coating on hot or cold foods.

GRATE: To rub food across a grating surface to make fine pieces.

GREASE: To coat a pan with a thin layer of butter, ghee, or coconut oil.

GRILL: To cook meat on a grate over a heat source.

GRIND: To cut food into smaller pieces using a food grinder or food processor.

KNEED: To work dough by pressing, folding and stretching.

LOW BOIL: The point between a simmer and a rolling boil.

MARINADE: A seasoned liquid in which meat or vegetables are soaked to flavor and tenderize them.

MARINATE: To soak food in a marinade.

MASH: To remove lumps by smashing or beating a food to make a smooth mixture.

COOKING TERMS

MELD: To merge or blend ingredients, thereby enhancing flavor.

MELT: To heat a solid food over low heat until it becomes liquid.

MINCE: To chop food into very fine pieces.

MIX: To combine two or more foods together by beating or stirring.

PAR BOIL: To boil a food until it is partially cooked.

PEEL: To remove the outer covering of a vegetable or fruit.

PINCH: A small amount of a dry ingredient that can be pinched between a finger and a thumb.

PREHEAT: To heat an oven, pan or griddle to a specific temperature.

PUREE: To mash or blend a food until it is as smooth as possible.

ROAST: To cook foods with a dry heat, uncovered in an oven.

ROLLING BOIL: When liquid boils and bubbles so rapidly that it can't be stirred down.

SAUTÉ: To cook food with butter, ghee, sesame or coconut oil in a skillet over medium- high heat.

SCALD: To heat a liquid to a temperature just below the boiling point.

SHRED: To rub food across a shredding surface to make narrow strips.

SIEVE: To separate liquids from solids.

SIMMER: To cook food in a liquid in which bubbles form slowly and burst just when reaching the surface.

STEAM: To cook a food over the vapor given off by boiling water.

STIR: To mix ingredients together with a spoon or fork.

STIR-FRY: To cook small pieces of food in a skillet over medium-high heat.

STOCK/BROTH: A strained clear liquid in which meat and vegetables are simmered in water.

STRAIN: To pour a liquid through a sieve, strainer or cheesecloth.

TEMPER: To slowly bring up the temperature of a cold ingredient by adding a small amount of hot liquid.

TOAST: Process of drying or browning food by exposing it to heat to develop flavor.

TOSS: To mix ingredients by lifting and dropping, using two utensils.

WHIP: To beat a food lightly and rapidly to add air into mixture and increase volume.

WHISK: To beat or stir with rapid, circular strokes.

CANNING

Have you ever considered canning fruits and vegetables? Canning is a way you can enjoy out-of-season foods throughout the winter months. Included are a few canning recipes that we hope will entice you to learn to preserve food. For the serious canning enthusiast, you may want to purchase the Ball Blue Book which will guide you, in detail, how to preserve different fruits and vegetables.

When beginning your canning experience, it's important to ensure quality food for controlling bacteria, molds, and yeasts. Start with top-quality fresh produce that is not diseased or damaged. Food should be canned within a few hours of being picked. The canning recipes in this book can be processed in a boiling-water canner.

You will need to purchase a boiling-water canner (stainless steel or enamel-coated), some glass canning jars (jelly, pint, or quart size) and some lids and bands (regular or wide-mouth sizes). Other utensils that are nice to have, but not essential, are a jar lifter and a jar funnel.

1 Start by filling your boiling-water canner half-full of water and bring to a simmer (this takes about 30 minutes). Next, wash (sterilize) your jars. A dishwasher works great. Jars need to be heated 10 minutes before filling to prevent jars from breaking. Place new lids in a saucepan and add water to cover. Bring to a simmer until ready to use (do not boil lids as this can cause seal failure).

2 Fill jars one at a time (leave 1/2 inch space from food to rim of jar and remove air bubbles with a table knife), wipe off rim of jar, place lid on jar and screw band on firmly. Place filled jars onto the canner rack until rack is full. Lower into simmering water (water level must cover jars by 1 to 2 inches—add boiling water if needed). Bring water to a rolling boil and set timer for processing recipe.

3 When processing time is completed, turn off heat and take lid off canner. Remove jars from canner and place on cooling rack. Let jars cool 12 to 24 hours and then check the seal. Gently press the center of the lid to see if it is concave. If the center does not pop back, the seal is good. If the center does pop back, refrigerate and use within a couple days. Gently remove band and wipe off jars. Label each jar with date canned and store in a cool, dry, dark place.

DEHYDRATING

Dehydrating is the oldest method of food preservation. This simple method removes 80 to 95 percent of moisture from fruits and vegetables. We have included some recipes using the dehydrating method for you to enjoy. Our dried fruit recipes make delicious, fun-to-eat snacks. And, for a great time saver, toss some dried vegetables into your favorite soup recipe.

There are three basic principles to dehydrating: Heat (high enough temperature to force out moisture without cooking food), Dry Air (ability to absorb the moisture released from food) and Air Circulation (ability to move the moisture away from food). When dehydrating fruits and vegetables, the enzyme action is slowed down but not stopped entirely. For vegetables, you can steam blanch (vegetables are placed in a colander or steamer basket above boiling water and heated by the steam) to retard the enzyme action and kill the growth of microorganisms. For fruits, it is recommended that you pretreat (keep fruit from turning brown) by dipping the fruit in a solution of lemon or lime juice mixed with water.

While a few dehydrating recipes can be made with your oven set at low temperatures, an electric dehydrator is the best piece of equipment for dehydrating. Other items needed include a sharp knife, vegetable peeler, colander or steamer basket and canning jars with lids and bands.

For more detailed dehydrating instructions, check out the Ball Blue Book.

1. To begin dehydrating vegetables, start with high-quality produce that is ripe. Wash and prepare vegetables according to recipe (cutting vegetables in thin, uniform slices helps with even drying and shorter drying time). Next, steam blanch vegetables if recipe calls for this step. Place vegetables in single layer on dehydrator trays. Drying time varies, so dehydrate according to the manufacturer's instructions. Pack in airtight canning jars, seal and label. Store in a cool, dry, dark place.

2. Some vegetables can be eaten dried; however, if you want to reconstitute, soak using equal parts water and vegetables (boiling water can speed up softening). Most dried vegetables can be added directly to the dish you are preparing (additional broth or water may be needed if using a lot of dried vegetables).

3. To dehydrate fruits, start with sweet, ripe fruit. Wash and prepare fruit by trimming, peeling or slicing according to recipe (cutting in thin, uniform slices helps with even drying and shorter drying time). If pretreatment is needed (like apples), dip fruit in a solution made up of one cup lemon juice to one quart of water. Do not soak fruit longer than 10 minutes. Drain. Place in single layer on dehydrator trays and process according to the manufacturer's instructions. Pack in airtight canning jars, seal and label. Store in a cool, dry, dark place.

FREEZING

Freezing fruits and vegetables is a great food preservation method that allows most food to keep its natural color, its fresh flavor and its nutritive qualities. We have chosen to include some recipes throughout this book using the freezing method. So, whether it is fruits or vegetables, give freezing a try and enjoy pulling out those frozen items and creating delicious meals during the winter months.

The principle of preservation by freezing is to expose food to extreme cold which slows down the growth of microorganisms (bacteria, yeasts and molds) and enzyme activity. When freezing vegetables, you want to inactivate the enzymes by a short heat treatment called blanching. If enzymes are not inactivated, it can cause vegetables to lose their fresh flavor and color. Controlling enzyme activity in fruits is best accomplished by adding a sweetener.

The equipment needed for freezing fruits and vegetables are items you typically find in your kitchen: a large kettle, a wire basket or metal strainer and some freezer containers or bags (pint, quart, half-gallon size).

For more detailed freezing instructions, check out the Ball Blue Book.

1. To begin freezing vegetables, start with unblemished, quality produce picked at its peak freshness. Wash, trim and cut vegetables according to recipe.

2. In a large kettle, bring water to a vigorous boil (this takes about 10 to 15 minutes). Place vegetables in a wire basket or metal strainer and lower into boiling water. Begin counting blanching time when vegetables are placed in water. Cover kettle. Remove vegetables from kettle as soon as blanching time is complete. Immerse in ice water and stir to cool. Drain. Immediately pack in airtight freezer containers or bags. Seal, label and freeze. Place in single layers in freezer.

3. Freezing fruit requires ripe, fresh, undamaged produce. Fruit should be frozen shortly after being picked. Wash in cold water. Drain. Prepare fruit according to recipe. Pack into freezer bags or freezer containers. Seal, label and freeze. Place in single layers in freezer.

Over time, frozen food loses its quality. Fruits (except citrus) and vegetables (except onions) can typically be stored up to 12 months if properly prepared for storage.

STEAMING

The method of steaming allows the rich nutrients to remain in vegetables and display their bright vibrant colors on the dinner plate. It is quick and easy!

To steam vegetables, you will need a medium saucepan with lid, steamer basket, knives and cutting board.

1. Wash and trim vegetables. Cut into uniform pieces. In a medium pan, add 1 to 2 inches of water and bring to a vigorous boil. Insert steamer basket (water should be below the basket).

2. Add vegetables and cover. Set timer. The smaller the chunks or slices, the less steaming time needed. Be careful to not over steam. Vegetables should be firm, but tender.

Vegetables steam at different rates. For example, spinach might take only 2 to 3 minutes, while carrots might take 10 minutes, depending on size. If you desire to steam mixed vegetables, start with the longer cooking vegetables first and then add others according to their steaming minutes.

APPLES

DIG INTO THIS!

Different apple varieties produce different flavors.

Some apples have been genetically modified by removing an enzyme that turns an apple brown when exposed to oxygen.

Apples may contain pesticide residue, so it's best to buy organic. Check the Environmental Working Group website to see how they rank on the "Dirty Dozen" list.

Apples contain no fat, sodium or cholesterol and are high in fiber.

Most of the vitamin C content of an apple is found just underneath the skin.

Apples are a natural mouth freshener.

HOW DOES YOUR GARDEN GROW...?

* Look for disease-resistant root stock when purchasing trees.

* Spring planting is recommended.

* An apple tree takes 3 to 7 years to produce fruit, depending on the variety and root stock.

* Choose a site with 6 or more hours of direct sun daily.

* To reliably set fruit, cross-pollination is required. Plant at least 2 varieties of apple trees with similar bloom time within 100 feet of each other.

* Plant tree with the graft union at least 2 inches above ground level.

* You can prune an apple tree at any time, but it is best to prune mature trees annually in the late dormant season (late winter just before spring growth starts).

* Discard any apples that have fallen off the tree (drops) to help with insect control.

* Pick apples early to late fall, depending on the maturity time of your apple variety.

* Store apples at temperatures between 32° F and 40° F.

* Enjoy researching and selecting your favorite apple variety at your local garden center.

To ensure healthy fruit, it's important to pick up and discard all infected apples. You may purchase organic sprays and sticky traps at your local nursery to help control apple maggots and codling moths, or try this homemade recipe.

MOLASSES INSECT CONTROL RECIPE

1/2 cup molasses
2 cups apple cider vinegar
4 cups water
2 one gallon milk jugs

Cut a 2 inch hole, opposite of handle, in each jug.

Mix ingredients together and pour half of mixture into each jug. Hang 2 jugs per large tree on bottom limbs. Check weekly, discard and refill as needed.

Grow it. Preserve it. Prepare it.

FREEZING APPLES

1. Wash apples in cold water; drain.

2. Remove any bruises. Core, peel and slice.

3. To prevent browning while working, place sliced apples in a large bowl of water with 1 teaspoon of lemon juice.

4. Place drained, sliced apples (measure out by cups needed in favorite recipes) in freezing bags.

5. Seal, label and freeze.

Always wash your fruits and vegetables before eating!

FRUIT AND VEGETABLE WASH

1 tablespoon lemon juice
1 tablespoon baking soda
1 cup water

Put in a spray bottle and spray produce. Let sit on produce 2 to 5 minutes and rinse off.

DEHYDRATING APPLES

1. Select apples (any sweet and flavorful variety).

2. Wash apples in cold water (any quantity you desire to dehydrate).

3. Peel if not using organic apples. Remove all bruises. Core and slice.

4. Place slices on rack. Sprinkle cinnamon on apple slices (optional).

5. Dehydrate according to manufacturer's instructions.

6. Apples can also be dried in oven set at 150° F. Arrange apples on cooling racks placed on baking sheets and dry 10 to 20 hours. Apples will be leathery when dried.

7. Let apples cool to room temperature. Place in storage bags or containers. Store in cool, dry, dark place. *(Refer to dehydrating, page 25)*

5 pounds fresh apples yields approximately 2 cups of dried apples.

DEHYDRATED APPLES

RECIPES

APPLE LEMONADE

3 apples, washed and quartered
1/2 lemon, washed

Juice all ingredients in a juicer.

Makes 1 serving

APPLE SMOOTHIE

3/4 cup milk or coconut milk
1-1/2 cups spinach, kale or lettuce
1 apple, peeled, cored and chopped
1 ripe banana, sliced
3/4 teaspoon ground cinnamon

Place all ingredients in a blender in order listed and blend to desired consistency.

Makes 1 serving

HELPFUL HINTS

A pound of apples is approximately 3 medium apples or 2 cups sliced.

APPLE SALSA

1 Granny Smith apple, washed, cored and diced
1 red apple, washed, cored and finely chopped
1 teaspoon lemon juice
1/2 cup dried cranberries
1/4 cup honey
1-1/4 teaspoons ground cinnamon

In a small bowl, mix all ingredients together and enjoy with cinnamon chips.

Makes 6 servings

CINNAMON CHIPS

6 brown rice tortillas
1/4 cup water
2 tablespoons honey
1 tablespoon ground cinnamon

Preheat oven to 350° F. Heat water, honey and cinnamon in a small pan over medium heat. Place tortillas on baking sheets and brush with glaze. Cut into squares with a pizza cutter. Bake 7 to 8 minutes until crispy.

Makes 6 servings

There are many varieties of delicious eating apples. Two of our favorites are Honeycrisp and Zestar. For a fun snack, core and slice apples and spread with peanut butter or almond butter. Or, place a slice of cheese between two apple slices to enjoy a delicious "apple sandwich."

CANNING APPLES

APPLESAUCE

6 pounds apples
2 teaspoons cinnamon
Water

1. Wash apples in cold water. Drain. Core, peel and slice.

2. Place apples in a large pot. Add 1/2 inch to 1 inch of water to bottom of pot to prevent sticking. Cover and cook on medium heat, stirring often until apples become soft (or puree them using an immersion blender).

3. Stir in cinnamon.

4. Ladle hot applesauce into jars. Process pints 20 minutes in a boiling water canner. *(Refer to canning, page 24)*

Makes 7 pints

We remember eating apple butter spread on freshly baked bread in Grandma's kitchen. Today we enjoy eating apple butter spread on pancakes and waffles.

APPLE BUTTER

6 pounds apples
2 cups raw apple cider
1/2 to 1 cup honey
(depending on apple tartness)
2-1/2 teaspoons ground cinnamon
1 teaspoon ground ginger
1/2 teaspoon ground cloves
1/2 teaspoon ground nutmeg

1. Wash, core and cut apples (leaving the skin on if organic).

2. Combine apples and cider in a large pot and bring to a boil. Reduce to a simmer. Cook about 20 minutes until apples are soft. Puree with an immersion blender, food processor or regular blender. Transfer to a slow cooker. Stir in honey and spices.

3. Cook on low setting, stirring occasionally, for 8 hours. Leave lid slightly open to let steam escape and allow the apple butter to thicken.

4. Ladle into jars and keep in refrigerator, or process in hot water bath 15 minutes. *(Refer to canning, page 24)*

Makes 6 to 7 half-pints

APPLE SPINACH SALAD

RECIPES

APPLE SPINACH SALAD

8 cups spinach, washed and drained
8 dates, diced
1 apple, chopped
2/3 cup chopped walnuts

DRESSING:
1/2 cup honey
1/4 cup Dijon mustard
3 tablespoons olive oil

Place salad ingredients in a large bowl. In a small bowl, blend together dressing ingredients. Pour over salad and toss to coat evenly.

Makes 8 servings

BAKED APPLES

6 large apples
1 tablespoon pumpkin pie spice *(page 189)*
3 tablespoons honey
1/4 cup plus 2 tablespoons butter or coconut oil
1/2 cup chopped walnuts, optional
1/3 cup water

Preheat oven to 350° F. Wash and core apples. Peel about 1 inch of skin off the top, cut the bottoms flat and arrange in a 9 x 13 glass baking dish. In a small bowl, combine spice, honey, butter and nuts. Fill each apple with a tablespoon of mixture. Pour water in baking dish and bake uncovered 40 to 50 minutes, basting 2 to 3 times.

VARIATION:
Cut apples in bite size chunks. Place in a large bowl with remaining ingredients (omitting water). Stir. Place in a covered 9 x 9 glass baking dish and bake 30 minutes.

Makes 6 servings

Accurate measuring is important. Level off your measuring spoons and cups—too much, or too little, will change the outcome of the recipe.

GLUTEN-FREE APPLE CRISP

4 cups sliced apples, fresh or frozen
1 tablespoon lemon juice
2 tablespoons butter, melted
1/3 cup honey
1 teaspoon ground cinnamon

CRUMBLE TOPPING:
1/2 teaspoon ground cinnamon
1/2 cup chopped walnuts
1 cup almond flour
2 tablespoons coconut flour
2 tablespoons honey
1 teaspoon vanilla
2 tablespoons butter

Preheat oven to 350° F. Place apples in a medium bowl. Add lemon juice, butter, honey and cinnamon. Stir. Pour into a 9 x 9 buttered glass baking dish. Mix topping together with a fork or pastry blender until it crumbles. Sprinkle topping evenly over filling.

Bake 30 to 45 minutes or until apples are soft. Eat warm or cold. Top with ice cream, whipped cream or yogurt if desired.

Makes 9 servings

GRANDMA'S APPLE CRISP

4 cups sliced apples, washed, peeled and cored
2/3 cup raw cane sugar, coconut sugar or date sugar
1/2 cup unbleached flour
1/2 cup rolled oats
3/4 teaspoon ground cinnamon
3/4 teaspoon ground nutmeg
1/3 cup butter, room temperature

Preheat oven to 350° F. Place apples in a buttered 9 x 9 glass pan. Stir remaining ingredients together in a medium bowl and sprinkle over apples. Bake uncovered 30 to 45 minutes until golden brown and bubbly. Delicious served warm with ice cream or whipped cream.

Makes 9 servings

OATMEAL SPICE CAKE

1/2 cup rolled oats
3/4 cup boiling water
3 eggs
3 tablespoons coconut oil
3/4 cup maple syrup
1-1/2 cups applesauce *(page 32)*
1/2 teaspoon salt
1 teaspoon baking soda
1 tablespoon vanilla
2 teaspoons ground cinnamon
1/3 cup plus 1 tablespoon coconut flour
1-1/2 cups rolled oats

Preheat oven to 350° F. Pour boiling water over 1/2 cup oats and let sit. In a large bowl, beat next 8 ingredients together with a mixer. Stir in coconut flour and dry oats. Lastly, fold in soaked oats.

Butter a 9 x 13 glass pan and sprinkle lightly with additional coconut flour. Pour batter into pan and bake 30 to 35 minutes until toothpick inserted comes out clean. Cool and frost with a double recipe of Caramel Coconut Frosting *(page 91)*.

Makes 24 servings

CARAMEL SAUCE

1/4 cup butter
2/3 cup maple syrup
1 cup heavy cream
1 teaspoon vanilla

In a medium saucepan, melt butter with maple syrup over medium-high heat. Bring to a low boil and cook 3 minutes. While stirring, slowly pour in cream.

Continue cooking and stirring at a low boil 15 to 20 minutes until thick. Stir in vanilla. Serve warm with apples or over ice cream. Pure deliciousness!

Makes 2 cups

Cooking time may vary on all our recipes based on the type of stove used – gas, glass top, electric coil, etc.

HELPFUL HINTS

A bushel of apples weighs about 42 pounds and will yield 20 to 24 quarts of applesauce.

EATING PURE

I was recently sitting around the table enjoying an evening meal with family, when my eight-year-old granddaughter asked, "Grandma, why do you buy organic food?" She continued to share with me how I could save money if I purchased cheaper food. And, yes, to her credit, it only seems logical when only comparing price. However, there are other facts to consider, such as the pesticide residue found on many fruits and vegetables. I personally like to follow the "Clean 15" and the "Dirty Dozen" lists put out by the Environmental Working Group. When out shopping, these lists can assist you in your produce selections and help you determine whether you should buy organically grown produce. Take a look at their website and read up on pesticide residue. If cost is still a concern, buying local is a great way to save money and still get clean, fresh food that supports your local farmers.

RECIPES

TRADITIONAL PIE CRUST

3 cups unbleached flour
2 teaspoons salt
1 cup lard
1/2 cup plus 2 tablespoons cold water

Place all ingredients in a food processor. Process until it's in a ball (or can be mixed with a pastry blender or fork). Divide into 4 evenly sized balls of dough.

Using your hands, slightly flatten each ball to about 1/2 inch thick. Place on well-floured surface. Sprinkle some flour over top of dough. Starting at the center, roll dough, working your way out until it's about 1/2 inch larger in diameter than your pie pan.

Gently fold in half and transfer to a pie pan. Unfold and carefully press dough against bottom and sides.

For a single crust pie, trim off excess dough along edge of pan with a knife. Finish edge. Prick bottom and sides with a fork. Bake 10 minutes at 425° F.

For a double crust pie, pour prepared pie filling into bottom crust. Roll out another ball of dough. After folding in half, make a few 1/2 inch slits at an angle in the center of the folded edge. Rub a little water on the top edge of the bottom crust.

Place top crust on filling and unfold to cover entire pie. Press the top crust firmly onto the bottom crust. Trim off excess dough along edge of pan with a knife. Finish edge.

Bake according to pie filling directions.

Makes 4 singles or 2 double-crusted 9 inch pie crusts.

RECIPES

TRADITIONAL WHIPPED CREAM

1 cup heavy cream
2 tablespoons honey
2 teaspoons vanilla

In a medium bowl, whip cream with a mixer until soft peaks form, add honey and vanilla.

Makes 2 cups

APPLE PIE

Pastry for double crust pie
6 cups thinly sliced tart apples, washed, peeled and cored
2 tablespoons unflavored gelatin
1/2 cup honey
1/2 teaspoon ground nutmeg
1 teaspoon ground cinnamon
1/8 teaspoon salt
2 tablespoons butter

Preheat oven to 400° F. Place pastry in a 9 inch pie plate. Stir together all ingredients and place in crust. Cover with top crust. Bake 15 minutes. Remove from oven. Carefully wrap edge of pie with foil. Reduce oven temperature to 350° F. Continue baking 50 to 60 minutes until crust is brown and juice is bubbling out. Place a rimmed baking sheet on the rack below the pie to prevent the need to clean the oven after baking.

Makes 6 to 8 servings

DAIRY-FREE WHIPPED CREAM

1 can of organic coconut milk
1 tablespoon maple syrup
1 teaspoon vanilla

Chill coconut milk overnight. Remove from refrigerator and turn can upside down so when you open it, the thick cream is on top. Scoop out the thick cream and place in a mixing bowl. Reserve remaining liquid for future recipes. With a mixer, whip the thick coconut cream until fluffy. Stir in remaining ingredients. Serve immediately.

Makes 1-1/2 cups

ICE CREAM

3 cups heavy cream
3 cups whole milk
2/3 cup maple syrup or honey
1/4 teaspoon salt
1 tablespoon vanilla

In a large pan, heat cream and milk to 180° F (scalding). Remove from heat and add remaining ingredients. Chill in refrigerator overnight.

Put in an ice cream freezer. Process according to manufacturer's instructions.

Makes 2 quarts

We use unflavored gelatin in several recipes as a gluten-free thickening agent, but did you know that gelatin is very nutritious for you? Unflavored gelatin is collagen protein and amino acids that are essential in helping heal damaged cell walls. Healthy digestion, hair and nails, reduced inflammation and joint pain, strong bones and better immune function are some of the benefits of including gelatin in your diet. It's important to know your source of gelatin.

ASPARAGUS

DIG INTO THIS!

Asparagus is one of the easiest vegetables to grow organically with little maintenance.

Asparagus can be green, white or purple.

April through June is the peak growing season.

Place asparagus between your forefinger and thumb and bend it until it snaps to find its natural breaking point.

Asparagus can be a detox as well as a laxative and may help with urinary tract problems.

Asparagus is high in fiber and vitamins A and C.

To store fresh asparagus, refrigerate stalks "standing up" in a shallow cup of water.

HOW DOES YOUR GARDEN GROW...?

✳ Asparagus is a perennial; it will come up each year. It takes 2 to 3 years before you can harvest. Typical asparagus beds can remain productive 15 to 20 years.

✳ Asparagus grows best next to basil, parsley or tomatoes.

✳ It's best not to plant next to garlic or onions.

✳ Plant in early spring. Place roots in the west or north part of the garden so the tall ferns do not shade other plants.

✳ Dig a trench about 6 to 8 inches deep. Add 1 inch of compost. Place asparagus crown in trench, spreading out the roots, approximately 12 to 18 inches apart.

✳ Cover with 2 inches of soil and continue to fill trench with soil as shoots emerge until trench is completely filled.

✳ Harvest fresh asparagus after two years from planting date. A typical harvest lasts 4 to 8 weeks. Let spears grow into ferns through the remaining summer months.

✳ Under ideal conditions, an asparagus spear can grow 6 or more inches in a 24-hour period. Make sure you check them daily.

✳ To prepare an asparagus bed for winter, cut back fern in mid-fall. Cover with 1 inch of compost, then top with 6 inches of mulch.

3 STAGES OF ASPARAGUS: ROOT, SPEARS AND FERNS

Grow it. Preserve it. Prepare it.

FREEZING ASPARAGUS

1. Select young and tender asparagus. Wash and sort into similar sizes.

2. Trim bottom of stalk and cut or snap into even spear lengths.

3. Blanch in boiling water— small spears 1-1/2 minutes, medium spears 2 minutes and large spears 3 minutes.

4. Drain off hot water, dip in ice water, drain and cool.

5. Pack into freezer bags. Seal, label and freeze.
   (Refer to freezing, page 26)

We enjoy our frozen asparagus throughout the winter in soups or steamed as a side dish.

CREAM OF ASPARAGUS SOUP

STEAMED ASPARAGUS

1 pound asparagus, washed and trimmed
1 tablespoon butter
1/2 teaspoon salt

Steam asparagus 5 to 10 minutes until tender (*refer to steaming, page 27*). Transfer to a bowl. Add butter and salt.

Makes 4 servings

CREAM OF ASPARAGUS SOUP

2 pounds asparagus, fresh or frozen (cut in 3/4 inch pieces)
1 large onion, chopped
3 carrots, chopped
3 cloves garlic, minced
3 tablespoons butter
6 cups chicken broth (*page 158*)
1-1/2 teaspoons salt
1/2 teaspoon pepper
1/2 cup heavy cream

Sauté onions, carrots and garlic in butter in a large pan over medium-low heat until soft. Add broth, asparagus pieces, salt and pepper.

Simmer 15 to 20 minutes until asparagus is tender. Puree soup with an immersion blender (or regular blender) until smooth. Stir in cream right before serving.

Makes 6 servings

SAUTÉED GARLIC ASPARAGUS

3 tablespoons butter
3 cloves garlic, minced
1 pound asparagus, washed and trimmed
1/2 teaspoon salt
1/8 teaspoon pepper
1/4 cup grated Parmesan cheese

Melt butter in a large skillet over medium heat. Add garlic and asparagus spears; cook 10 minutes, uncovered. Stir occasionally until asparagus is tender. Sprinkle with salt, pepper and Parmesan cheese.

Makes 4 servings

ASPARAGUS SALAD

2 pounds asparagus, washed and trimmed
1/2 cup chopped red bell pepper
1/3 cup chopped pecans
1/2 teaspoon butter
Olive oil dressing (*page 150*)

Cut asparagus into 1 inch pieces. Boil asparagus in a large pot of salted water until tender-crisp. Rinse with cold water and drain.

Toast pecans in butter in a small skillet, stirring constantly until brown. In a large bowl, combine all ingredients and toss with olive oil dressing.

Makes 4 to 6 servings

It's important to read the entire recipe beforehand to make sure you have the necessary ingredients and understand the preparation of them. Some substitutions may be in order if your pantry needs to be restocked. Good substitutions for butter are coconut oil when baking or sesame oil when sautéing and roasting. Vegetables can also be substituted in many recipes; for instance, if a stir-fry calls for carrots and broccoli and you have zucchini and cauliflower on hand, make the substitution.

BACON WRAPPED ASPARAGUS

1 pound asparagus, washed and trimmed
1/4 cup butter, melted
4 slices bacon
Pepper

Preheat oven to 400° F. Place bacon on rimmed baking sheet and bake 5 to 7 minutes. Cool slightly and save bacon grease for drizzle.

Using a pastry brush, lightly coat asparagus spears with butter. Divide asparagus into 4 bundles.

Wrap each bundle with 1 slice of the partially cooked bacon. Place each bundle back on rimmed baking sheet. Sprinkle with pepper and drizzle with the leftover bacon grease.

Bake 12 minutes. Flip asparagus bundles and cook until bacon is crispy.

Makes 4 servings

ASPARAGUS DIPPING STICKS

1 pound asparagus, washed and trimmed
1 egg
3/4 cup almond flour
1 tablespoon Italian seasoning *(page 125)*
1/2 teaspoon salt
1/2 teaspoon garlic powder
1/3 cup grated Parmesan cheese

Preheat oven to 450° F. Whisk egg in a pie plate. Mix almond flour, Italian seasoning, salt, garlic powder and cheese in another bowl. Dip the asparagus into the egg and then into the flour mixture, coating evenly.

Lay asparagus on a cooling rack that has been placed on a rimmed baking sheet. Arrange so they're not touching. Bake 20 minutes until golden.

Serve plain or with pizza sauce *(page 257)*.

Makes 8 servings

HELPFUL HINTS
A pound of asparagus is approximately 16–20 spears and equals 3 cups chopped

BACON WRAPPED
ASPARAGUS

FRIED RICE AND ASPARAGUS

1 cup brown rice
2 eggs, beaten
4 teaspoons butter, divided
1/2 pound asparagus, washed
and cut into 1 inch pieces
1 red bell pepper, chopped
3/4 cup chopped red onion
2 cloves garlic, minced
1 tablespoon minced fresh ginger
1/4 cup coconut aminos
2 tablespoons apple cider vinegar
1 teaspoon sesame oil
Hot pepper sauce, to taste *(page 175)*

Rinse rice and place in a pan of boiling, salted water. Reduce heat and simmer 20 to 30 minutes until tender. While rice is cooking, cook eggs in a skillet with 2 teaspoons butter. Remove eggs, cover and set aside.

Place remaining 2 teaspoons butter in a skillet and sauté asparagus 2 minutes over medium-high heat. Add pepper, onion, garlic and ginger. Cook 5 minutes until tender-crisp. Add cooked rice, coconut aminos and vinegar. Cook 1 minute until liquid is absorbed. Fold in cooked eggs. Stir in sesame oil and hot sauce before serving.

Makes 4 servings

ASPARAGUS BAKE

2 cups sliced fresh mushrooms
1 onion, chopped
2 tablespoons butter
1/2 cup beef broth *(page 158)*
1/4 cup heavy cream
1 teaspoon salt
1/8 teaspoon ground nutmeg
1/8 teaspoon pepper
1 pound asparagus,
washed and cut into 1 inch pieces
1/4 cup chopped red bell pepper
3/4 teaspoon lemon juice

Preheat oven to 350° F. In a large skillet, sauté mushrooms and onions in butter over medium-high heat 10 minutes. Mix broth, cream and seasonings together in a large bowl. Stir in sautéed mixture and remaining ingredients. Pour into an 8 x 8 glass baking dish. Bake uncovered, 45 minutes until tender.

Makes 4 servings

EATING PURE

In our recipes, we chose to use Coconut Aminos in place of soy sauce. Coconut Aminos is a soy-free sauce made from coconut tree sap, which comes out of the tree with vital, active and alive nutrients. This sap is very low on the glycemic index. Many of the conventional soy sauces on the market today are made with non-organic, genetically modified soybeans to which mold, yeast and bacteria cultures have been added during the fermentation process. Use Coconut Aminos like soy sauce in dressings, marinades and stir-fries.

RECIPES

CHICKEN ASPARAGUS STIR-FRY

2 chicken breasts, cut in 1 inch pieces
3/4 cup chopped green onions
2 cloves garlic, minced
2 tablespoons butter
1 pound asparagus, washed
and cut into 1 inch pieces
1 cup frozen peas
2 cups cherry or grape tomatoes, halved
1 teaspoon salt
1/2 teaspoon pepper
1/4 cup fresh chopped parsley
1/4 cup grated Parmesan cheese

In a large skillet, sauté chicken, onions and garlic in butter 5 minutes over medium heat. Add asparagus, peas, tomatoes, salt and pepper. Continue cooking an additional 5 to 7 minutes until tender. Add parsley and cheese. Serve alone or on top of brown rice noodles or zucchini noodles.

Makes 4 servings

Free-range chickens live naturally, eating grass and scavenging for seeds, bugs and grubs. These chickens are the tastiest and provide the best nutrition. They are part of the farm's natural ecosystem and are less likely to have growth hormones and antibiotics in them. Check out the Eat Wild website to find a small, local farm near you to purchase free-range chicken.

FRESH BEANS

DIG INTO THIS!

Green beans are also called string beans and snap beans.

Bean pods can be green, yellow, purple or speckled with red.

Kids love watching purple beans turn bright green when cooking!

Green, navy, kidney and black beans are called "common beans."

Green beans continue to cook after you remove them from boiling water. If using beans in a cold dish, dip them in cold water after cooking.

Eat raw beans with your favorite dip.

HOW DOES YOUR GARDEN GROW...?

❋ Days to maturity: 50 to 60.

❋ Beans grow best next to beets, cabbage, cauliflower, cucumbers, peas or potatoes.

❋ It's best not to plant next to basil, kohlrabi or onions.

❋ Plant when soil temperature reaches 60° F.

❋ Plant seeds 1 inch deep.

❋ Bush beans should be planted 4 inches apart with 6 inches between rows.

❋ Pole beans are planted in hills with 4 plants per hill with a stake in the center—leave 15 inches between hills.

❋ Seeds will begin to grow in 7 to 10 days.

❋ Pick beans when they are about the thickness of a pencil.

❋ If picked regularly, beans will continue producing all summer.

❋ Green beans can be refrigerated up to 6 days after harvesting.

Most popular varieties include yellow wax beans, green beans and purple beans.

Grow it. Preserve it. Prepare it.

FREEZING BEANS

1. Wash and drain beans. Remove stem end and leave whole or break into 1 inch pieces.

2. Blanch 3 minutes in boiling water. Drain off hot water, dip in ice water, drain, and cool.

3. Pack into freezer bags. Seal, label and freeze. *(Refer to freezing, page 26)*

Frozen green or yellow beans can be tossed into soups and casseroles. It is best to limit the freezer storage of beans to about 3 months to obtain the highest concentration of multiple nutrients.

HELPFUL HINTS
1 pound of green beans equals 3 cups chopped.

CANNING BEANS

DILL PICKLED GREEN BEANS

2 pounds green beans
4 heads of dill
(or 4 teaspoons dill seed)
6 cloves garlic, peeled
2-1/2 cups water
2-1/2 cups apple cider vinegar
1/4 cup salt
1/2 teaspoon cayenne pepper
3/4 teaspoon red pepper flakes

1. Wash the dill and place 1 head in bottom of each pint jar along with 1-1/2 cloves of garlic.

2. Wash and drain green beans. Remove stem end and pack into jars.

3. Combine water, vinegar, salt, cayenne and pepper flakes in a medium pan and heat to boiling. Pour over beans and process in hot water bath 10 minutes. *(Refer to canning, page 24)*

4. Allow pickled beans to sit 10 days after processing before eating.

Makes 4 pints

DILL PICKLED GREEN BEANS

FRESH GREEN BEAN SALAD

2 cups chopped green beans, fresh
1/4 cup chopped red onion
1 large cucumber, peeled and chopped
1 cup cherry or grape tomatoes, halved
2 tablespoons olive oil
2 tablespoons lemon juice
1/2 teaspoon salt
1/4 teaspoon pepper

Steam green beans 4 minutes *(refer to steaming, page 27)*. Run beans under cold water and drain well. Combine beans, onions, cucumbers and tomatoes in a large bowl. Mix remaining ingredients in a small bowl and pour over salad. Toss to coat evenly.

Makes 4 servings

SAUTÉED GREEN BEANS

3 tablespoons butter
3 cups green beans, fresh or frozen
1/2 cup slivered almonds or cashew pieces
1/2 teaspoon salt
1/8 teaspoon pepper

Melt butter in a large skillet over medium heat. Add nuts and sauté until golden brown. Add green beans. Cover and cook 5 to 8 minutes until tender. Remove from skillet and sprinkle with salt and pepper.

Makes 4 servings

STEAMED GREEN BEANS

3 cups green beans, fresh or frozen
1 tablespoon butter
1/2 teaspoon salt

Steam green beans (washed and stemmed) in a covered pan 3 to 5 minutes until tender *(refer to steaming, page 27)*. Transfer to a bowl. Add butter and salt.

Makes 4 servings

CRISPY BACON AND GREEN BEANS

6 pieces bacon
2 tablespoons bacon grease
3 handfuls fresh green beans, washed and stemmed
2 cloves garlic, minced
3/4 cup chopped onion
1 cup chicken broth *(page 158)*
1/2 red bell pepper, chopped
1/2 teaspoon salt
1/4 teaspoon pepper

Fry bacon until crisp. Place 2 tablespoons of bacon grease in a skillet. Add garlic and onions and sauté 5 minutes. Add green beans and cook until beans turn bright green. Add chicken broth, red pepper, salt and pepper.

Turn heat to medium-low and cover with lid, leaving lid cracked to allow steam to escape. Cook until liquid evaporates and beans are a bit crisp and caramelized. Serve with bacon crumbled on top.

Makes 6 servings

If you are baking another dish in your oven, try this easy method for making beans. Simply toss green beans in a glass baking dish with butter, salt, pepper and a little minced garlic. Roast at 350° F 20 minutes or until tender.

GREEN BEAN CASSEROLE

4 cups chopped green beans, fresh or frozen
1/2 cup chopped onion
8 mushrooms, sliced
1/4 cup butter, melted
2 tablespoons quinoa flour
1 cup chicken broth *(page 158)*
1/4 teaspoon garlic powder
1 teaspoon salt
1/4 teaspoon pepper
1/4 cup grated Parmesan cheese

Preheat oven to 350° F. Place beans, onions and mushrooms in a large bowl. Melt butter in a sauce pan over medium heat. Stir in quinoa flour to make thick paste. Add broth and cook, stirring constantly, until thick.

Remove from heat and stir in garlic powder, salt and pepper. Pour over green bean mixture. Stir and pour into an ungreased 9 x 9 glass pan. Sprinkle cheese on top. Bake uncovered 1 hour.

Makes 4 to 6 servings

You will see many recipes using one of our favorite ingredients—raw cheese. Cheese is only as good as the milk it's made from. Look for good quality cheese that is undyed, organic, or is made from raw milk. By researching and reading labels, you will be able to purchase the best cheese for your family.

ROASTED MEDLEY

20 button mushrooms,
washed, trimmed and cut in half
3 Yukon gold potatoes, cut in 1 inch chunks
1 large onion, cut into wedges
1/4 cup butter, melted
2 cups chopped green beans, fresh or frozen
1-1/4 teaspoons salt
1/4 teaspoon pepper
1-1/2 teaspoons dried thyme
1/2 cup grated Parmesan cheese

Preheat oven to 400° F. In a large bowl combine mushrooms, potatoes and onions. Drizzle vegetables with melted butter. Toss to coat evenly and spread in an even layer on a rimmed baking sheet. Roast 20 minutes. Remove from oven, stir and add green beans. Continue roasting another 20 minutes until slightly browned. Sprinkle with salt, pepper, thyme and cheese. Roast an additional 5 minutes until cheese is melted.

Makes 4 to 6 servings

HASH BROWN CASSEROLE

2 pounds ground beef
1 medium onion, chopped
1 clove garlic, minced
1 cup chicken broth *(page 158)*
1 cup sour cream
1 cup shredded raw cheddar cheese
2 cups chopped green beans, fresh or frozen
1-1/2 teaspoons salt
1/2 teaspoon pepper
6 cups frozen hash browns, thawed

Preheat oven to 350° F. In a large skillet, brown ground beef, onion and garlic over medium-high heat. Add next 6 ingredients and stir. Place in a 9 x 13 glass pan. Top with hash browns. Bake 1 to 1-1/2 hours uncovered.

Makes 6 servings

BEETS

DIG INTO THIS!

Beets are in the same plant family as spinach.

Red or golden beets are the two most common varieties.

Beet greens are an excellent source of vitamin A.

Beet roots provide vitamin C and potassium.

Beets are a good source of dietary fiber and antioxidants.

Red coloring from beets is used to improve the color of tomato paste, sauces and jams.

Cooked and pureed beets are great to incorporate into your baby's diet as you introduce solid food. Freeze beet puree in ice cube trays. Thaw and warm up cubes as needed.

HOW DOES YOUR GARDEN GROW...?

* Days to maturity: 48 to 55.
* Beets grow best next to cabbage, leeks, lettuce, onions or radishes.
* It's best not to plant next to pole beans.
* Plant from early spring to early July.
* Plant seeds 1/2 inch deep, in rows 8 inches apart.

* Seeds will begin to grow in 5 days.
* Thin plants to 1 plant every 3 inches.
* Water regularly so soil doesn't dry out.
* Harvest when they are 1-1/2 to 2-1/2 inches in diameter—large beets may be tough.
* Harvest by pulling or digging the roots and then twisting off the tops.
* Store unwashed beet greens 2 to 3 days in refrigerator. Beet roots can be stored in a separate bag several weeks.

Deer are common in our area and they love beets! Because of this we have tall fences surrounding our gardens.

Grow it. Preserve it. Prepare it.

FREEZING BEETS

1. Select uniformed size, deep red, tender beets.

2. Trim greens to 2 inches from beet, keeping root intact. Wash and boil on stove until beets are tender (or bake in 350° F oven, covered, 2 to 2-1/2 hours).

3. Cool. Cut off stem and root. Remove skin. Leave whole, quarter, slice or dice and put into freezer containers.

4. Seal, label and freeze.
   (Refer to freezing, page 26)

HELPFUL HINTS

1 pound of beets equals 5 medium beets or 4 cups chopped, and 8–10 cups of greens.

BEETS: The Food Coloring Alternative!

Wash a small beet. Cut off ends and peel. Quarter and put in a food processor. Line a bowl with cheesecloth and pour chopped beets into it. Wearing rubber gloves, gather ends together and twist tightly as juice runs out into a container. This is best used in foods that remain cold such as yogurts, smoothies, whipped cream, cream cheese, etc.

CANNING BEETS

PICKLED BEETS

10 pounds beets, small to medium size
8 cups apple cider vinegar
4 cups water
2 cups honey
1 tablespoon salt
7 tablespoons pickling spice

1. Trim greens to 2 inches from beet, keeping root intact. Wash and boil on stove until beets are tender (or bake in 350° F oven, covered, 2 to 2-1/2 hours).

2. Cool. Cut off stem and root. Remove skin.

3. Cut into wedges or bite size chunks and pack into jars.

4. Add 1 tablespoon of pickling spice to each quart (1-1/2 teaspoons per pint).

5. In a medium pan, bring vinegar, water, honey and salt to a rolling boil. Pour over beets. Process in boiling water bath 30 minutes.
   (Refer to canning, page 24)

Makes 14 pints or 7 quarts

PICKLED BEET

BEET JUICE DRINK

1 or 2 large carrots
2 stalks celery
1/4 of a very small beet
1/2 of an apple

Wash and cut ends off all vegetables.
Juice all ingredients in a juicer.

Makes 1 serving

DILLED BEET SOUP

8 cups beef broth *(page 158)*
1 large onion, chopped
4 large beets, peeled and chopped
4 large carrots, peeled and chopped
2 cups shredded cooked beef
2 cups cabbage, thinly sliced
3/4 cup chopped fresh dill or 1/3 cup dried dill weed
2 tablespoons lemon juice
1 teaspoon salt
1/2 teaspoon pepper

In a large pot, boil onions, beets and carrots in broth
30 minutes until tender. Stir in beef, cabbage and dill.
Cook an additional 15 minutes until cabbage is tender.
Stir in lemon juice, salt and pepper. Don't be deceived;
this is delicious!

Makes 8 servings

HARVARD BEETS

4 medium beets
1/3 cup apple cider vinegar
1/4 cup honey
1/2 teaspoon pectin
(from Pomona's Universal Pectin)
1/2 teaspoon calcium water
(from Pomona's Universal Pectin)
3 tablespoons butter
1 teaspoon salt
1/4 teaspoon pepper

Wash beets. Trim greens to 2 inches from beet,
keeping root intact. Place beets in a medium pan,
cover with water and bring to a boil. Reduce heat,
cover and keep at a low boil 20 to 30 minutes
until tender.

While beets are cooking, combine vinegar and honey
in a small saucepan. Stir in pectin and calcium water.
Bring to a boil, reduce heat and simmer uncovered,
20 to 30 minutes, stirring frequently until thick. Add
butter, salt and pepper. Once beets are done, drain
and run under cold water. Remove skins. Cut off
ends and slice or cube. Place in a serving bowl. Pour
thickened mixture over all and stir to coat evenly.

Makes 4 servings

VARIATION:
For traditional buttered beets, remove skins after
boiling. Slice and place in a serving bowl. Toss with
butter, salt and pepper.

Pectin is considered one of the most
natural thickening agents. It is found in peels
of apples and other citrus fruits. We use it
as a base for jams, desserts and our delicious
Harvard Beets recipe.

RECIPES

ROASTED BEETS AND SAUTÉED BEET GREENS

6 to 8 small beets with greens
1/4 cup butter, divided
2 cloves garlic, minced
Salt and pepper to taste
1 tablespoon apple cider vinegar, optional

Preheat oven to 350° F. Wash beets. Trim greens to 2 inches from beet, keeping root intact. Rinse greens, removing any large stems and set aside. Place beets in a small baking dish or roasting pan. Cover and bake 45 to 60 minutes until tender.

Peel, slice and toss with 2 tablespoons butter, salt and pepper. If desired, sprinkle on apple cider vinegar for added zip.

Heat 2 tablespoons butter in a skillet over medium-low heat. Add garlic and cook 1 minute. Tear the beet greens into 2 to 3 inch pieces and add to skillet. Cook and stir until greens are wilted and tender. Season with salt and pepper. Serve alongside roasted beets.

Makes 4 servings

Did you know different colors of fruits and vegetables provide different nutrients? To receive maximum nutritional benefits each day, eat a rainbow of fruits and vegetables. Make it fun by letting your children help you do menu planning based on colors. You will be creating beautiful plates of color as well as keeping your body healthy!

BLUEBERRIES

DIG INTO THIS!

Blueberries are one of nature's convenience foods because there is no need for peeling, hulling or pitting.

Dried blueberries make a great travel snack for toddlers.

Fresh blueberries are packed with disease-fighting antioxidants, nutrients and dietary fiber.

Blueberries have a low glycemic index value.

Blueberries are one of the only natural foods that are truly blue in color.

Blueberry bushes can be incorporated into your landscaping. They provide pretty flowers in the spring, edible fruit during summer and beautiful fall color.

HOW DOES YOUR GARDEN GROW...?

❋ Plant blueberries in soil that is acidic, high in organic matter, and well-drained, yet moist. Soil pH should ideally be between 4 and 5.

❋ Purchase started plants from your local nursery.

❋ Plant in early spring.

❋ Dig holes 20 inches deep and 18 inches wide, spaced about 5 feet apart.

❋ Apply a 2 to 4 inch layer of woodchips, saw dust or pine needles after planting. This will keep the shallow root systems moist.

❋ Water 1 to 2 inches per week.

❋ Apply fertilizer 1 month after planting.

❋ Do not allow bush to produce fruit the first couple years. Pinch back blossoms to stimulate growth.

❋ After 4 years from planting, prune to stimulate growth of new shoots.

❋ Prune plants in late winter, preferably just before growth begins.

❋ Drape netting (available at your local nursery) over ripening blueberries to protect from birds.

❋ Blueberries will be ready for picking in late July through mid-August.

❋ Pick berries a couple days after they turn blue. They should pull off easily into your hand.

❋ Full production is reached after 6 years.

❋ Store unwashed blueberries in refrigerator 5 to 10 days.

Plump, juicy berries are now easy to grow in your backyard on bushes that are resistant to most pests and diseases, and they can produce up to 20 years!

Grow it. Preserve it. Prepare it.

FREEZING BLUEBERRIES

Blueberries are one of the easiest fruits to freeze!

1. Wash blueberries; drain. Allow to dry thoroughly.

2. Measure out by cups as you put into freezer bags. Seal, label and freeze.

Look at your favorite recipes before freezing and bag up the number of cups needed to make your favorite blueberry recipes.

DEHYDRATING BLUEBERRIES

1. Wash blueberries. Plunge into boiling water 25 to 30 seconds until skins start to crack.

2. Remove and dip into ice water until completely cool. Drain well.

3. Place in single layer on dehydrator trays. Dehydrate according to manufacturer's instructions. Store in cool, dry, dark place in airtight glass jars.

BLUEBERRY BANANA MUFFINS

RECIPES

BLUEBERRY SMOOTHIE

1 cup vanilla or plain yogurt *(page 236)*
1 tablespoon honey
1 cup frozen blueberries

Place all ingredients in a blender in order listed and blend to desired consistency.

Makes 1 serving

BLUEBERRY PINK LEMONADE

1/2 cup lemon juice
7 cups water, divided
2/3 cup honey
1-1/2 cups fresh or frozen blueberries, divided

Mix lemon juice with 6 cups water in a 2 quart pitcher. In a small pan, combine honey, 1/2 cup blueberries and 1 cup water. Cook 5 minutes on medium-high heat, stirring occasionally. Pour mixture through strainer and add to pitcher. Chill. Fill tall glasses with ice cubes. Add chilled lemonade. Toss remaining blueberries into glasses.

Makes 6 servings

BLUEBERRY FRUIT POPS

1/4 cup water
1 cup yogurt *(page 236)*
2 tablespoons honey
1 ripe banana
1 cup frozen blueberries

Place all ingredients in a blender and blend until smooth. Pour into liquid frozen pop molds or an ice cube tray and freeze at least 4 hours.

Makes 4 servings

BLUEBERRY SAUCE

2 cups blueberries
2 tablespoons honey
2 tablespoons lemon juice

In a small pan, simmer all ingredients 10 minutes on medium heat until slightly thick. Delicious served on pancakes, ice cream, yogurt, etc.

Makes 2 cups

BLUEBERRY BANANA MUFFINS

3 eggs
1/4 cup honey
3 tablespoons butter or coconut oil, melted
2 teaspoons lemon juice
2 ripe bananas, mashed
1/2 teaspoon salt
1/2 teaspoon baking soda
2-1/2 cups almond flour
1 tablespoon coconut flour
1-1/2 cups blueberries

OPTIONAL TOPPING:
1/2 cup chopped pecans
1 tablespoon butter
1/2 teaspoon cinnamon

Preheat oven to 350° F. Line muffin tin with paper liners. In a large bowl, beat eggs with a mixer. Add next 4 ingredients and mix well. Stir in dry ingredients. Fold in blueberries and pour into muffin liners.

Optional Topping: In a small bowl, mix all ingredients together, sprinkle on top and gently press into each muffin. Bake 25 to 30 minutes, or until a toothpick comes out clean from the muffin.

Makes 12 muffins

Our Blueberry Banana Muffins are no ordinary muffins! In baking these muffins you will discover they have a little different appearance. They tend to be a little denser than your average muffins, but have the same delicious flavor you would expect.

BLUEBERRY PARFAIT

1 cup blueberries
2 cups plain or vanilla yogurt *(page 236)*
2 bananas, sliced
1/2 cup almonds, sliced
2 cups granola

Divide all ingredients evenly and layer in 4 individual serving dishes for a beautiful, healthy and delicious breakfast, snack or dessert.

Makes 4 servings

GRANOLA

2 cups pumpkin seeds
2 cups sunflower seeds
2-1/2 cups shredded coconut
1/2 teaspoon salt
1 tablespoon ground cinnamon
1 cup honey
1 tablespoon vanilla
1/2 cup dried cranberries
1/2 cup raisins

Preheat oven to 350° F. Line 2 rimmed baking sheets with parchment paper. Mix first 5 ingredients in a large bowl. Warm honey and vanilla in a small pan and pour over dry mixture. Toss well and spread on baking sheets. Bake 25 to 30 minutes, stirring occasionally. Remove from oven and add dried fruit. Stir while cooling. Break apart and store in airtight container at room temperature.

Makes 8 cups

GLUTEN-FREE PIE CRUST

1-1/2 cups almond flour
3 tablespoons coconut flour
1/4 teaspoon salt
1/2 teaspoon ground cinnamon
1 egg
1/4 cup butter
1 teaspoon vanilla
2 tablespoons honey

HELPFUL HINTS
One pint blueberries equals 2 cups.

Preheat oven to 350° F. In a medium bowl, mix all ingredients together and press into a 9 inch pie pan. Bake 15 to 20 minutes until golden brown.

BERRY PIE

3 cups fresh blueberries, divided
3 cups fresh raspberries, divided
1/3 cup honey
1 tablespoon unflavored gelatin
1 tablespoon lemon juice
1 pie shell, cooked and cooled *(page 62)*
Whipped cream *(page 37)*

Wash berries and gently pat dry. Place 1/2 cup blueberries and 1/2 cup raspberries in a 2 quart pan. Add honey. Sprinkle gelatin over all. Bring to a boil on medium heat and cook 5 minutes, stirring constantly. Remove from heat and add lemon juice. Refrigerate until mixture begins to thicken around edges. Fold in remaining berries. Pour mixture into baked pie shell and chill 2 to 3 hours. Top with whipped cream before serving.

Makes 8 servings

BLUEBERRY CRISP

4 cups frozen blueberries
2 tablespoons lemon juice
2 tablespoons honey
1 tablespoon unflavored gelatin
TOPPING:
3/4 cup almond flour
2 tablespoons coconut flour
1/2 teaspoon salt
1 cup shredded coconut
3/4 cup chopped pecans
1/2 cup coconut oil
1/4 cup honey

Preheat oven to 350° F. In a medium bowl, stir blueberries, lemon juice, honey and gelatin together. Place in a 9 x 9 glass pan. Bake 30 minutes. Mix flours, salt, coconut and pecans together in a medium bowl. Warm coconut oil and honey in a small pan over low heat. Stir into dry ingredients. Sprinkle over berries. Bake an additional 20 to 25 minutes until golden brown. Cool 1 hour before serving.

Makes 9 servings

EATING PURE

Have you ever heard the phrase, "Butter is better?" Well, as it turns out, it really is! Butter is a natural healthy fat our bodies need every day. Bright yellow organic butter from grass-fed cows is the most nourishing.

Our grandson cannot have dairy, so we make ghee (clarified butter), which is pure milk fat and contains no milk protein or lactose. To make ghee, you simply bake unsalted butter in a glass pan for 1 hour at 225° F. The milk protein will separate and be at the bottom of the pan. A rich golden liquid (ghee) will be on the top. A crust usually forms on the very top, which I scoop off with a spoon and throw away. I then pour the ghee through a cheese cloth or a small strainer into a 2 cup glass jar, being careful to stop pouring before the white milk protein flows into the jar. Making ghee was one of the easiest things to incorporate into my schedule. I either do it as soon as I get up in the morning or right after supper when I'm in the kitchen cleaning up and preparing for the next day. It's amazing how fast that hour goes by, and the next thing you know, you're pouring it through the strainer. Ghee can be stored in your kitchen cabinet (several weeks) and can be used in any recipe calling for butter.

BROCCOLI

DIG INTO THIS!

Broccoli is a member of the cruciferous vegetable family and is closely related to cauliflower.

One cup raw chopped broccoli supplies your daily needed vitamin C.

Broccoli is very high in vitamin A and is rich in calcium, which helps maintain healthy skin, bones and teeth.

When cooking broccoli, fresh is best. The older the broccoli, the stronger the odor.

Save that stalk of broccoli! Use it shredded in slaws or chopped with florets.

If you have a hard time digesting raw broccoli, enjoy eating it cooked.

HOW DOES YOUR GARDEN GROW...?

* Days to maturity from transplant: 55 to 70.
* Broccoli grows best next to beets, carrots, cucumbers, lettuce, potatoes, spinach or tomatoes.
* It's best not to plant next to beans or strawberries.
* Start seedlings 4 to 6 weeks prior to planting. Sow 1/4 inch deep in starter mix and water well. Place in a sunny window.
* Seeds will begin to grow in 4 to 7 days.
* Broccoli plants can be purchased from your local nursery.
* Transplant seedlings in spring to mid-summer.
* Soil high in organic matter with soil pH around 7.0 is best.
* Plant about 18 inches apart in every direction as mature plants grow about 2-1/2 feet tall.
* Keep broccoli plants well watered.
* Harvest when head reaches the size of a large fist. (It will produce buds and yellow flowers if you wait too long.)
* Cut the head with about 4 inches of stalk.
* Some varieties of broccoli will continue to produce side shoots for several weeks after the main head has been harvested.
* Store fresh-washed broccoli in an open bag in the refrigerator up to 10 days.

Cabbage loopers are common pests of the brassica family of plants, including broccoli. There are several methods you can use to protect your plants: use row covers, hand pick insects, purchase organic insect spray at your local nursery, or use this spray.

NATURAL INSECT PEST SPRAY

10 cloves garlic, crushed
2 tablespoons cayenne pepper
4 cups water
1 tablespoon pure soap

Put the garlic, pepper and water in a pan and bring to a boil. Turn off burner and let sit 1 hour. Strain and put in a spray bottle. Add soap. Spray on leaves of plant once a week.

Grow it. Preserve it. Prepare it.

FREEZING BROCCOLI

1. Remove leaves and woody portions.

2. Separate heads and immerse in a brine (1 cup salt to 1 gallon water) 30 minutes to remove insects. Rinse and drain.

3. Blanch 3 minutes in boiling water. Drain and immerse in cold water until completely cool.

4. Drain and pack into freezer bags or containers.

5. Seal, label and freeze. *(Refer to freezing, page 26)*

Frozen broccoli can be tossed into soups and casseroles.

INSECT VEGETABLE WASH

1/4 cup vinegar
2 tablespoons salt

Put the vinegar and salt in a sink, half filled with cold water. Soak vegetables 5 to 10 minutes. Rinse with cold water and drain. This does not affect the flavor of the fruits or vegetables. The vinegar cleans and the salt draws out any dirt or small insects.

CREAM OF BROCCOLI SOUP

RECIPES

STEAMED BROCCOLI

1 large head broccoli
2 tablespoons butter
1 teaspoon lemon juice
1 teaspoon salt
1/4 teaspoon pepper

Wash broccoli and cut into florets. Steam 5 to 6 minutes in a covered pan *(refer to steaming, page 27)*. Broccoli is done when you can pierce it with a fork. Be careful not to overcook it. Transfer to a bowl. Toss with butter, lemon juice, salt and pepper.

Makes 4 to 6 servings

ROASTED BROCCOLI

1 large head broccoli
3 tablespoons butter or coconut oil, melted
1 clove minced garlic or 1/2 teaspoon garlic powder
Salt to taste

Preheat oven to 400° F. Wash, drain and separate broccoli into bite-sized florets (the smaller the pieces, the faster and crispier they will cook). Toss the chopped broccoli with melted butter or coconut oil and the garlic. Spread in a single layer on a rimmed baking sheet. Bake 15 to 20 minutes or until slightly brown around the tips. Sprinkle with salt and toss to coat evenly.

Makes 4 to 6 servings

VEGETABLE DILL DIP

3/4 cup plain yogurt *(page 236)*
3/4 cup sour cream
2 tablespoons dried dill weed
1 teaspoon onion powder
2 teaspoons seasoned salt *(page 125)*
1/8 teaspoon garlic powder

Mix all ingredients together in a medium bowl. Refrigerate 4 to 6 hours to allow flavors to meld. Serve with broccoli, carrots, cauliflower, etc.

Makes 2 cups

CREAM OF BROCCOLI SOUP

3 tablespoons butter
1 medium onion, chopped
1 celery stalk, chopped
1 large carrot, chopped
5 cups chicken broth *(page 158)*
5 cups broccoli, fresh or frozen
1-1/2 teaspoons dried thyme
1 clove garlic, minced
1 teaspoon salt
1/2 teaspoon pepper
1/2 cup heavy cream
1-1/2 cups shredded raw cheddar cheese
2 cups shredded cooked chicken, optional

In a large pot, sauté onions, celery and carrots in butter over medium heat 10 minutes. Add broth, broccoli and thyme. Cook an additional 10 to 15 minutes. Add garlic.

With an immersion blender, blend the soup until creamy. Add salt, pepper, cream and cheese. Add chicken if desired and reheat.

Makes 6 servings

DAIRY-FREE ALTERNATIVE:

Use ghee in place of butter (page 63). Omit cheddar cheese. Replace heavy cream by soaking 1 cup raw cashews in 1 additional cup of chicken broth while the soup cooks. Puree cashews and broth in a blender and add to soup.

HELPFUL HINTS

One pound of fresh broccoli equals 2 cups chopped.

BROCCOLI SALAD

1 large head broccoli
2 cups red grapes, halved, optional
3/4 cup raw cashews
6 slices crisp cooked bacon, crumbled
1/4 cup chopped red onion

DRESSING:

1 cup yogurt (page 236)
2 tablespoons apple cider vinegar
1/4 cup honey

Wash broccoli and separate into florets. Combine salad ingredients in a large serving bowl.

In a separate bowl, whisk together dressing ingredients. Add dressing to salad and toss to mix well. Chill 2 to 3 hours before serving.

Makes 4 to 6 servings

Bacon and other preserved meats that are cured using time-honored, traditional methods are the healthiest choices. We like to buy bacon made from pigs raised by local farmers. Visit the Local Harvest website to find a farmer near you.

BROCCOLI STIR-FRY

2 chicken breasts, cut in 1 inch pieces
1 small onion, sliced
2 cloves garlic, minced
3 tablespoons butter
2 tablespoons coconut aminos
1 tablespoon sesame oil
1/2 teaspoon ground ginger
2 teaspoons salt
1/4 teaspoon pepper
1/8 teaspoon cayenne pepper
5 cups broccoli florets
1/4 cup maple syrup

In a large skillet, sauté chicken, onion and garlic in butter 10 minutes. In a small bowl, mix together coconut aminos, sesame oil and spices. Pour over chicken. Add broccoli. Continue cooking 5 minutes. Pour maple syrup over all to glaze. Stir thoroughly. Heat through 2 to 3 minutes before serving. Serve alone, with cauliflower rice *(page 96)*, or with brown rice.

Makes 4 servings

ROASTED BROCCOLI AND SHRIMP

5 cups broccoli florets
1-1/2 pounds shrimp, peeled and deveined
2 tablespoons sesame oil
1-1/2 tablespoons lemon juice
1 teaspoon salt
1/4 teaspoon pepper
1/4 teaspoon crushed red pepper

Preheat oven to 425° F. Steam broccoli in a covered pan 3 minutes *(refer to steaming, page 27)*. In a large bowl, toss shrimp and broccoli with remaining ingredients. Place broccoli and shrimp in single layer on a rimmed baking sheet. Bake 8 minutes or until shrimp are done.

Makes 4 servings

EATING PURE

What is more picturesque than a herd of cows grazing in a thick, lush green pasture on a hillside? I married a dairy farmer a number of years ago and, oh, did I learn what life is like on a dairy farm! One memory I have is the daily arrival of fresh milk to the kitchen. We filled containers with milk straight from the bulk tank after the cows were milked! No pasteurization, no homogenization…just plain, raw milk full of rich vitamins, proteins and fats.

Today there is much debate regarding milk, whether it is good for you or bad for you. I encourage you to do some of your own research. Check out the pasteurization and homogenization processes for a possible loss of enzymes and beneficial bacteria that could occur when milk is processed. Growth hormones in milk is another controversial subject. Organic raw milk does not contain growth hormones found in most "regular" milk.

BRUSSELS SPROUTS

DIG INTO THIS!

Brussels sprouts are named after the city of Brussels; thus Brussels is always capitalized and ends with an "s".

Brussels sprouts grow on a tall stalk and can be stored up to 30 days if left on the stalk in a cool place.

Brussels sprouts are a great source of essential nutrients and proteins that fill you up, without filling you out.

Over boiling Brussels sprouts makes them soggy and tasteless.

Over steaming Brussels sprouts may cause them to become bitter tasting.

Each Brussels sprouts plant yields approximately a quart of sprouts.

HOW DOES YOUR GARDEN GROW...?

* Days to maturity: 90 to 110.
* Brussels sprouts grow best next to beets, carrots, cucumbers, lettuce, peas, potatoes, radishes, spinach or tomatoes.
* It's best not to plant next to strawberries or pole beans.
* Start seedlings 4 to 6 weeks before last frost. Sow seeds 1/4 inch deep in starter mix and water well. Place in a sunny window.
* Seeds will begin to grow in 5 to 8 days.
* Started plants can be purchased from your local nursery.
* Transplant seedlings in mid to late spring.
* Plant 18 to 20 inches apart in a staggered pattern with rows 24 inches apart.
* Fertilize every 3 to 4 weeks with an organic fertilizer such as fish emulsion.

* Harvest when the buds are firm and marble size (1/2 to 1 inch). Sprouts will mature starting from the bottom of the stalk.
* Remove the leaves below the sprout first, then snap the sprouts off the stalk.
* Store Brussels sprouts in a plastic bag in refrigerator up to 10 days.

Grow it.   Preserve it.   Prepare it.

FREEZING BRUSSELS SPROUTS

1. Remove coarse outer leaves; wash and sort into small, medium and large sprouts.

2. Blanch small sprouts 3 minutes, medium sprouts 4 minutes and large sprouts 5 minutes in boiling water.

3. Drain and immerse in cold water until completely cool.

4. Drain and pack into freezer bags or containers.

5. Seal, label and freeze.
   (Refer to freezing, page 26)

It is important to use a vegetable wash (page 66) **on Brussels sprouts to remove grit and critters between leaves.**

HELPFUL HINTS

One pound Brussels sprouts equals about 4 cups whole sprouts.

ROASTED BRUSSELS SPROUTS

STEAMED BRUSSELS SPROUTS

1-1/2 pounds Brussels sprouts
1 teaspoon salt
1/4 teaspoon pepper
3 tablespoons butter

Wash, trim and cut Brussels sprouts in quarters. Steam 6 to 8 minutes in a covered pan, tossing halfway through *(refer to steaming, page 27)*. Transfer to a bowl. Toss with butter, salt and pepper.

Makes 6 servings

SAUTÉED BRUSSELS SPROUTS WITH BACON

8 slices bacon, cooked
2 tablespoons reserved bacon drippings
2 tablespoons butter
2 pounds Brussels sprouts, sliced in food processor
1 small red onion, chopped
1-1/2 teaspoons salt
1/2 teaspoon pepper

Fry bacon in a skillet, cool and crumble. In the same skillet, sauté Brussels sprouts with chopped onion in butter and bacon drippings, covered, on low to medium heat 20 minutes. Remove cover and continue cooking until slightly browned. Toss in bacon, salt and pepper.

Makes 6 to 8 servings

ROASTED BRUSSELS SPROUTS

1-1/2 pounds Brussels sprouts
3 tablespoons butter, melted
3/4 teaspoon salt
1/2 teaspoon pepper

Preheat oven to 400° F. Wash and cut off brown ends of Brussels sprouts and pull off any yellow outer leaves. Put in a bowl with the rest of ingredients and toss to coat. Roast on a rimmed baking sheet 35 to 40 minutes until crisp on the outside and tender on the inside. *Note: Shake pan from time to time to brown evenly.*

Makes 6 servings

CHEESY BRUSSELS SPROUTS

2 tablespoons butter
3-1/2 cups shredded Brussels sprouts
1 teaspoon salt
1/4 teaspoon red pepper flakes
1/2 teaspoon pepper
3/4 cup heavy cream
3/4 cup shredded raw cheddar cheese
1/4 cup grated Parmesan cheese

Preheat oven to 400° F. Melt butter in an 8 x 8 glass baking dish for 2 minutes as oven is preheating. Bring water to a boil in a medium pot. Add salt and Brussels sprouts. Cover and boil 5 minutes. Drain. Transfer to baking dish. Sprinkle with red pepper flakes and pepper. Pour cream on top and sprinkle with cheese. Bake uncovered 25 to 30 minutes until golden brown.

Makes 4 to 6 servings

Years ago, every farm kitchen had lard on hand at all times. Today, many people don't know that good quality, pure lard is still a good source of vitamin D. Use it occasionally for frying and sautéing on medium-high heat.

CABBAGE

DIG INTO THIS!

Drinking a few sips of cabbage juice before a meal aids digestion and assists in healing stomach and intestinal ulcers.

Cabbage is very low in calories and high in fiber and iron—a winning combination.

How to cut and core a cabbage: Cut the stem off cabbage head. Cut in half through the stem, then in half again through the stem. Now you have a wedge with the core at one end. Stand cabbage on core end and cut core out.

Use a stainless steel knife when cutting cabbage to prevent cabbage from turning black.

Once cabbage is cut, use within 2 days, or trim off dark areas.

HOW DOES YOUR GARDEN GROW...?

* Days to maturity: 65 to 95 depending upon variety.

* Cabbage grows best next to beets, bush beans, carrots, cucumbers, lettuce, onions, potatoes or spinach.

* It's best not to plant next to pole beans, strawberries or tomatoes.

* Start seedlings 4 to 6 weeks before last frost. Sow seeds 1/4 inch deep in seed starter mix and water well. Place in a sunny window.

* Seeds will begin to grow in 5 days.

* Cabbage plants can be purchased from your local nursery.

* A healthy cabbage plant requires full sun to grow. Transplant seedlings in early spring on a cloudy day to prevent wilting.

* Plant early and late varieties to ensure harvest throughout the season.

* Plant 12 to 18 inches apart, depending on variety.

* Plant oregano and rosemary near cabbage to keep cabbage moths away.

* Overwatering can lead to damaged plants or split heads.

* To prevent bug infestation, spray weekly with insect spray until 1 week from harvest. *(page 65)*

* Cabbage heads are prone to crack under stresses such as weather and growing too large. To prevent splitting, twist the head and pull up to slightly dislodge roots and slow plant's growth.

* Harvest early varieties of cabbage when head reaches softball size by cutting at the base with a sharp knife.

* Harvest late varieties of cabbage by cutting at the base and removing the limp lower leaves.

* Store cabbage in a plastic bag in refrigerator several weeks.

Grow it.   Preserve it.   Prepare it.

FREEZING CABBAGE

1. Choose a solid cabbage head with crisp green leaves. Wash and discard the outer leaves.

2. Cut head into wedges and core. Shred coarsely if desired.

3. Blanch wedges 3 minutes or shredded 1-1/2 minutes in boiling water.

4. Drain and immerse in cold water until completely cool.

5. Drain and pack into freezer bags or containers.

6. Seal, label and freeze.
   (Refer to freezing, page 26)

Frozen cabbage can be tossed into soups and casseroles.

HELPFUL HINTS

1 medium head of cabbage is about 2 pounds. 2 pounds of cabbage equals approximately 10 cups shredded.

COLESLAW

COLESLAW

4 cups shredded cabbage
1 cup shredded carrots

DRESSING:
1/2 cup plain yogurt *(page 236)*
1/2 cup mayonnaise *(page 77)*
1 tablespoon apple cider vinegar
2 tablespoons honey
1/2 teaspoon salt
1/4 teaspoon pepper
1/8 teaspoon celery seed
1/8 teaspoon garlic powder

Place cabbage and carrots in a medium bowl. In a separate bowl, whisk together dressing ingredients. Stir into cabbage and carrots.

Makes 6 servings

VARIATION:

For a colorful twist, stir prepared dressing into 1 cup shredded red cabbage, 2 cups shredded broccoli stalks, 1 cup sliced Brussels sprouts and 1 cup shredded carrots.

MAYONNAISE

1 egg yolk, use organic store bought
1 teaspoon cold water
1 tablespoon apple cider vinegar
1/4 teaspoon dry mustard
1 tablespoon honey
Pinch of garlic powder
1/2 teaspoon salt
1/8 teaspoon pepper
1/2 cup olive oil
1/4 cup sesame oil

Place all ingredients, in order listed, into a small bowl. With an immersion blender, slowly blend until creamy. Store in a glass container in refrigerator up to 2 weeks.

Makes 1 cup

VARIATION:

To make avocado mayonnaise, substitute 3/4 cup avocado oil for the olive and sesame oils. It's a great way to incorporate another healthy fat into your diet!

Do you experience gas and bloating when eating cabbage, broccoli, or beans? These are a few of the foods that contain an indigestible sugar that cannot be broken down in our small intestines. It gets passed to our large intestines where bacteria will try to break it down. You may experience more or less gas depending on the health of your gut bacteria. Try eating more yogurt, kefir or probiotics to boost the good bacteria, making digestion easier with minimal gas.

SAUERKRAUT

1 head cabbage
2 tablespoons salt
Half-gallon jar

Wash cabbage, remove outer leaves (save for later). Cut into thin shreds with food processor or sharp knife. (Make sure all tools are sanitized with boiling water before starting.)

Put cabbage shreds into a large glass bowl. Add salt and let sit 15 minutes. With clean hands or a wooden spoon, press down and massage cabbage until it breaks down and juice is flowing well.

Pack tightly into a half gallon jar. Place large outer leaves on top. Make sure cabbage is completely submerged under juice. Put lid on jar, screw down loosely. Place jar on a plate and place in dark corner of kitchen for one week.

It's not uncommon for a layer of mold to develop on the outer leaves. This does not mean your sauerkraut is ruined. Simply discard the layer of mold and everything underneath the brine should be safe. However, if it smells bad, don't eat it.

After one week, allow sauerkraut to mellow for one month in refrigerator before eating. Sauerkraut will keep many months in refrigerator.

Heating raw, naturally fermented sauerkraut will destroy all the probiotic benefits in a matter of seconds. Eat it cold to receive the natural occurring rich probiotics.

ROASTED CABBAGE

1 head of cabbage, washed
1/2 cup butter, melted
1-1/2 teaspoons salt
1/2 teaspoon pepper

Preheat oven to 375° F. Slice cabbage into 6 to 8 wedges. Lay wedges on a rimmed baking sheet. Drizzle with butter and season with salt and pepper. Bake 20 to 30 minutes until tender and golden brown. Serve immediately.

Makes 6 to 8 servings

SAUTÉED CABBAGE AND BACON

3 slices bacon, chopped
1/2 head of cabbage, shredded
2 tablespoons water
1 teaspoon honey
1/2 teaspoon salt
1/8 teaspoon pepper
1 tablespoon apple cider vinegar, optional

Place bacon in a large skillet. Fry over medium-high heat until crisp. Remove bacon and set aside. Add cabbage to bacon grease. Stir in water, honey, salt and pepper. Cook 15 minutes until cabbage wilts. Stir in bacon and sprinkle with vinegar before serving.

Makes 6 servings

VEGETABLE BEEF SOUP

1-1/2 lbs. ground beef
1 onion, chopped
2 cloves garlic, minced
2 quarts beef broth *(page 158)*
1 teaspoon salt
1/2 teaspoon pepper
1/2 head cabbage, cored and chopped
2 cups sliced carrots
3 stalks of celery, sliced
2 cups tomato juice *(page 254)*
2 bay leaves
1 cup green beans, fresh or frozen
1 cup garden peas, fresh or frozen
1 tablespoon dried parsley, optional

In a large skillet, brown beef with onion and garlic over medium-high heat. Transfer to a large stock pot and add all ingredients except green beans, peas and parsley. Bring to a boil over medium-high heat. Reduce heat, cover and simmer 45 to 60 minutes. Add green beans, peas and parsley. Continue cooking an additional 10 minutes. Remove bay leaves before serving.

This is an excellent soup to cook in a slow cooker on low 8 to 10 hours. Toss in green beans and peas 5 to 10 minutes before serving.

Makes 8 servings

EATING PURE

Probiotics is a term you hear more and more. It is live, healthy bacteria which aide in digestion. People received that good bacteria years ago from eating fermented foods. The term "fermented" is a preservation method that breaks down carbohydrates and proteins using microorganisms such as bacteria, molds and yeast. This process produces delicious foods like kimchi, kombucha, raw cheese, raw olives, raw pickles, sauerkraut and yogurt. The probiotics found in homemade sauerkraut can far exceed over-the-counter processed probiotics.

ORIENTAL SALAD

3 cups shredded cabbage
1 cup shredded carrots
2/3 cup slivered almonds
2/3 cup cashews
2/3 cup sunflower seeds
2 tablespoons sesame oil

DRESSING:

1/2 cup sesame oil
3 tablespoons maple syrup
2 tablespoons red wine vinegar
1 tablespoon coconut aminos
1 teaspoon salt
1/4 teaspoon pepper
1/8 teaspoon ground ginger
1/4 teaspoon turmeric
1/4 teaspoon onion powder

Place cabbage and carrots in a large bowl. In a large skillet, roast nuts and seeds in oil over medium-low heat. Stir constantly 10 minutes until golden brown. Add to salad. In a small bowl, whisk together dressing ingredients and pour over salad before serving.

This is a great salad to make ahead of time—store salad and dressing in separate containers in refrigerator and toss together right before serving.

Makes 4 to 6 servings

ORIENTAL SALAD

RECIPES

SAUSAGE AND CABBAGE STIR-FRY

1 pound ground pork or beef

3 cloves garlic, minced

1 teaspoon grated fresh ginger

1-1/2 teaspoons poultry seasoning *(page 127)*

1/4 teaspoon cayenne pepper

1 teaspoon salt

2 tablespoons coconut aminos

3 tablespoons honey

5 cups shredded cabbage

3/4 cup shredded carrots

1/2 cup chopped celery

Asian Sauce, optional *(see below)*

In a large skillet, brown pork with next 5 ingredients. Stir in coconut aminos and honey. Add cabbage, carrots and celery. Cook over medium heat until vegetables are cooked through, but still have some crunch. Serve alone or with rice. Top with Asian Sauce if desired.

Makes 4 servings

ASIAN SAUCE

1/2 cup cold water

1/2 teaspoon unflavored gelatin

1/4 cup orange juice

1/4 cup maple syrup

1/4 cup red wine vinegar

1 tablespoon coconut aminos

1 tablespoon sesame oil

In a small saucepan, sprinkle gelatin over water. Let stand 1 minute to soften. Cook over low heat until dissolved. Remove from heat. Stir in remaining ingredients. Store in a glass container in refrigerator. This is good drizzled over cabbage stir-fry, rice, noodles, or a lettuce wrap with shredded chicken, carrots and cashews.

Makes 1 cup

CABBAGE SALAD

4 cups shredded cabbage

1 cup shredded carrots

1/2 cup green onions, thinly sliced

1 shredded green apple, optional

DRESSING:

1 tablespoon sesame oil

1/4 cup lime juice

2 tablespoons honey

1-1/2 teaspoons apple cider vinegar

1/4 teaspoon ground ginger

1/4 teaspoon salt

Combine dressing ingredients in a blender and blend until smooth.

Place salad ingredients in a large bowl. Toss with dressing. Marinate 30 minutes in refrigerator.

Makes 4 servings

To prepare fresh ginger root, simply peel with a paring knife and grate or mince into your favorite vegetables, stir-fries, teas, juice drinks, etc. Ginger root is immune boosting, anti-inflammatory, and aids in digestion. If left unpeeled, ginger root can be stored in the refrigerator up to 3 weeks or in the freezer for 6 months.

CANTALOUPE

DIG INTO THIS!

Guess what? Grandma was right! They aren't really "cantaloupe." The melon that's most widely recognized in the U.S. is actually a muskmelon. It has netted skin and a strong scent. The true cantaloupe has ribbed pale green skin and is rarely grown outside of Europe. Since most people refer to muskmelon as cantaloupe, we'll continue to refer to them as such.

Cantaloupe is packed full of beneficial nutrients such as vitamins C, A and K, potassium and magnesium.

An average size melon contains just 100 calories. Who knew something so sweet could be good for you?!

Cantaloupe are the most popular melon in the United States.

HOW DOES YOUR GARDEN GROW...?

❋ Days to maturity from direct seed: 85 to 90. Days to maturity from transplant: 75 to 80.

❋ Cantaloupe does best planted next to sweet corn.

❋ It's best not to plant next to potatoes.

❋ Melons love heat and the soil temperature should be 70° F to 90° F when planting.

❋ Seeds can be planted in hills. Space hills 24 inches apart with 3 seeds per hill, thinning later to 1 plant per hill.

❋ Plant seeds 1/2 inch deep, 16 inches apart.

❋ Seeds will begin to grow in 3 to 5 days.

❋ Started plants can also be purchased from your local nursery.

❋ Melons are particular about soil pH. Use a complete organic fertilizer—fish emulsion or kelp from the time you transplant until fruit sets on the vine.

❋ Water evenly, but not too much throughout the season. Check soil moisture frequently—it should not be too dry or too wet.

❋ Most melons are ripe when the rind changes from gray-green to yellow-buff and gentle thumb pressure easily separates the vine from the stem.

❋ Store cantaloupe in refrigerator 5 to 10 days or up to 15 days if freshly picked.

Successful gardeners will tell you planning and preparing your garden starts in the fall. Pick the right location for your plants. Sunshine and good quality soil are key. Most plants require at least six hours of full sun to produce a good crop. Leafy crops, like lettuce and spinach, can tolerate less sun than fruit bearing crops such as tomatoes and peppers.

Next, consider the garden soil. A soil test can help you determine the levels of nutrients in your soil. This easy-to-use kit can be purchased at your local nursery or your local extension office. In the fall, work in organic matter, like leaves and pine needles, to create an optimal seed bed for spring planting.

Grow it. Preserve it. Prepare it.

Fruit flies are attracted to ripened fruits and vegetables in our kitchen and like to breed in drains, garbage disposals, trash bins, open bottles, etc. Try to keep things as clean as possible and if you still experience them, use this recipe to get rid of the little pests.

FRUIT FLY RECIPE

1/2 cup apple cider vinegar
1 tablespoon honey, or small piece of over ripe, old fruit
3 drops dishwashing soap

Place vinegar, honey and soap in a small jar. Puncture 1/8 inch holes in lid, screw on securely and set on counter. (You can also use plastic wrap with holes punctured in it and secured to jar top with a rubber band.)

If you use ripe fruit instead of honey, place vinegar and soap in jar. Add the fruit, making sure it sticks out of the liquid. Cover and place where you would normally see fruit flies.

Every 2 to 3 days, dump contents and make a fresh batch until you no longer see fruit flies.

HELPFUL HINTS

An average cantaloupe equals approximately 4 to 6 cups cubed.

CANTALOUPE
BLACKBERRY SALAD

MELON PEACH
SMOOTHIE

MELON PEACH SMOOTHIE

1/2 cup vanilla yogurt *(page 236)*
1/2 teaspoon vanilla
2 medium ripe peaches, sliced
2 cups cubed cantaloupe
1/2 cup ice cubes

Place all ingredients in a blender in order listed and blend until smooth. This is also good with whole blueberries tossed in after blending.

Makes 2 servings

CANTALOUPE AND GRILLED CHICKEN SALAD

2 boneless, skinless chicken breasts
1 teaspoon salt
8 cups salad greens, washed and chopped
1/2 cantaloupe, cut in 1 inch chunks
1 cup fresh raspberries
2 kiwis, sliced
1/3 cup chopped walnuts
Raspberry vinaigrette *(page 150)*

Preheat grill. Cut chicken breasts into 1 inch strips. Sprinkle salt on chicken and grill 10 minutes, turning once. Remove from grill and chop into bite size pieces. Place remaining ingredients in a large bowl. Add chicken and toss with dressing.

Makes 4 servings

CANTALOUPE BLACKBERRY SALAD

1/2 cantaloupe, cut in 1 inch chunks
2 cups blackberries
1 tablespoon honey
1 teaspoon fresh, grated ginger
1 tablespoon lime juice

Place cantaloupe and blackberries in a large bowl. In a separate bowl, mix together honey, ginger and lime juice. Pour over salad and toss. Cover and let sit 30 minutes.

Makes 4 servings

DOUBLE CHOCOLATE CHIP COOKIES

2 eggs
1/4 cup coconut oil
1/4 cup water
1 tablespoon vanilla
1 cup date sugar
1/4 cup cocoa
1/2 teaspoon salt
1 teaspoon baking soda
1 cup almond flour
2 cups rolled oats, ground
1/2 cup dark chocolate chips
1/2 cup chopped walnuts, optional

Preheat oven to 350° F. In a large bowl, beat eggs with mixer until frothy. Mix in oil, water and vanilla. Add next 6 ingredients and beat well—dough will be stiff. Stir in chips and walnuts. Drop by large teaspoonfuls onto parchment lined baking sheet. Flatten slightly. Bake 10 minutes. Remove from oven and let sit on baking sheet 5 minutes before placing on cooling rack.

Makes 2-1/2 dozen

We're back to reading labels again. Gluten is a hidden ingredient in many foods. Oats, vanilla and chocolate are three examples where cross-contamination can occur in processing facilities. Labels can tell you if it has been processed in a facility that also processes wheat, barley and rye.

CARROTS

DIG INTO THIS!

Carrots come in a variety of colors–orange, purple, white, yellow and red.

Carrots are loaded with beta-carotene and vitamin E. You will receive the greatest health benefits from these antioxidants when you eat carrots raw.

Cooking carrots breaks down fiber, making it more usable to the body. However, overcooking destroys some nutrients.

Carrots that become dry with a white appearance can be rehydrated by soaking in cold water for a short period of time.

Pureed carrots are one of the first solid foods to introduce into your baby's diet.

To peel or not to peel? If not organically grown, it is best to peel carrots.

HOW DOES YOUR GARDEN GROW...?

* Days to maturity: 55 to 75.
* Plant carrots next to beans, Brussels sprouts, cabbage, leeks, onions, peas, peppers or tomatoes.
* It's best not to plant next to dill, celery or parsnips.
* Sow seeds 1/4 inch to 1/2 inch deep in early spring through early July.
* Plant in rows 6 to 8 inches apart.
* Seeds will begin to grow in 6 to 10 days.
* Keep soil moist throughout the germination period.
* Thin to 2 inches apart.
* Harvest by pulling carrots from ground (pre-loosen soil with garden fork if tops break off) and cutting off the greens leaving about 1 inch of stem.
* Store in refrigerator away from apples, pears and potatoes as these may cause carrots to become bitter.

Wondering how to store carrots for a longer period of time? Place unwashed carrots in a large plastic container with holes drilled in lid. Spread 1 inch of damp sand on bottom and lay carrots in single layer so they aren't touching.

Cover with another inch of sand and repeat layer by layer. Store in cool, dark place (32° F to 40° F) and check often to make sure sand is damp, but not wet.

Grow it. Preserve it. Prepare it.

FREEZING CARROTS

1. Wash, peel and wash carrots again.

2. Slice or quarter carrots.

3. Blanch sliced carrots 3 minutes, or quartered carrots 5 minutes in boiling water.

4. Drain and immerse in cold water until completely cool.

5. Drain and pack into freezer bags or containers.

6. Seal, label and freeze. *(Refer to freezing, page 26)*

HELPFUL HINTS

One pound of fresh carrots equals 6 to 8 medium carrots, 4 cups shredded, or 6 cups sliced.

One of the most convenient snack foods for children are baby carrots. We recommend cutting whole carrots into snack-size sticks to receive the most nutrients and avoid the solutions used in processing baby carrots.

CARROT PINEAPPLE JUICE DRINK

RECIPES

CARROT PINEAPPLE JUICE DRINK

2 carrots
2 stalks celery
1/8-1/4 small beet
1/8 pineapple

Wash and cut ends off carrots, celery and beet. Cut pineapple in half lengthwise, quarter and cut off outside skin leaving inside core. Juice all ingredients in a juicer.

Makes 1 serving

Bromelain in fresh (not canned) pineapple has been shown to promote joint health.

PINEAPPLE CARROT SALAD

2 cups shredded carrots
2/3 cup chopped pineapple
1/2 cup raisins

DRESSING:

2 tablespoons coconut milk
1/4 teaspoon turmeric
1 tablespoon honey
1 tablespoon lemon juice
1 tablespoon olive oil

Place carrots, pineapple and raisins in a large bowl. In a small bowl, whisk dressing ingredients together. Pour over salad and mix well.

Makes 4 servings

CARROT RAISIN SALAD

2 cups shredded carrots
1/2 cup raisins
1/4 cup mayonnaise *(page 77)*
1 tablespoon honey
1 tablespoon coconut milk

Place carrots and raisins in a medium bowl. In a small bowl, combine remaining ingredients and pour over salad. Stir and serve.

Makes 4 servings

CARROT GINGER SOUP

2 tablespoons butter, melted
1-1/2 to 2 onions, peeled and quartered
5 cloves garlic
6 cups chicken broth *(page 158)*
6 cups sliced carrots
2 tablespoons grated fresh ginger
1 teaspoon salt
1/2 teaspoon pepper
2 teaspoons ground coriander, optional
1 cup coconut milk

Preheat oven to 400° F. Place quartered onions and garlic in a 9 x 9 glass pan and pour melted butter on top. Bake 20 to 30 minutes until slightly brown.

Place broth, carrots, ginger and spices in a stockpot. Cover and bring to a boil. Reduce heat and simmer 15 to 20 minutes until carrots are tender. Add onions and garlic. Continue simmering until all are tender. Add coconut milk. Puree with an immersion blender (or regular blender) until smooth.

Makes 6 to 8 servings

New on the scene are coconut products— milk, water, oil, flour and sugar. Coconuts add healthy nutrients to your diet including lauric acid, which is antiviral, antibacterial, antifungal and boosts the immune system. Lauric acid, is also found in mother's breast milk, making coconut milk an excellent addition when you begin incorporating food into your baby's diet. For a delicious morning treat, add a little coconut milk with a dash of vanilla to your coffee.

RECIPES

STEAMED CARROTS

1 pound carrots, sliced
2 tablespoons butter
1 teaspoon salt
1/4 teaspoon pepper

Steam washed and prepared carrots in a covered pan 8 to 10 minutes until crisp-tender *(refer to steaming, page 27)*. Transfer to a bowl. Add butter, salt and pepper.

Makes 4 servings

ROASTED CARROTS

10 to 12 carrots, peeled, halved and cut lengthwise
3 tablespoons butter, melted
1 teaspoon salt
1/4 teaspoon pepper

Heat oven to 400° F. In a medium bowl, toss together carrots, butter, salt and pepper. Arrange carrots in a 9 x 13 glass pan. Bake 30 minutes. Take pan out of oven and stir. Roast additional 10 minutes until carrots are lightly browned.

Makes 4 to 6 servings

GLAZED CARROTS

3 cups sliced carrots
1/2 cup water
1/2 teaspoon salt
3 tablespoons butter
3 tablespoons maple syrup
1/3 cup chopped pecans, optional

Place all ingredients except pecans in a large skillet. Bring to a boil. Reduce heat and simmer 12 minutes until liquid evaporates. Continue cooking 2 to 3 minutes, stirring constantly, to caramelize. Sprinkle with pecans.

Makes 4 servings

SUMMER GARDEN CASSEROLE

4 to 5 medium red potatoes, sliced
2 carrots, sliced
2 cups green beans, fresh or frozen
3 cups shredded cabbage
1 pound ground beef
1 medium onion, chopped
1 teaspoon salt
1/2 teaspoon pepper
1 small to medium zucchini, sliced
2 cups tomato sauce *(page 256)*

Preheat oven to 350° F. In a large skillet, brown beef with onion. Wash and slice vegetables. In a 6 quart covered baking dish, place ingredients in layers in order listed. Bake covered, 1 to 1-1/2 hours. Stir and serve.

Makes 6 to 8 servings

CARAMEL COCONUT FROSTING

2 tablespoons coconut oil
2 tablespoons butter
1/4 cup maple syrup
1/4 cup heavy cream or coconut milk
1 teaspoon vanilla
1/2 cup shredded coconut
1/4 cup chopped walnuts

In a small pan, low boil coconut oil, butter, maple syrup and cream 15 minutes on medium-high heat. Stir in vanilla, coconut and walnuts. Cool before spreading on cake.

Frosts 8 x 8 cake

CARROT CAKE

4 large eggs
1/4 cup coconut oil
1/4 cup coconut milk
5 Medjool dates, pitted and chopped
1 cup shredded carrots
1 cup shredded apple *(approx. 2 medium apples)*
1/2 cup date sugar
2 teaspoons vanilla
1/3 cup coconut flour
1/2 teaspoon ground cinnamon
1-1/2 teaspoons pumpkin pie spice *(page 189)*
3/4 teaspoon baking soda
1/2 teaspoon salt
1/4 cup walnuts

Heat oven to 350° F. In a large bowl, beat eggs with mixer until frothy. Mix in oil and milk. Add dates, carrots, apples, sugar and vanilla. Mix in remaining dry ingredients and nuts. Pour in an 8 x 8 buttered glass pan. Bake 40 to 45 minutes. Cool and frost with Caramel Coconut Frosting.

Makes 9 servings

VARIATION:
This recipe can also be used for muffins. Place muffin baking liners in muffin tin and fill liners with mixture. Bake 25 minutes at 350° F.

Makes 8 to 10 muffins

Note: A food processor can be used to chop dates, shred carrots and shred apples.

By doubling recipes and freezing one, you can have a meal prepared in advance when you're in a pinch for time. Both the baked Summer Garden Casserole and Carrot Cake are great recipes to double and freeze.

CAULIFLOWER

DIG INTO THIS!

Cauliflower is one of the cruciferous vegetables which should be included in your diet several times a week to receive fantastic health benefits.

Antioxidants are nature's way of providing nutrients to your cells, and cauliflower is full of antioxidants to help fight free-radicals in your body.

Sautéing cauliflower, rather than boiling or steaming, prevents it from becoming waterlogged, mushy and flavorless.

Cauliflower is a low calorie vegetable.

Cooked cauliflower spoils quickly. Consume within 2 to 3 days.

Store full heads of cauliflower in a bag in refrigerator up to 7 days. Store precut florets 1 to 2 days.

HOW DOES YOUR GARDEN GROW...?

* Days to maturity: 65 to 80.
* Cauliflower grows best next to beets, bush beans, carrots, cucumbers, lettuce, onions, potatoes, spinach or tomatoes.
* It's best not to plant next to pole beans or strawberries.
* Start seedlings 4 to 6 weeks before last frost. Sow seeds 1/4 inch deep in seed starter mix and water well. Place in a sunny window.
* Seeds will begin to grow in 6 days.
* Started plants can be purchased from your local nursery.
* Transplant seedlings in late spring.
* Space 20 inches apart.

* Cauliflower requires consistent soil moisture. Water 1 to 1-1/2 inches each week.
* Fertilize frequently with compost tea (see below) or diluted solutions of fish emulsion or kelp fertilizers.
* To prevent unappealing yellow or "ricey" texture heads, fold some of the leaves over the head (when it's 2 to 3 inches wide) and secure leaves together at top with rubber bands or twine, or plant a variety where this occurs naturally.
* In warm weather, harvest heads about 4 to 7 days after securing leaves over cauliflower. In cool weather, harvest in about 10 days. Keep checking heads daily to prevent rotting.

COMPOST TEA

Compost tea can be made from 2 quarts mature compost and 2 quarts water mixed in an ice cream pail. Place in a cool spot and stir daily up to 5 days before using. Strain liquid from compost and use immediately without further dilution.

Compost tea should be made from mature, earthy-smelling compost that's at least a year old. If there is an unpleasant odor, don't use it. **NEVER APPLY COMPOST TEA TO ANY VEGETABLE WITHIN 3 WEEKS OF HARVEST.**

Grow it. Preserve it. Prepare it.

FREEZING CAULIFLOWER

1. Remove outer leaves and cut into florets about 1 inch across. Wash and drain.

2. Place cauliflower in brine made up of 1 cup salt to 1 gallon of water. Soak 30 minutes (to remove insects). Rinse and drain.

3. Blanch 3 minutes in boiling water. Drain and cool completely.

4. Pack into freezer bags or containers. Seal, label and freeze. *(Refer to freezing, page 26)*

Frozen cauliflower can be tossed into soups and casseroles.

HELPFUL HINTS

An average cauliflower head is 2 pounds and equals 6 cups shredded cauliflower.

Overcooking vegetables leads to valuable nutrients getting destroyed. To avoid losing their healthy properties, it is best to eat vegetables raw. The next best method is lightly steamed.

CAULIFLOV
BROCCOLI SA
AND CHICKEN T

SAUTÉED CAULIFLOWER

1 large head cauliflower
1/3 cup butter
1 clove garlic, minced
2 tablespoons lemon juice
1/4 teaspoon salt
1 tablespoon chopped fresh parsley

Wash cauliflower, remove outer leaves and cut into florets. In a large skillet, sauté cauliflower and garlic in butter 8 to 10 minutes. Place in a serving bowl and sprinkle with lemon juice, salt and parsley.

Makes 6 servings

ROASTED CAULIFLOWER

1 medium head cauliflower,
washed and cut into 1-1/2 inch florets
1/4 cup sesame oil
2 cloves garlic, sliced
2 tablespoons lemon juice
1 teaspoon salt
1/2 teaspoon pepper
1/4 cup grated Parmesan cheese
Chopped chives, optional

Preheat oven to 400° F. Toss cauliflower with oil, garlic, lemon juice, salt and pepper. Place on a rimmed baking sheet. Bake 15 minutes, stirring occasionally. Remove from oven and sprinkle with cheese. Roast 5 minutes. Garnish with chives.

Makes 6 servings

CAULIFLOWER BROCCOLI SALAD

4 cups cauliflower florets
4 cups broccoli florets
1 cup raisins, optional
1 cup sunflower seeds
1/2 cup chopped red onion
6 slices crisp cooked bacon, crumbled
1 cup shredded raw cheddar cheese, optional

DRESSING:

1 cup yogurt *(page 236)*
or mayonnaise *(page 77)*
1/4 cup honey
2 tablespoons apple cider vinegar
1/4 teaspoon salt
1/8 teaspoon pepper

Wash cauliflower and broccoli, remove outer leaves and cut into florets. Combine all salad ingredients in a large bowl. Stir dressing ingredients together in a small bowl and pour over salad. Toss and enjoy!

Makes 6 to 8 servings

STEAMED CAULIFLOWER

1 large head cauliflower
2 tablespoons butter
1 teaspoon salt

Wash cauliflower, remove outer leaves and cut into florets. Steam cauliflower in a covered pan 5 to 7 minutes or until tender *(refer to steaming, page 27)*. Transfer to a bowl. Add butter and salt.

Makes 4 to 6 servings

For a thick, rich yogurt to use in dressing or dip recipes, let yogurt drip overnight.
Place a strainer on top of a bowl. Insert a natural brown coffee filter and fill with yogurt.
Let yogurt drip overnight in the refrigerator. You will be amazed the next day to discover how much
liquid (whey) has dripped out! The yogurt will now have a thick consistency like sour cream.

VEGGIE
RICE

RECIPES

CAULIFLOWER RICE

1 head cauliflower
2 tablespoons butter
1/3 cup chopped onion
2 cloves garlic, minced
1/3 cup water
1 teaspoon salt

Wash cauliflower, remove outer leaves and cut into large florets. Shred in a food processor or with a hand grater. In a large skillet, sauté onion and garlic in butter over medium-high heat 3 minutes. Add cauliflower and sauté 5 minutes. Add water and salt. Cover and continue cooking 5 to 8 minutes until water is absorbed.

Makes 4 to 6 servings

VARIATION: Add your favorite spices and ingredients to make Mexican rice or fried rice.

VEGGIE RICE

2 tablespoons butter
1/2 cup chopped onion
1/2 large head cauliflower, shredded
1 small head broccoli, chopped
1/2 red bell pepper, chopped
1 carrot, chopped
3/4 teaspoon salt
1/4 cup water
1 tablespoon apple cider vinegar
1 teaspoon toasted or plain sesame oil

In a large skillet, sauté onion in butter 5 minutes over medium-high heat. Add cauliflower, broccoli, red pepper and carrot. Continue cooking 5 minutes. Add salt and water. Cover and cook 5 to 8 minutes until water is absorbed. Combine vinegar and sesame oil. Stir into rice and serve.

Makes 6 servings

MASHED CAULIFLOWER

1 head cauliflower, washed and cut into florets
5 cloves garlic
1/4 cup butter
1 teaspoon salt
1/8 teaspoon pepper

Steam florets and whole garlic cloves 10 to 15 minutes until tender. Place in a food processor or a blender with remaining ingredients. Blend until smooth. Delicious!

Makes 4 to 6 servings

VARIATION:
Kids love cheese and crumbled bacon added to this dish.

EASY EGG BAKE

4 cups shredded cauliflower, fresh or frozen
2 cups shredded raw cheddar cheese
1 pound bacon, cooked and crumbled
1/2 cup chopped onion
1 cup chopped red pepper, optional
1 teaspoon salt
1/4 teaspoon pepper
12 eggs, beaten
1/4 cup chopped chives, optional

Preheat oven to 350° F. In a large bowl, stir together all ingredients except eggs and chives. Place in a buttered 9 x 13 glass pan. Pour eggs evenly over mixture and sprinkle with chives. Cover and bake 50 to 60 minutes. Allow dish to set 8 minutes before serving.

Makes 10 to 12 servings

CAULIFLOWER AND CHEESE CASSEROLE

1 large head cauliflower, washed and cut into small florets
1 tablespoon butter
1/2 cup heavy cream
1 1/2 teaspoons seasoned salt *(page 125)*
2 tablespoons quinoa flour
1 cup shredded raw cheddar cheese

Preheat oven to 400° F. Combine all ingredients in a large bowl. Place in a 2 quart covered casserole. Bake 40 to 60 minutes until tender. (Uncover last 15 minutes.) Remove from oven and stir. Allow dish to set 5 minutes before serving.

Makes 6 servings

VARIATION:
For a colorful vegetable dish, add 1 cup sliced carrots, 1 cup broccoli florets and an additional 1/2 teaspoon seasoned salt and 1/2 cup shredded raw cheddar cheese.

CAULIFLOWER RICE USES: Substitute cauliflower rice in any recipe that is served over a bed of rice, or as thickening in soups, stews and sauces.

CELERY/CELERIAC

DIG INTO THIS!

Celery contains properties that may help lower blood pressure.

The leaves of celery are very high in nutrients and make great garnishes. Add them to stock, broth, soups or salads.

Seeds of celery contain high amounts of iron so use celery seed freely.

Add celery to your stir-fry for a delicious crunchy taste.

For fun, try planting the tail end of celery in soil to grow your own stalk!

An average celeriac (celery root) is approximately the size of a softball.

HOW DOES YOUR GARDEN GROW...?

❋ Days to maturity from transplant: 80.

❋ Celery can be grown next to almost everything, although it's best not to plant celery next to carrots or parsnips.

❋ Start celery indoors 8 to 10 weeks before last frost date.

❋ Celery seeds need light to germinate. Sow seeds by sprinkling on top of a potting mixture with organic matter and then lightly cover with potting mix. Moisten, cover with plastic and place in warm area with indirect light.

❋ Seeds begin to grow in 7 days.

❋ Plant outdoors after temperatures stay above 55° F.

❋ Space transplants 8 inches apart.

❋ Celery has a small root system; add plenty of compost to the bed and to the planting hole when transplanting. Use fish emulsion during the growing season to replenish soil nutrients.

❋ Water heavily throughout season.

❋ Harvest whole celery plants or individual stalks by cutting them at the soil line.

❋ Celery will keep in refrigerator up to 14 days.

CELERIAC

❋ Days to maturity from transplant: 95 to 100.

❋ Celeriac is a close relative to celery and is grown for its root rather than its stalk. Harvest after the first few light frosts in fall.

❋ To harvest, use a garden fork and lift the plant free from the soil. Cut the tops an inch or two above the root. Trim roots. Store in refrigerator.

Grow it. Preserve it. Prepare it.

FREEZING CELERY

1. Choose crisp, tender stalks, free from coarse strings.

2. Pull celery apart and wash thoroughly. Trim and cut into desired lengths.

3. Blanch 3 minutes. Drain off hot water, dip in ice water, drain, cool.

4. Pack into freezer bags. Seal, label and freeze. *(Refer to freezing, page 26)*

HELPFUL HINTS

Remember: celery loses its crispness when frozen and, therefore, is best for cooked recipes.

FUN KIDS' CRAFT:

Chop the end off of a celery stalk 1-1/2 inches from root to create a celery rose stamp. Dip in your favorite craft paint to make a beautiful rose.

CELERY STIR-FRY

RECIPES

CELERY JUICE DRINK

4 green apples, washed and quartered
4 celery stalks, washed and trimmed

Juice all ingredients in a juicer for a refreshing drink.

Makes 1 large serving

MASHED CELERIAC

3 tablespoons butter
1/2 cup chopped onions
3 celeriac, peeled and cut into 1 inch chunks
2 large Yukon Gold potatoes,
peeled and cut into 1 inch chunks
1 Granny Smith apple, peeled,
cored and cut into 1 inch chunks
3 cloves garlic, minced
2 teaspoons salt
1/2 teaspoon pepper
4 cups chicken broth *(page 158)*

Heat butter in a large saucepan and sauté onions 3 minutes until translucent. Add remaining ingredients and simmer on low 30 minutes. Blend with an immersion blender or a regular blender and serve.

Makes 6 to 8 servings

BEEF STEW

1 pound beef stew meat
4 medium carrots, sliced
4 celery stalks with leaves, sliced
4 medium potatoes, cubed
1 medium onion, chopped
3 cloves garlic, minced
1 cup tomato juice *(page 254)*
2 cups beef broth *(page 158)*
1/4 cup quinoa flour
2 teaspoons salt
1 teaspoon pepper

Preheat oven to 350° F. Place all ingredients in a 6 quart covered baking dish. Bake 2 to 3 hours.

Makes 6 servings

HONEY ROASTED CASHEWS

3 cups cashews
2 tablespoons honey
2 tablespoons maple syrup
2 tablespoons butter
1 teaspoon vanilla
1 teaspoon salt

Preheat oven to 350° F. Line a rimmed baking sheet with parchment paper. Melt honey, maple syrup and butter in a small saucepan. Add vanilla. Place cashews in a medium bowl. Pour honey mixture over nuts. Toss to coat. Spread in single layer on prepared sheet. Bake 15 to 20 minutes, stirring every 5 minutes. Remove from oven and pour into bowl. Toss with salt and let cool, stirring occasionally. When completely cool, store in glass jar with airtight lid.

Makes 3 cups

VARIATION:

For a great snack, substitute almonds for cashews and add 1/2 teaspoon cinnamon with the salt.

CELERY STIR-FRY

2 chicken breasts, cut in 1 inch pieces
1/2 teaspoon salt
1/4 teaspoon pepper
1 tablespoon plus 1 teaspoon honey
5 cloves garlic, chopped
2 tablespoons sesame oil
6 celery stalks, sliced
3 carrots, sliced
1/2 cup honey roasted cashews

In a small bowl, mix together salt, pepper, honey and garlic. Pour over chicken and marinate 10 minutes. In a large skillet, sauté celery and carrots in oil. Cook 5 minutes over medium-high heat. Add chicken mixture. Cook 10 minutes until chicken is tender and no longer pink. Stir in honey roasted cashews and serve alone or with brown rice.

Makes 4 servings

RECIPES

CHICKEN SALAD

2 cups shredded cooked chicken
1/2 cup finely chopped celery
1/2 cup sour cream
1/4 cup chopped onions
1/4 teaspoon onion powder
1/8 teaspoon garlic granules
1/2 teaspoon salt
1/4 teaspoon pepper
1/2 cup cashews, optional

In a medium bowl, mix all ingredients together and chill 2 hours to blend flavors. Delicious served on top of lettuce!

Makes 4 servings

Spread almond butter, cashew butter or peanut butter into the center of a celery stalk. Place raisins at even intervals to make "ants on a log."

CUCUMBERS

DIG INTO THIS!

Cucumbers are popular in facials as they may help to reduce swelling when applied topically.

Pickling cucumbers are small and have thin skins. Slicing cucumbers are larger with thick skins.

Snack on cucumbers to help curb hunger as well as help with your daily water intake as they are made up of 95% water.

Cucumber vines like to climb. You will find cucumbers are straighter, a more uniform shape and less likely to rot or experience insect damage if grown on a trellis. Growing cucumbers on a trellis can also save some garden space.

HOW DOES YOUR GARDEN GROW...?

* Days to maturity: 48 to 60.

* Cucumbers grow best next to bush beans, cabbage, corn, eggplant, lettuce, peas, radishes and tomatoes.

* It's best not to plant next to potatoes.

* Radishes planted near cucumbers can help deter cucumber beetles.

* Apply an inch of compost to cucumber bed before planting and work it into the top few inches of soil.

* Soil temperature needs to be at least 70° F.

* Sow seed 1/2 inch to 1 inch deep, 6 to 10 inches apart. Seeds can be planted in hills. Space hills 24 inches apart with 3 seeds per hill, thinning later to 1 plant per hill.

* Seeds will begin to grow in 3 to 4 days.

* When seedlings emerge, begin to water frequently, and increase to a gallon per week after fruit forms.

* Inconsistent watering leads to bitter-tasting fruit. Water slowly in morning or early afternoon. A soaker hose works well.

* Harvest cucumbers whenever they are large enough to use. Slicing cucumbers should be 6 to 8 inches, dills 4 to 6 inches, and baby dills 2 inches. Small cucumbers are more flavorful than large ones.

* At peak harvesting, you should be picking every couple of days. Keep them picked and they will keep producing.

* Cucumbers keep best if wrapped individually in paper towels, and placed in plastic storage bags in refrigerator 7 to 10 days.

Grow it. Preserve it. Prepare it.

FREEZING CUCUMBERS

Who knew you could freeze cucumbers? A typical blanching process is not used. Instead, you prepare a brine as if you're making pickles.

Small cucumbers work best, 4 to 6 inches long and about 1-1/2 inches in diameter. Peeling is optional.

1. Wash cucumbers and slice uniformly. Slice 1 medium onion per 8 cups sliced cucumbers.

2. In a large bowl, combine cucumbers and onion with 1 to 2 tablespoons of salt. Stir. Cover and let sit at room temperature 2 hours.

3. Drain. Transfer cucumbers back to bowl.

4. In a separate bowl, combine 1/2 cup apple cider vinegar with 3/4 cup honey. Pour over cucumbers and stir well to evenly coat.

5. Spoon cucumbers into freezer containers. Seal, label and freeze.

6. Wait at least one week before eating. Thaw cucumbers overnight in refrigerator before serving.

Cucumbers retain a nice crunch when frozen this way. Eat these like traditional pickles, or add to salads or dips. You can chop them and use as relish or blend chopped cucumbers with mayonnaise to make your own tartar sauce.

Try freezing cucumbers by juicing or pureeing with a little water. Freeze in ice cube trays and store frozen cubes in a freezer bag. These make great additions to green smoothies or can be added to chilled water.

SLICED REFRIGERATOR PICKLES

RECIPES

CUCUMBER JUICE DRINK

1 cucumber, washed and peeled
2 stalks celery, washed and trimmed
1 carrot, washed and trimmed
1 apple, washed and quartered
1/4 lemon wedge, washed

Juice all ingredients in a juicer.

Makes 1 serving

SLICED REFRIGERATOR PICKLES

7 cups sliced cucumbers *(don't peel)*
1 green pepper, sliced
1 large onion, sliced
1 cup honey
1 cup apple cider vinegar
1 teaspoon celery seed
2 tablespoons salt

Wash cucumbers and slice. Place cucumbers, peppers and onions in a large 2 quart jar. Combine honey, vinegar, celery seed and salt in a medium pan. Bring to a boil. Reduce heat to low and simmer 10 to 15 minutes. Pour over cucumbers. Stir and refrigerate 3 days before eating. Pickles can be stored in refrigerator for several weeks.

Makes 2 quarts

CUCUMBER DIP

2 cups yogurt *(page 236)*
1 cucumber, grated
1 clove garlic, minced
1-1/2 teaspoons dried dill weed
or 1 tablespoon fresh dill
1/4 teaspoon salt
1-1/2 tablespoons lemon juice

Stir all ingredients together in a medium bowl. Chill 1 hour to allow flavors to meld. This is also a great dressing on salads!

Makes 3 cups

CUCUMBERS AND SOUR CREAM

2 cups cucumbers, peeled and thinly sliced
1 teaspoon salt
1/2 cup sour cream
1 tablespoon apple cider vinegar
1 tablespoon dried chives
or 2 tablespoons fresh chopped chives
1 teaspoon dill seed
1/8 teaspoon pepper

In a medium bowl, sprinkle salt on cucumbers and let stand at room temperature 30 minutes. Drain. Combine remaining ingredients in a small bowl. Stir and pour over cucumbers. Chill 30 minutes.

Makes 4 servings

Apple cider vinegar is made from crushed fermented apples versus white vinegar made from corn. Organic, raw, unfiltered apple cider vinegar contains nutrients which provide many health benefits. Throughout our recipes, we always use Bragg's Apple Cider Vinegar. You might notice that the pickles look cloudy, but the health benefits far outweigh the appearance.

CANNING CUCUMBERS

DILL PICKLES

8 pounds cucumbers
4 cups apple cider vinegar
4 cups water
3/4 cup salt
7 large fresh dill heads
7 cloves garlic

1. Wash cucumbers.

2. Combine salt, vinegar and water in a large sauce pot. Bring to a boil.

3. Gently break apart each dill head. Place 1/2 head of fresh dill and 1 garlic clove at bottom of each jar. Pack cucumbers in jar. Add another 1/2 head of fresh dill at top of jar leaving 1/2 inch head space.

4. Ladle hot liquid over cucumbers. Remove air bubbles.

5. Process pints and quarts 15 minutes in a boiling water canner. *(Refer to canning, page 24)*

   Makes 7 pints

VARIATION:
For Kosher-Style pickles add 1 bay leaf, 1 clove garlic, 1 piece hot red pepper and 1/2 teaspoon mustard seed to each jar.

CUCUMBER SALAD WITH CAJUN CRACKERS

OVERNIGHT CUCUMBERS

2 large cucumbers, washed and thinly sliced
1 small onion, thinly sliced
2 tablespoons honey
1/2 cup apple cider vinegar
1 cup water
1 teaspoon salt
1/2 teaspoon pepper

Place cucumbers and onions in a medium bowl. Combine rest of ingredients in a small saucepan.

Bring to a boil over medium-high heat 1 minute. Remove from heat. Cool 5 minutes. Pour over cucumbers and onions. Mix well. Refrigerate overnight and serve the next day.

Makes 4 to 6 servings

CUCUMBER SALAD

2 cucumbers, diced
4 tomatoes, diced
1/4 cup chopped onion
2 tablespoons olive oil
2 tablespoons lemon juice
1/2 teaspoon salt
1/8 teaspoon pepper

In a medium bowl, stir all ingredients together to coat evenly. Serve chilled or at room temperature.

Makes 4 servings

HELPFUL HINTS

One pound of cucumbers equals 2 medium or 3 cups sliced. A bushel of cucumbers is 48 to 50 pounds and makes 24 quarts of dill pickles.

EATING PURE

In the kitchen, salt is a key ingredient. It is used to preserve food, aid in fermenting food and to enhance flavors of many dishes. In our recipes, we use unrefined Celtic sea salt or Himalayan salt. These salts are hand-mined and dried naturally by the sun and wind. You ask why we choose to use these salts? For their purity. These two salts contain many beneficial minerals that are not found in ordinary table salt. These salts range in color from white to varying shades of pink and can be used in the same manner as table salt. The next time you are shopping for salt, check out unrefined sea salt or Himalayan salt to enjoy the nutritional benefits of each. Himalayan Pink Salt can also be used in making bath salts, body scrubs, and homemade soaps.

CREAMY CUCUMBER SALAD

4 large cucumbers, peeled and sliced
1/2 medium onion, sliced
2 teaspoons salt
1 cup mayonnaise (page 77)
2 tablespoons honey
1/4 teaspoon pepper
1/2 teaspoon dried dill weed, optional

Place cucumbers and onion in a medium bowl. Add salt. Stir to mix well and let sit at room temperature 1 hour. Drain and rinse cucumbers. With clean hands, gently squeeze all water out of cucumbers (this step is important). In a small bowl, mix remaining ingredients and toss with cucumbers to coat.

Makes 4 servings

PRETTY SLICED CUCUMBERS

Wondering how they make cucumbers look fancy with ridges displayed on veggie trays? Easy! Wash the cucumber. Take a fork and run down sides of cucumber lengthwise. Slice and spread in circles on your platter. Simple touches make a difference!

EGGPLANT

DIG INTO THIS!

Eggplants are known as aubergines in other parts of the world.

Eggplants should be firm and about the size of a large pear. An eggplant should feel heavy for its size and is tastiest at less than 1-1/2 pounds. Look for smooth, shiny dark purple skin with a green stem.

For best flavor, use an eggplant before the stem turns light brown.

The inside flesh of a fresh eggplant is light colored and should contain few seeds.

Although eggplants don't have an overwhelming supply of any one nutrient, they do have an impressive array of many vitamins and minerals including powerful antioxidants.

HOW DOES YOUR GARDEN GROW...?

❋ Days to maturity from transplant: 58 to 65.

❋ Eggplant grows best next to bush beans, peas, peppers and potatoes.

❋ Sow seeds indoors 6 to 8 weeks before transplant date.

❋ Seeds will begin to grow in 7 days.

❋ Started eggplants can also be purchased from your local nursery.

❋ Eggplants are sensitive to transplant shock, so start in 4 inch pots, 2 to 3 seeds per pot. Germinate with bottom heat at 80° F soil temperature and reduced to 70° F after seedlings emerge.

❋ Thin to one plant per pot by cutting the extras with a scissors.

❋ Transplant when the soil temperature and daytime air temperature reaches 70° F, and night air temperature is above 60° F.

❋ Water heavily throughout season.

❋ Potato beetles/larvae thrive on eggplant. Be prepared to hand pick the insects off as soon as they appear.

❋ A month before the first frost, snip off any blossoms to encourage existing fruit to ripen.

❋ Harvest after they've reached half their mature size. Cut from the stems with shears leaving some stem attached.

❋ Eggplants bruise easily and should be harvested with care.

❋ Eggplant does not store well. Eat within 1 to 3 days.

To promote hardy transplants as they grow indoors, place a fan on low speed in front of plants a few hours each day. The moving air will strengthen the stems in preparation for planting outdoors.

Grow it. Preserve it. Prepare it.

FREEZING EGGPLANT

1. Wash and peel eggplant. Slice into 1/3 inch thick rounds.

2. Blanch one eggplant at a time, 4 minutes in water containing 1/2 cup lemon juice.

3. Drain and cool completely.

4. Pat dry and pack into freezer containers separating slices with freezer wrap. Seal, label and freeze. *(Refer to freezing, page 26)*

HELPFUL HINTS

A large eggplant is about 1-1/2 pounds and equals 4 to 5 cups diced and is approximately 4 to 6 servings.

EGGPLANT PARMIGIANA

RECIPES

ROASTED EGGPLANT DIP

1 medium eggplant, washed and peeled
2 red bell peppers
1 medium onion
2 cloves garlic
1 tablespoon butter
1 tablespoon water
1 teaspoon salt
1/4 teaspoon pepper
1/4 teaspoon cayenne pepper
2 tablespoons lemon juice

Preheat oven to 400° F. Cut eggplant, peppers and onion into 1 inch chunks. Place in a large bowl and toss with garlic, butter and water. Place in single layer on a rimmed baking sheet. Roast 40 to 45 minutes, stirring occasionally until lightly browned. Place in a food processor or a blender with remaining ingredients. Puree until smooth. Delicious served with your favorite veggies or crackers!

Makes 6 to 8 servings

SAUTÉED EGGPLANT

2 tablespoons butter
1 onion, chopped
1-3/4 pound small eggplants
1 teaspoon salt
1/4 teaspoon pepper
2 cups canned tomatoes *(page 252)*
2 tablespoons fresh basil, chopped
1 cup shredded raw cheddar cheese

Wash, peel and slice eggplant into 1/3 inch thick slices. In a large skillet, sauté onion in butter over medium heat 2 minutes. Add eggplant, salt and pepper. Cover and cook 5 minutes. Flip. Add tomatoes. Cover and simmer over medium-low heat 15 to 20 minutes until eggplant is tender. Stir in basil. Top with cheddar cheese and serve.

Makes 4 servings

EGGPLANT PARMIGIANA

2 eggplants
2 eggs, lightly beaten
3/4 cup grated Parmesan cheese, divided
1/4 cup milk
1 teaspoon dried parsley
1/2 teaspoon garlic powder
1/2 teaspoon dried basil
1 teaspoon salt
1/8 teaspoon pepper
1/2 cup butter
1 pound ground beef
1 quart spaghetti sauce *(page 257)*
2 cups shredded raw cheddar cheese

Preheat oven to 350° F. Wash, peel and cut eggplants into 1/3 inch thick slices. In a medium bowl, combine eggs, 3 tablespoons Parmesan cheese, milk and next 5 ingredients.

Melt butter in a large skillet. Dip eggplant slices in egg mixture and fry over medium heat until golden on each side. Drain on paper towels.

Brown beef and add spaghetti sauce. Arrange half of eggplant slices in a greased 9 x 13 pan. Pour half of hamburger sauce mixture over eggplant and sprinkle with half of remaining Parmesan cheese. Repeat layers.

Bake uncovered 40 minutes. Sprinkle with cheddar cheese and bake 5 to 10 minutes until cheese melts. Remove from oven and let rest 10 minutes before serving.

Makes 6 to 8 servings

This dish is a great gluten-free replacement for traditional lasagna.

GARLIC

DIG INTO THIS!

Garlic is both a vegetable and an herb.

When selecting garlic, look for firm, tight, heavy, dry bulbs.

Garlic has been used medicinally for centuries. Its antioxidant properties may help the well-being of the heart and immune systems.

We've tested—and proven—garlic smell can be removed from hands by running under cold water while rubbing a stainless steel object for 10 seconds!

Drinking lemon juice or eating a few slices of lemon will help combat garlic breath.

One garlic bulb can have 4 to 15 cloves, depending on the variety.

HOW DOES YOUR GARDEN GROW...?

* Garlic grows best next to beets and lettuce.
* It's best not to plant next to beans or peas.
* Plant in fall.
* Purchase garlic bulbs from your local nursery.
* Plant garlic clove 2 inches deep with the pointed end up, 8 inches apart.
* Mulch with a thick layer of straw or leaves before the ground freezes to protect the bulbs.
* Remove mulch in early spring.
* Don't water unless the ground gets very dry.
* Keep weeds under control with shallow cultivation.
* Snip off flowers as they appear to promote larger bulbs.

Garlic and onions planted in your garden will help with insect control.

* Harvest in late July when half of the leaves have turned yellow or the tops fall over. Use a broad digging fork to loosen the soil and pull the bulbs.
* Cure garlic 2 to 3 weeks in a dark, dry, well-ventilated area until the skins are dry and the necks are tight. Cut tops leaving 1-1/2 inches of stem and store in a cool, dry place.
* After harvesting and curing, select the largest bulbs for replanting. Separate cloves before planting.

Grow it. Preserve it. Prepare it.

DEHYDRATING GARLIC

GARLIC POWDER

1. Peel and thinly slice garlic cloves.

2. Spread in single layer on dehydrator trays or cookie sheets.

3. Dehydrate according to manufacturer's instructions or bake at 170° F 2 to 3 hours until garlic is dry and crumbles easily when crushed in your hand.

4. Cool. Crush in grinder to desired consistency. Store in a glass jar or freeze.

Roasting garlic is easy and delicious. Toss unpeeled garlic cloves in melted butter. Place in a glass baking dish and roast at 400° F 10 to 15 minutes. Gently squeeze garlic cloves out of skins. Great for making garlic butter, garlic oil or can be used in your favorite recipes.

YUMMY GARLIC POTATOES

RECIPES

GARLIC MARINADE

1/2 cup sesame oil
3/4 cup lemon juice
5 cloves garlic, minced
2 teaspoons salt
1 teaspoon pepper
2 tablespoons dried rosemary, optional

In a small bowl, mix all ingredients together. Pour over chicken or turkey and marinate 4 to 8 hours before grilling or baking.

Makes 1 cup

GARLIC AVOCADO VINAIGRETTE

3 cloves garlic, minced
3 tablespoons lemon juice
2 tablespoons grated Parmesan cheese
1/2 teaspoon salt
1/4 teaspoon pepper
1/4 cup avocado oil

In a small bowl, combine all ingredients except oil. Slowly pour in the avocado oil while whisking. Serve on your favorite salad greens.

Makes 2 servings

HELPFUL HINTS

One clove garlic equals 1/4 teaspoon garlic powder. Three cloves equals 1-1/2 tablespoons of minced garlic.

YUMMY GARLIC POTATOES

8 medium red potatoes, quartered
5 cloves garlic, minced
1 teaspoon salt, divided
1/4 cup butter
1/2 cup heavy cream
1/3 cup grated Parmesan cheese

Place washed potatoes, garlic and 1/2 teaspoon salt in a large saucepan. Cover with water and bring to a boil. Reduce heat, cover and simmer 20 minutes until tender. Drain. Transfer to a bowl. Add butter, cream and 1/2 teaspoon salt. Mash. Stir in cheese.

Makes 4 to 6 servings

GARLIC FRIES

4 medium potatoes
3 cloves garlic, minced
3 tablespoons butter, melted
1/2 teaspoon pepper
1 teaspoon salt

Preheat oven to 400° F. Wash potatoes and cut into pencil-size fries. Place in a bowl of ice water and let stand 30 minutes. Drain and pat dry. Toss potatoes with remaining ingredients and place on a buttered jelly roll pan. Bake 45 to 60 minutes, stirring occasionally, until golden brown and crispy. Cool 5 minutes before serving.

Makes 4 servings

The role of a marinade is to add flavor and tenderize meat.
Place meat and marinade in a resealable plastic bag and refrigerate.
Discard marinade before grilling or baking.

ROASTED GARLIC SOUP

12 cloves garlic, unpeeled
2 cups cauliflower florets
2 cups chopped zucchini
1/2 cup butter, divided
1 large onion, chopped
2 teaspoons salt
1/2 teaspoon pepper
1/8 teaspoon cayenne pepper, optional
2 teaspoons dried basil
4 cups chicken broth *(page 158)*

Preheat oven to 400° F. Place garlic, cauliflower and zucchini in a large bowl. In a small pan melt 1/4 cup butter and pour over vegetables. Stir to coat. Place in single layer on a rimmed baking sheet. Roast 25 minutes until lightly brown.

While vegetables are roasting, sauté onions in a stock pot with remaining butter over medium-high heat until tender. Stir in seasonings and chicken broth. Take roasted vegetables out of oven, cool. Remove skins from garlic cloves. Add vegetables to soup. Puree with an immersion blender until smooth. Cook an additional 10 minutes.

Makes 4 servings

WHITE CHICKEN CHILI

2 cups chopped cooked chicken
1 tablespoon butter
3/4 cup chopped onion
2 cloves garlic, minced
5 cups chicken broth *(page 158)*
4 cups prepared lima or navy beans *(page 121)*
2 teaspoons salt
1 teaspoon ground cumin
1/8 teaspoon cayenne pepper
3/4 teaspoon chili powder
1/8 teaspoon pepper
1-1/2 teaspoons dried oregano
1 green chili pepper, optional

Sauté onion and garlic with butter in a stockpot 3 to 5 minutes over medium-high heat. Add remaining ingredients. Reduce heat, cover and simmer 30 minutes. This can also simmer in a slow cooker on low several hours.

Makes 4 servings

EATING PURE

We have learned that dried beans, lentils and other legumes are generally very hard to digest. To help with digestion of beans, it's important to soak beans for at least 12 hours before cooking. Put two cups of dried beans in a two quart glass jar. Fill with six cups lukewarm water and two tablespoons of lemon juice. Soak 12 to 24 hours. Drain and rinse well until water runs clear. Cook beans on low (approximately 2 hours until soft) skimming off and discarding the impurities in the foam that rises to the top. Drain and use in your favorite recipe or put in glass containers and freeze. Beans and lentils are staples we like to have in the freezer at all times to pull out and add to broth or a casserole for a quick meal.

Navy beans, lima beans, lentils and split peas would be the best choice if you're trying to limit your starch and sugar intake.

HERBS

DIG INTO THIS!

Chives are one of the earliest plants to appear in spring and are a treat to add to salads.

Store fresh basil in a glass of water at room temperature.

Italian (flat-leafed) parsley has a stronger, richer flavor than curly parsley.

Parsley is a natural breath freshener and aids in digestion.

Parsley is thought to contain twice the amount of iron as spinach.

Oregano has been used for centuries as a health boosting herb.

Did you know curry powder is a blend of several spices including turmeric, coriander, cumin and chili powder?

HOW DOES YOUR GARDEN GROW...?

BASIL

* Plant next to tomatoes to control insects.
* Pinch or snip off growing basil tips to increase yield.
* Harvest basil leaves when they are large enough to use.
* Use basil in pesto, tomato sauces, soups, and seasoning mixes.

CHIVES

* Plant on the edge of your vegetable or flower garden for an attractive border.
* When leaves of chives are large enough to use, snip off with scissors.
* Use fresh chives in place of onions in salads, dips and spreads.

CILANTRO

* Cilantro is best seeded in the garden rather than transplanted. Plant multiple times to have cilantro all season long.
* Pick as needed when it's 8 inches tall. Cilantro loses its potent flavor when dried or stored more than a few days.

* Coriander is the spicy seeds of cilantro. When cilantro goes to seed and seedheads turn from yellow to brown, snip entire head and store upside down in a brown bag. Close bag and place in warm, dry place. Seeds will ripen and drop to bottom of bag.
* Use cilantro to add zip to your salsas, dips and salads.

DILL

* Plant dill in your garden to help with insect pest control, but not next to carrots.
* Snip fresh leaves when plants are at least 12 inches tall.
* Harvest dill flower umbels for pickles before they go to seed.
* Dill seeds can be harvested when the heads turn from yellow to tan. Turn seedheads upside down in brown bag and collect seeds as they fall to bottom of bag.
* Use dill in dips, salads, soups, beets, eggs and fish.

Grow it. Preserve it. Prepare it.

HERBS

HOW DOES YOUR GARDEN GROW...?

MARJORAM

* Marjoram is sweeter than oregano and partners well in any Italian dish.

* Harvest leaves when plants are 4 to 6 inches tall. Pick individual leaves for immediate use or clip entire stems for drying and storage.

* Use marjoram in soups, tomato sauces and seasoning mixes.

MINT

* Mint tea is wonderful to calm a queasy stomach.

* Cut mint and hang stems to dry leaves. Crumble leaves and store in airtight jar.

* Use mint in lemonades, teas and salads.

OREGANO

* Cut oregano plants off about 2 inches above ground before they flower to get another harvest at the end of the season.

* Use oregano to add zest to tomato and pizza sauces as well as Mediterranean and Italian dishes.

PARSLEY

* Harvest parsley beginning with larger, outer leaves. Cut whole stem to maintain production.

* Use parsley as a garnishment in salads, soups and meats. Basically it's great in just about everything.

ROSEMARY

* This herb is ornamental, fragrant and delicious. Both leaves and flowers are edible.

* Snip off pieces of stem as needed.

* Use rosemary on pork, chicken, turkey and in seasoning mixes.

SAGE

* Sage helps repel harmful insects.

* Sage is most flavorful when leaves are harvested just as the flowers begin to open.

* Use sage in poultry and meat seasonings.

THYME

* Thyme is part of the mint family and is easy to grow with little maintenance. The flowers attract butterflies and bees.

* To collect thyme, cut just before flowers open and hang upside down in brown bag.

* Use thyme with fish, chicken and roasted vegetables.

DEHYDRATING HERBS

1. Harvest herbs for drying when they are in the bursting bud stage just before flowers open. Gather herbs in the early morning after dew has evaporated.

2. Rinse in cool water, gently shake off excess water, discarding all bruised and imperfect leaves and stems.

3. Place in single layer on dehydrator trays. Dry according to manufacturer's instructions. Herbs are dry when stems break and leaves crumble easily.

To dry herbs in oven, bake at 170° F until dry and crumbly. Cool and place in airtight jars.

Rosemary, Sage, Thyme, Savory, Cilantro, Dill and Parsley can be dried without a dehydrator. Simply tie in small bundles and hang to air dry.

FREEZING DILL

Pick dill when heads are green and place in freezer bag. Seal, label and freeze. When ready to use, take out of freezer, run under water to thaw and place in pickle jars.

RECIPES

PESTO

2 cups packed fresh basil leaves
2 cloves garlic
3 tablespoons olive oil
1/2 teaspoon salt
1/4 teaspoon pepper
1/4 cup grated Parmesan cheese

Puree all ingredients in a food processor. Use immediately or freeze in ice cube trays. When frozen, transfer cubes to freezer bag. Try this pesto on grilled chicken, burgers, brown rice noodles or as a spread.

Makes 1 cup

SEASONED SALT

1/4 cup salt
2 teaspoons paprika
2 teaspoons onion powder
1 teaspoon garlic powder
1/2 teaspoon turmeric
1/2 teaspoon pepper

Combine all ingredients in a small bowl and store in airtight container. This is good on just about anything!

ITALIAN SEASONING

1/4 teaspoon pepper
1 tablespoon dried parsley
1 tablespoon dried rosemary
1 tablespoon dried thyme
2 tablespoons dried basil
1 tablespoon dried marjoram
2 tablespoons dried oregano

Combine all ingredients in a small bowl and store in airtight container. This is a great seasoning mix to use in Italian dishes, tomato sauces, salads, and dressings.

TACO SEASONING

2 tablespoons chili powder
1/2 teaspoon garlic powder
1/2 teaspoon onion powder
1 teaspoon dried oregano
1-1/2 teaspoons paprika
1 tablespoon ground cumin
1 tablespoon salt
1-1/2 teaspoons pepper

Combine all ingredients in a small bowl and store in airtight container. Use 2-1/2 teaspoons per pound of meat.

RANCH SEASONING

2 tablespoons dried parsley
2 teaspoons dried dill weed
1 teaspoon dried basil
1 teaspoon garlic powder
2 teaspoons onion powder
1/2 teaspoon pepper
1 teaspoon salt

Combine all ingredients in a small bowl and store in airtight container.

RANCH DRESSING

In a small bowl, combine 2 tablespoons Ranch Seasoning mix, 1/3 cup milk and 1 cup mayonnaise *(page 77)*.

RANCH DIP

In a small bowl, combine 1 tablespoon Ranch Seasoning mix and 1/2 cup sour cream.

Dried herbs are 3 to 4 times stronger than fresh herbs. To substitute dried herbs for fresh, use 1/4 to 1/3 the amount listed in the recipe.

GUACAMOLE

RECIPES

CAJUN SEASONING

2 teaspoons salt
1-1/4 teaspoons pepper
2 teaspoons garlic powder
1 teaspoon onion powder
2-1/2 teaspoons paprika
3/4 teaspoon cayenne pepper
1 teaspoon dried oregano
1 teaspoon dried thyme
3/4 teaspoon red pepper flakes

Combine all ingredients in a small bowl and store in airtight container. Use this on chicken, fish and beef.

CAJUN CRACKERS

1-1/2 cups shredded raw cheddar cheese
1/4 cup grated Parmesan cheese
1 egg
1-1/2 cups almond flour
1 teaspoon Cajun seasoning
1 tablespoon water
Salt to taste

Preheat oven to 350° F. In a medium bowl, stir first 5 ingredients together with a fork. Add water and stir. Form mixture into a ball with your hands. Flatten dough into a large patty. Place between 2 layers of parchment paper cut to the size of your baking sheet. Roll into a thin layer. Remove top sheet of paper.

Using a pizza cutter, cut into 2 inch diagonal pieces. Slide crackers and parchment paper on to a baking sheet. Sprinkle with salt. Bake 15 minutes. Remove from oven, cool slightly and flip over. Bake 10 to 15 minutes until brown and crispy.

Makes 4 to 6 servings

RECIPES

GUACAMOLE

4 avocados, peeled and mashed
1/2 cup chopped tomatoes
1/3 cup chopped onion
1 Jalapeño, seeded and chopped
1 tablespoon lime juice
1 teaspoon salt
1/4 teaspoon pepper
1/8 teaspoon cayenne pepper
1/4 cup chopped fresh cilantro

In a medium bowl, combine all ingredients. For a smooth guacamole, blend with an immersion blender. Chill 30 minutes to blend flavors. If storing overnight, place in refrigerator with an avocado pit in the guacamole to help with discoloration.

Makes 4 to 6 servings

Delicious served with eggs, burgers, tacos, fajitas or just plain dip in and eat it with a spoon— yummy!

HELPFUL HINTS

It's best to purchase spices in small amounts to obtain their peak flavor. Replenish them often.

CHICKEN RUB

1 teaspoon salt
1/2 teaspoon pepper
2 teaspoons paprika
1-1/2 teaspoons onion powder
1/2 teaspoon garlic powder
1 teaspoon dried thyme

Combine all ingredients in a small bowl. Rub on 3 to 4 pound chicken. Place in a slow cooker. Add 1/4 inch water to bottom of slow cooker. Cook on high 4 to 5 hours.

POULTRY SEASONING

1-1/2 tablespoons dried sage
1 tablespoon dried parsley
1 tablespoon dried thyme
1 tablespoon dried marjoram
2 teaspoons dried rosemary
1/4 teaspoon ground nutmeg
1/4 teaspoon ground cumin
1/4 teaspoon pepper

Combine all ingredients in a small bowl and store in airtight container. This can be used with pork, chicken and turkey.

EATING PURE

When we think of herbs and spices, our thoughts turn to how they enhance the flavor of the foods we eat. However, the more articles we read, the more we discover that studies are suggesting that herbs and spices have a lot to offer in the way of health benefits. For centuries some of these herbs and spices have been used for medicinal purposes. Wondering how you can benefit by adding some of these herbs and spices to your diet? Check out cinnamon, turmeric, garlic, oregano, thyme and basil to list a few. We know for ourselves, if we can receive some health benefits while adding flavor to our food, it is a winning combination.

Over time, we have come to appreciate the many herbs and spices used in cooking. When preparing dishes, it is important to start with pure ingredients, including your spices. The best herbs and spices should be grown in conditions where pesticides or herbicides are not used.

CHICKEN TENDERS WITH HONEY DIJON DRESSING

For this recipe, we like to chop the onion in an immersion blender attachment so it's almost like a thick liquid.

BREAKFAST SAUSAGE

1 pound ground pork or beef
1 small onion, finely chopped
1 egg
1/2 teaspoon pumpkin pie spice *(page 189)*
1/8 teaspoon cayenne pepper
1-1/2 teaspoons poultry seasoning *(page 127)*
1 teaspoon dried basil
1/2 teaspoon salt
1/8 teaspoon pepper

In a large bowl, mix all ingredients together. Shape into patties and fry in a large skillet over medium-high heat until no longer pink in center.

Makes 8 patties

FISH STICKS

3 fillets of cod, cut into strips
1 egg
1 tablespoon milk
1/4 cup coconut flour
2 teaspoons seasoned salt *(page 125)*
2 tablespoons butter, melted

Preheat oven to 425° F. Cut fish into thin strips. Whisk egg and milk together in a shallow dish. Place coconut flour and seasoned salt into a large storage bag. Shake to mix thoroughly. Pour melted butter in a rimmed baking sheet. Dip fish in egg mixture, place in bag and toss to coat. Do one or two pieces of fish at a time. Lay in single layer on pan. Bake 15 to 20 minutes. Remove from oven and flip pieces over. Continue baking 15 to 20 minutes until brown and crispy.

Makes 4 to 6 servings

Looking for a tasty, quick meal? Make a double batch of these tenders and freeze half for later. Just pop in the oven and reheat.

CHICKEN TENDERS

4 boneless, skinless chicken breasts
1 egg
1 tablespoon milk
1/4 cup butter, melted
2 tablespoons coconut flour
1 cup grated Parmesan cheese
1-1/2 teaspoons seasoned salt *(page 125)*

Preheat oven to 425° F. Cut chicken into thin strips approximately 3/4 inch x 4 inches. Whisk egg and milk together in a shallow dish. Place coconut flour, cheese and seasoned salt into a large storage bag. Shake to mix thoroughly. Pour melted butter in a rimmed baking sheet. Dip chicken in egg mixture, place in bag and toss to coat. Do one or two pieces of chicken at a time. Lay in single layer on pan. Bake 15 to 20 minutes. Remove from oven and flip pieces over. Continue baking 15 to 20 minutes until brown and crispy.

Makes 4 to 6 servings

Growing your own herbs is fun and easy! We grow basil, parsley, rosemary, mint and oregano in a pot on the patio. It's wonderful to have fresh herbs available to use as you are cooking. In the fall, simply move the pot into the house, place it in a sunny spot and enjoy using your herbs all winter.

MARINATED PORK TENDERLOIN

1/2 cup lemon juice
1/4 cup sesame oil
3 cloves garlic, minced
1 teaspoon poultry seasoning *(page 127)*
1 teaspoon Dijon mustard
1 teaspoon salt
1/4 teaspoon pepper
2 pork tenderloins, 1 pound each

Place all ingredients in a small bowl except tenderloins. Pour marinade into a gallon storage bag. Add tenderloins and gently shake to coat. Refrigerate 3 to 8 hours. Remove pork from bag and discard marinade.

Place on a preheated grill and grill 20 to 30 minutes until done. Tenderloins can also be baked in a covered baking dish 1 hour at 350° F.

Makes 6 servings

CAJUN ROAST BEEF

3 pound beef roast
3/4 cup ketchup *(page 255)*
1/4 cup apple cider vinegar
1/2 cup water
2 teaspoons Cajun seasoning *(page 126)*
2 tablespoons honey

Place roast in a slow cooker. In a small bowl, combine remaining ingredients and pour over roast. Cook 3 to 4 hours on high. Shred and serve.

Makes 6 servings

KALE

DIG INTO THIS!

Kale is one of the cruciferous vegetables that should be included in your diet 2 to 3 times per week for its health benefits.

The benefits from eating kale are so extensive that some claim kale to be the perfect food.

Kale is a good source of calcium.

A light frost produces sweeter kale leaves. For this reason, it's more widely available mid-winter through early spring.

There are several varieties of kale which differ in appearance, taste and texture.

HOW DOES YOUR GARDEN GROW...?

❋ Days to maturity from direct seed: 50 to 60. Days to maturity from transplant: 40 to 55.

❋ Plant kale next to beets, bush beans, cabbage, cucumbers, lettuce, onions or potatoes.

❋ It's best not to plant next to pole beans or tomatoes.

❋ Fast growing kale is the tastiest, so work compost into the soil at least a month before planting.

❋ Plant seed 1/2 inch deep in late spring, 6 inches apart.

❋ Seeds will begin to grow in 5 to 7 days.

❋ Thin plants to 12 inches apart.

❋ Started seedlings can be purchased from your local nursery.

❋ Transplant seedlings 12 inches apart, in rows 18 to 24 inches apart.

❋ Fertilize every 3 to 4 weeks with an organic fertilizer such as fish emulsion.

❋ Water heavily during growing season.

❋ Individual kale leaves can begin to be harvested as soon as they are large enough to use.

❋ Harvest entire plant by cutting the stem about an inch above the ground. This is best done after the leaves have been nipped by frost when the flavor is at its peak.

❋ Store kale in a storage bag in the refrigerator 2 to 4 weeks.

To begin your gardening experience, the best place to start is container gardening. In selecting a container, you will need to consider size, drainage and soil. Keep in mind what material the container is made of to eliminate any toxic exposure to your plants. Larger containers allow for more root space and soil will not dry out as fast. Place some rocks in the bottom of your container for good water flow. Fill with high quality soil and enjoy watching your plants grow.

Grow it. Preserve it. Prepare it.

FREEZING KALE

1 Soak kale leaves in 1 to 3 tablespoons of vinegar in a sink full of water 20 to 30 minutes. Drain, rinse and remove leaf blades from stems (fold in half and tear or cut the middle stem out).

2 Roughly tear or chop leaves. Blanch leaves 2-1/2 minutes. *(Refer to freezing, page 26)*

3 Place leaves in ice water until completely cool. Drain. Remove excess water with a clean dry towel.

4 Place kale leaves individually on a parchment lined baking sheet. Freeze. Place in freezer storage bag. Seal, label and return to freezer. Blanched, frozen kale will last up to 12 months and is great for grabbing a handful for a smoothie or tossing into your favorite soup.

You can also freeze kale without blanching. However, unblanched kale develops a bitter flavor so it's best to use this within 4 to 6 weeks.

KALE CHIPS

RECIPES

KALE PINEAPPLE SMOOTHIE

1/2 cup yogurt *(page 236)*
3/4 cup fresh pineapple, peeled and cored
1 ripe banana, sliced
2 leaves kale, torn in pieces
1/4 cup sliced or slivered almonds, raw
1/4 cup ice

Place all ingredients in a blender in order listed and blend until smooth.

Makes 1 serving

KALE CHIPS

1 bunch kale
2 tablespoons sesame oil
2 tablespoons apple cider vinegar
1/4 teaspoon salt
1/4 teaspoon garlic powder

Preheat oven to 350° F. Wash and tear kale into 2 inch pieces removing the woody center. Dry and put in a large bowl. Whisk together oil, vinegar and spices in a small bowl. Toss with kale to coat evenly. Spread in single layer on rimmed baking sheets. Bake 15 to 20 minutes until crispy. Adjust seasonings to your liking.

Kale chips can also be made in a dehydrator by following manufacturer's instructions.

Makes 4 servings

HELPFUL HINTS
1 pound of kale equals 4 to 6 cups sliced leaves.

STEAMED KALE

1 bunch kale
1 small onion, sliced
1 tablespoon lemon juice
3 tablespoons olive oil
1 clove garlic, minced
1/2 teaspoon salt
1/8 teaspoon pepper

Wash and remove tough stem and ribs of kale. Chop into 1/2 inch pieces. Place kale and onions in a steamer basket. Steam in a covered pan 5 minutes *(refer to steaming, page 27)*.

In a small bowl, whisk together lemon juice, olive oil, garlic, salt and pepper. Place kale in a serving bowl. Toss with dressing.

Makes 2 servings

SAUTÉED KALE

1 pound kale, stems removed, leaves torn in pieces
2 tablespoons butter
1 clove garlic, minced
1/3 cup beef broth *(page 158)*
3/4 teaspoon salt
1/4 teaspoon pepper
2 tablespoons apple cider vinegar

In a large skillet, sauté garlic in butter over medium-high heat 1 minute. Add broth and kale. Cover and cook 5 to 7 minutes. Remove cover and continue to cook until all liquid is evaporated. Season with salt, pepper and vinegar.

Makes 4 servings

RECIPES

EASY BEEF AND KALE

2 cups cubed butternut squash

1 tablespoon butter

1 pound ground beef

1/2 cup chopped onion

1-1/2 teaspoons Italian seasoning *(page 125)*

3 cups chopped kale

1-1/2 teaspoons salt, divided

1/2 teaspoon pepper

Preheat oven to 425° F. Melt butter in an 8 x 8 glass baking dish 2 minutes as oven is preheating. Toss squash into melted butter to coat. Sprinkle with 1/2 teaspoon salt. Roast 20 to 30 minutes until soft.

While squash is baking, place beef, onion and Italian seasoning in a large skillet. Brown over medium-high heat. Add kale and remaining salt and pepper. Cover and cook 7 minutes.

Add squash and serve.

Makes 4 servings

To obtain the correct flavor and best results when cooking, it's important to understand how to read a recipe.

When a recipe reads "1/2 cup chopped onion," it means 1/2 cup of pre-chopped onion. If the recipe reads "1/2 cup walnuts, chopped," you measure out 1/2 cup of walnuts and then chop the walnuts, leaving you with less than 1/2 cup of walnuts.

ABOUT TURMERIC

There has been a lot of information regarding the health benefits of adding turmeric to your diet to help fight inflammation. While turmeric is a new spice that we have begun to use in different dishes, we thought we should do some research and find out more about turmeric.

Turmeric is a bright yellow spice that has a peppery bitter flavor and is typically found in curries. Turmeric can be added to egg salad to give it a bold yellow color, sprinkled on steamed cauliflower, mixed in dips and added to curries.

It is important to note that adding turmeric to a recipe can change the color of the food to a distinct yellow. Don't be alarmed; the added flavor is delicious.

ONE DISH CHICKEN AND KALE

2 tablespoons butter
1 medium onion, sliced
2 boneless, skinless chicken breasts, cut into 1 inch pieces
2 cloves garlic, minced
1 tablespoon grated fresh ginger or 1 teaspoon ginger powder
1 teaspoon turmeric
1 teaspoon ground coriander
1/2 cup chicken broth *(page 158)*
4 cups chopped kale, fresh or frozen
4 cups sliced cabbage
2 tablespoons apple cider vinegar
1 tablespoon olive oil
1 teaspoon salt
1/4 teaspoon pepper

In a large skillet, sauté onion in butter over medium heat 5 minutes. Add chicken and garlic. Cook 5 minutes. Sprinkle ginger, turmeric and coriander over chicken. Cook 3 minutes. Add broth, kale and cabbage. Cover and simmer 5 minutes, stirring occasionally until tender. Remove from heat. Toss in remaining ingredients. Stir and serve.

Makes 4 servings

EATING PURE

Cruciferous vegetables, also known as Brassica, are extremely high in vitamins, minerals, proteins, carbs, fats and fiber. Some of the vegetables in this family include broccoli, Brussels sprouts, cabbage, cauliflower, kale, kohlrabi, radish, rutabaga and turnip. Their bitter taste has actually been linked to the properties which give them their wide variety of health benefits. Check it out for yourself and maybe the next time you eat kale, you'll be thinking of all the fantastic health benefits it provides!

KOHLRABI

DIG INTO THIS!

Kohlrabi grows above the ground and is not a root vegetable. The bulb is actually a swollen stem.

Kohlrabi comes in white, purple or light green colors.

Eat kohlrabi raw or cooked.

For the mildest flavor, use smaller kohlrabi bulbs.

Kohlrabi greens can be cooked any way you would cook kale.

1/2 cup raw kohlrabi has about 19 calories.

Kohlrabi is considered a "heart healthy" vegetable as it contains no fat or cholesterol.

Kohlrabi is a great source of vitamin C.

Kohlrabi is a cruciferous vegetable that belongs to the Brassica family.

HOW DOES YOUR GARDEN GROW...?

* Days to maturity: 40 to 45.
* Kohlrabi grows best when planted next to beets, bush beans, cucumbers, lettuce, onions, potatoes or tomatoes.
* It's best not to plant next to pole beans.
* One week before planting, till in compost to prepare seedbed.
* Plant seeds 1/4 to 1/2 inch deep in late spring.
* Seeds will begin to grow in 5 to 7 days.
* Thin seedlings to 6 inches apart when plants have at least 3 leaves.
* Keep the soil moist and fertilize with a fertilizer such as fish emulsion.
* Harvest when stems are 2 to 3 inches in diameter. Kohlrabi will begin to get tough and bitter the bigger it grows. Pull the entire plant and remove leaves.
* Store kohlrabi in the refrigerator 1 to 2 months.

It is said that if a plant is showing signs of wilt, the plant has already been stressed due to lack of water. The plant will now produce a smaller, less juicy fruit.

A plant receives its nutrients from the soil through the water that is surrounding the plant's roots. In most cases your plants need to receive at least an inch of water a week from rainfall, or watering, to ensure they are receiving the proper nutrients to produce fruit.

When watering, make sure the water is reaching the plant's roots. The amount of water needed for each plant may be different through the plant's life cycle. You may want to purchase a moisture meter at your local nursery to determine the effectiveness of your watering.

Grow it. Preserve it. Prepare it.

FREEZING KOHLRABI

Kohlrabi freezes well, making it a great candidate for preservation.

1. Wash, peel and slice 1/3 inch thick.

2. Blanch 2 to 3 minutes. Drain. Immerse in cold water, drain again and cool completely.

3. Pack into freezer jars or freezer containers. Seal, label and freeze. *(Refer to freezing, page 26)*

Frozen kohlrabi makes a great addition to soups.

HELPFUL HINTS

1 pound of kohlrabi equals 2 medium bulbs, which equals 1-3/4 cups cooked cubes.

Cut kohlrabi in thin sticks to eat raw with your favorite dip!

HAM AND KOHLRABI BAKE

RECIPES

SHREDDED KOHLRABI SLAW

1 large kohlrabi, peeled and shredded
2 carrots, shredded
1/4 cup sliced green onions
3 tablespoons red wine vinegar
2 tablespoons honey
1/8 teaspoon pepper
1/8 teaspoon celery seed

In a small bowl, whisk together vinegar, honey, pepper and celery seed. Toss with shredded vegetables. Refrigerate 30 minutes before serving.

Makes 2 servings

ROASTED KOHLRABI

2 large kohlrabi, peeled and diced
1 tablespoon coconut oil
3 cloves garlic, minced
1/2 teaspoon salt
2 tablespoons apple cider vinegar

Preheat oven to 425° F. Toss the kohlrabi, oil, garlic and salt in a bowl. Spread evenly on a rimmed baking sheet. Roast 25 to 35 minutes, stirring every 5 minutes. Sprinkle with vinegar and serve.

Makes 2 servings

BAKED KOHLRABI

4 kohlrabi, peeled
2 tablespoons butter
1/4 teaspoon garlic granules
1 teaspoon salt
1/4 teaspoon pepper
1/2 cup grated Parmesan cheese

Preheat oven to 450° F. Cut kohlrabi bulbs in half. Cut each half into 1/4 inch thick slices. Combine butter, garlic, salt and pepper in a large bowl. Toss in kohlrabi and stir to coat. Place kohlrabi in single layer on a rimmed baking sheet. Bake 15 minutes. Remove from oven and turn pieces over. Bake 10 to 15 minutes until light brown. Remove from oven and sprinkle with cheese. Bake 5 minutes to brown cheese.

Makes 4 to 6 servings

BUTTERED KOHLRABI

4 medium kohlrabi, unpeeled
1 cup chicken broth *(page 158)*
1/4 cup butter
1/2 teaspoon dried thyme
1/2 teaspoon salt
1/8 teaspoon pepper

Wash, cut ends and remove spikes and leaves from kohlrabi. Cut into 1/2 to 3/4 inch cubes. Place all ingredients in a large skillet. Cover and cook over medium-high heat 15 minutes, stirring occasionally, until tender.

Makes 4 servings

HAM AND KOHLRABI BAKE

1/4 cup butter
4 kohlrabi, peeled and sliced
1 cup diced ham
2 tablespoons fresh chopped parsley
2/3 cup heavy cream
1/3 cup shredded raw cheddar cheese
1/8 teaspoon ground nutmeg
1/2 teaspoon salt
1/4 teaspoon pepper

Preheat oven to 350° F. Melt butter in a large skillet. Add kohlrabi and cook 10 to 12 minutes. In a small pan, heat cream over low heat. Stir in cheese, nutmeg, salt and pepper. Place half of kohlrabi in a buttered casserole. Add ham and parsley. Top with remaining kohlrabi. Pour sauce over all. Bake uncovered 30 to 35 minutes until lightly browned.

Makes 4 servings

LEEKS

DIG INTO THIS!

Leeks are cousins to onions, shallots and garlic.

Leeks contain healthy amounts of folic acid and vitamins A and K.

Leeks are thought to have diuretic, laxative and anti-septic properties.

Leeks sweeten as they cook and have a milder, more herbal flavor than onions.

March to October are the best months to find leeks at the market.

Select leeks with clean, crisp, white bottoms and fresh-looking tops. Small to medium size leeks are the most tender.

Leeks can be used as onions in many recipes.

HOW DOES YOUR GARDEN GROW...?

✳ Days to maturity from transplant: 90 to 120.

✳ Leeks grow best next to carrots and tomatoes.

✳ It's best not to plant next to beans or peas.

✳ Leeks prefer deep, rich soil.

✳ Purchase seedlings from your local nursery or start inside 4 to 6 weeks before last frost.

✳ Seeds begin to grow in 5 to 7 days.

✳ Transplant seedlings in late spring.

✳ To transplant, remove seedlings from growing flat and gently pull roots apart. With a hoe, dig a trench about 8 inches deep. Set leeks in trench, spacing 4 to 6 inches apart. Fill trench with soil and gently press soil around leeks.

✳ When plants are the size of a pencil, mound soil around the base of the plant and repeat procedure every few weeks. The below ground stalks will be long and creamy white.

✳ Harvest when base reaches 1 inch in diameter.

✳ To harvest, loosen soil with garden fork and gently pull from ground. Harvest as needed as leeks keep 2 to 3 weeks in the refrigerator.

At times gardening can become another job to do. Watering, weeding, fertilizing, thinning, mounding, pruning, mulching and you name it. Sometimes we begin to wonder if it is worth the effort. But as we watch the plants grow and produce amazing fruit, we realize there is nothing tastier than fresh picked fruits and vegetables. Now we can enjoy the fruits of our labor!

Grow it. Preserve it. Prepare it.

FREEZING LEEKS

DEHYDRATING LEEKS

Leeks do not need to be blanched prior to freezing.

1. Wash and remove outer skin. Cut root end off. Slice in 1/4 inch slices and drain until all moisture is removed.

2. Arrange slices in single layer on a parchment lined baking sheet. Freeze.

3. Pour into freezer bags, label and return to freezer.

Frozen leeks can be tossed into your favorite stir-fry, soup or casserole. Frozen leeks will keep 3 to 6 months.

1. Wash and remove outer skin. Cut root end off. Slice in 1/4 inch slices and drain until all moisture is removed.

2. Lay leeks flat on dehydrator trays. Dehydrate according to manufacturer's instructions. *(Refer to dehydrating, page 25)*

Use in soups, stews, or toss into your favorite stir-fry.

Prepare leeks by removing outer skin. Cut root end off along with 1/4 inch of white base. Cut green top end off at the point where the first leaves branch away from the main stem. Slice the leeks in half lengthwise. Run under cold water making sure all dirt is removed between layers. Drain and proceed with recipe.

GLAZED CARROTS AND LEEK.

GLAZED CARROTS AND LEEKS

2 leeks, washed and sliced

4 carrots, sliced

1/3 cup chicken broth *(page 158)*

3 tablespoons butter

1 tablespoon honey

1/2 teaspoon dried thyme

1 teaspoon salt

1/4 teaspoon pepper

Place all ingredients in a large skillet and bring to boil. Reduce heat and simmer 15 minutes until liquid evaporates. Continue cooking an additional 2 to 3 minutes, stirring occasionally until lightly browned.

Makes 4 servings

POTATO LEEK SOUP

5 leeks, washed and chopped

4 Yukon gold potatoes, peeled and diced

1/4 cup butter, melted

4 cups chicken broth *(page 158)*

2 cups heavy cream

1 teaspoon salt

1/2 teaspoon pepper

1 tablespoon chives, optional

Preheat oven to 400° F. In a large bowl, combine leeks and potatoes. Add melted butter and stir to coat evenly. Place in single layer on a rimmed baking sheet. Bake 20 to 25 minutes, stirring occasionally, until slightly brown. Heat broth in a large saucepan. Add leeks and potatoes. Cook over medium-high heat until soft. Puree with an immersion blender until smooth. Stir in cream, salt and pepper. Heat through. Garnish with chives.

Makes 6 servings

CHICKEN CASSEROLE

1 cup raw cashews

2 cups chicken broth *(page 158)*

2 tablespoons sesame oil

2 leeks, washed and sliced

4 cloves garlic, minced

1/2 cup chopped red pepper

2 cups broccoli florets

4 cups shredded cauliflower

3 cups shredded cooked chicken

1 tablespoon Italian seasoning *(page 125)*

2 teaspoons salt

1/2 teaspoon pepper

2 cups shredded raw cheddar cheese, optional

Preheat oven to 350° F. In a small bowl, soak cashews in chicken broth 15 minutes. In a skillet, sauté leeks and garlic in sesame oil 5 minutes over medium heat.

Blend cashews and broth in a blender until smooth. In a large bowl, stir together cashew mixture, sautéed leeks and garlic, and all remaining ingredients. Place mixture in a 9 x 13 glass baking pan. Bake, uncovered, 30 to 45 minutes.

Makes 6 to 8 servings

HELPFUL HINTS
One pound of leeks equals 2 cups chopped.

BACON AND LEEK PIZZA

CRUST:

1 tablespoon butter, soft

2 cups shredded raw cheddar cheese

2 eggs

1/4 teaspoon pepper

1/4 cup grated Parmesan cheese

TOPPING:

6 slices bacon, cut into 1/2 inch pieces

2 leeks, washed and sliced

1/4 cup grated Parmesan cheese

Preheat oven to 350° F. Mix crust ingredients in a medium bowl. Spread on pizza stone or in a buttered 9 x 13 glass baking pan. Bake 10 to 15 minutes until golden brown. Cool 10 minutes.

While crust is baking, fry bacon in a large skillet. Drain grease from bacon and set aside. Sauté leeks in 2 tablespoons bacon grease until soft, about 10 minutes. Sprinkle bacon and leeks over cooked crust. Top with remaining 1/4 cup Parmesan cheese. Bake an additional 5 to 7 minutes. Let sit 2 minutes before slicing.

Makes 2 to 4 servings

CARAMELIZED LEEKS

2 leeks, washed

3 tablespoons butter

1 tablespoon honey

1/8 teaspoon salt

1/8 teaspoon pepper

Slice leeks into 1/4 inch half rings. Place butter and honey in a skillet and melt over medium heat. Add leeks and stir to coat. Add salt and pepper. Cook stirring constantly until color turns darker. Add a small amount of water if necessary to "deglaze" leeks that are sticking to bottom of pan. The water will evaporate almost immediately while loosening the slices. Continue this process of cooking and deglazing until the leeks reach a rich brown color. Toss caramelized leeks on pizzas, burgers or steak.

SAUSAGE LEEK QUICHE

2 leeks, washed

4 tablespoons butter, divided

1 pound ground pork or beef

1 tablespoon Italian seasoning *(page 125)*

1 teaspoon salt

1/4 teaspoon pepper

2 tablespoons grated Parmesan cheese

1 cup shredded raw cheddar cheese, divided

2 cups heavy cream

6 eggs

1/8 teaspoon ground nutmeg

Preheat oven to 350° F. Place 2 tablespoons butter in a 9 x 9 glass pan. Put in oven a couple minutes to melt butter. Remove and set aside.

Cut leeks into 1/4 inch half rings. Place leeks and 2 tablespoons butter in a large skillet. Sauté over medium heat until golden brown. Transfer leeks to a bowl and set aside. Brown meat with Italian seasoning, salt and pepper. Set aside.

Sprinkle Parmesan cheese evenly on top of melted butter in pan. Spread 1/2 cup cheddar cheese over Parmesan cheese. Layer with browned meat, remaining cheddar cheese and leeks. In a medium bowl, whisk together cream, eggs and nutmeg. Pour egg mixture over all and bake 40 to 50 minutes. Cool 10 minutes to set before serving.

Makes 6 to 8 servings

LETTUCE

DIG INTO THIS!

Lettuce leaves that are darker in color contain more vitamins and minerals.

Romaine lettuce is an excellent source of vitamins A and K.

Romaine lettuce is considered a "heart healthy" green due to its vitamin C and beta-carotene content.

Iceberg lettuce is the least nutritious.

Grow lettuce in gardens, tuck it into flowerbeds, or grow in pots and containers.

Place a handful of lettuce in a smoothie or juice drink for added health benefits.

To make a quick snack, wrap sliced meat, cheese, tuna or egg salad in lettuce leaves.

HOW DOES YOUR GARDEN GROW...?

※ Days to maturity from direct seed: 28 leaf lettuce, 45 to 60 head varieties. Days to maturity from transplant: 35 to 50.

※ Lettuce is a cool season crop that grows well in the spring and fall.

※ Summer Crisp varieties do well in the warmest part of the growing season.

※ One week before planting, till in compost to prepare seedbed.

※ Soil should be well drained and moist, but not soggy. Since the seed is so small, the soil should be well-tilled before planting. Large clumps of dirt will reduce germination.

※ Your local nursery may have lettuce available to transplant.

※ Leaf lettuce: plant seeds 1/4 to 1/2 inch deep in rows 4 inches apart.

※ Romaine and loose-head types: plant seeds 1/4 to 1/2 inch deep with seeds 8 inches apart.

※ Butterhead and iceberg types: plant seeds or transplants 12 inches apart.

※ Your rows of plants should be 16 inches apart.

※ Lettuce seeds will begin to grow in 7 to 14 days.

※ Consider planting rows of chives or garlic between your lettuce to control aphids.

※ Fertilize with a slow-release fertilizer.

※ An organic mulch will help conserve moisture, suppress weeds, and keep soil temperatures cool throughout the warmer months.

※ Water regularly (leaves will wilt when they need water).

※ Cut leaf lettuces about an inch above the soil as soon as leaves are salad sized. The plant will continue to produce.

※ Harvest head types as soon as plants are mature, but still young and tender.

※ Store leaf lettuce, unwashed, in closed plastic bag in refrigerator up to 1 week.

※ Wash and dry romaine, butterhead and iceberg lettuce and store in plastic bag in refrigerator up to 1 week.

Grow it. Preserve it. Prepare it.

There are hundreds of varieties of lettuce in a wide range of shapes, colors, forms and tastes. Leaf lettuce, summer crisp, iceberg, romaine, butterhead and bibb are some of the most common varieties.

LEAF LETTUCE:
Loose leaves are tender and sweet tasting.

ROMAINE:
Oblong leaves form fairly loose upright heads with a slightly tart flavor. Romaine leaves come in shades of green and red.

BUTTERHEAD AND BIBB:
This class of lettuce forms heads of beautiful tender, wavy leaves with a delicate flavor and creamy texture.

SUMMER CRISP:
Both leaf and head type lettuces are combined to produce crisp leaves with good flavor.

HELPFUL HINTS
One head of romaine lettuce equals 5 cups. One pound of lettuce equals 8 to 10 cups.

Children love to help wash and spin lettuce dry in a salad spinner!

RECIPES

OLIVE OIL DRESSING
2 tablespoons olive oil
1 tablespoon Dijon mustard
3 tablespoons lemon juice
1/2 teaspoon salt

Whisk all ingredients together in a small bowl. Serve with your choice of greens.

Makes 1/3 cup

GARLIC AVOCADO VINAIGRETTE
3 cloves garlic, minced
3 tablespoons lemon juice
2 tablespoons grated Parmesan cheese
1/2 teaspoon salt
1/4 teaspoon pepper
1/4 cup avocado oil

In a small bowl, combine all ingredients except oil. Slowly pour in avocado oil while whisking. Serve on your favorite salad greens.

Makes 1/2 cup

RASPBERRY VINAIGRETTE
2 tablespoons lemon juice
1/4 cup olive oil
1/2 cup raspberries, fresh or frozen
1 tablespoon honey
1/4 teaspoon pepper
1/4 teaspoon salt

Blend all ingredients in a blender or a food processor until smooth. Great with salads, grilled chicken or used as a marinade.

Makes 1 cup

CRANBERRY VINAIGRETTE
2 tablespoons red wine vinegar
1/4 cup olive oil
1 tablespoon Dijon mustard
3 tablespoons honey
1/4 teaspoon garlic granules
1/2 teaspoon salt
1/8 teaspoon pepper
1/2 cup cranberries, fresh or frozen

Blend all ingredients except cranberries in a blender or a food processor. Add cranberries and process until smooth. Great with salads, grilled chicken or used as a marinade.

Makes 1 cup

ITALIAN DRESSING
3 tablespoons apple cider vinegar
1 teaspoon Dijon mustard
1/4 cup sesame oil
1/4 teaspoon honey
1 teaspoon minced onion
2 cloves garlic, minced
1/4 teaspoon dried thyme
1/2 teaspoon dried basil
1/2 teaspoon dried oregano
1 teaspoon salt
1/2 teaspoon pepper

In a small bowl, whisk all ingredients together. Use on your favorite salad or as a marinade.

Makes 1/2 cup

FRENCH DRESSING

3/4 cup sesame oil
3/4 cup honey
1/3 cup ketchup *(page 255)*
1/3 cup apple cider vinegar
1/3 cup chopped onion
4 cloves garlic, minced
1 teaspoon salt
1/8 teaspoon cayenne pepper
1 teaspoon paprika
1/2 teaspoon celery seed

Blend all ingredients in a blender. Store in refrigerator 2 to 3 weeks. Great on all types of salad greens.

Makes 2 cups

CAESAR DRESSING

1 egg yolk at room temperature *(this is important)*
1 tablespoon apple cider vinegar
1/3 cup olive oil
1/2 teaspoon prepared mustard
1 tablespoon lemon juice
3 cloves garlic, minced
2 tablespoons grated Parmesan cheese
1/2 teaspoon salt
1/4 teaspoon pepper

Blend egg yolk, vinegar and oil in a blender on low speed until creamy. Add remaining ingredients and blend well. Try this on wedge salads.

Makes 1/2 cup

HONEY DIJON DRESSING

1/2 cup honey
1/4 cup Dijon mustard
3 tablespoons olive oil

Place all ingredients in a blender and blend until smooth. For best flavor, refrigerate overnight. This is good on spinach greens with bacon.

Makes 3/4 cup

BUTTERHEAD LETTUCE SALAD

1 head butterhead lettuce
1 cup cherry tomatoes, sliced in half
1 cup shredded raw cheddar cheese
2 boiled eggs, sliced *(page 152)*
2 avocados, diced
5 fresh basil leaves, chopped

Wash and dry lettuce. Tear lettuce into pieces and place in a large salad bowl with remaining ingredients. Drizzle Olive Oil Dressing *(page 150)* over salad and toss well.

Makes 4 servings

MOM'S CREAMY LEAF LETTUCE

5 cups leaf lettuce
1/2 cup heavy cream
2 tablespoons apple cider vinegar
2 tablespoons honey
1/4 teaspoon salt, optional
1/8 teaspoon pepper, optional

Wash, dry and tear lettuce into bite size pieces. In a small bowl, whisk together remaining ingredients. Pour dressing over lettuce. Toss well and serve immediately.

Makes 4 servings

WEDGE SALAD

1 head iceberg lettuce
1 cup cherry tomatoes, sliced in half
1/2 cup crisp fried bacon pieces
1/4 cup sunflower seeds

Wash and remove outside lettuce leaves. Cut into 4 wedges. Cut off core from each wedge. Serve on individual salad plates. Top with remaining ingredients. Drizzle with Caesar or French dressing.

Makes 4 servings

EGG SALAD WRAPS AND RADISH ROSE GARNISH

RECIPES

GRILLED CHICKEN SALAD

2 boneless, skinless chicken breasts
1 teaspoon seasoned salt *(page 125)*
1 head romaine lettuce, washed and chopped
1 cucumber, diced
1 cup cherry tomatoes, cut in half
1/2 green bell pepper, diced
1/2 red bell pepper, diced
1 cup prepared black beans *(page 121)*
1/2 cup black olives
1 cup shredded raw cheddar cheese
1 avocado, chopped
1 cup corn, optional
1/3 cup barbecue sauce *(page 257)*
1/3 cup Ranch dressing *(page 125)*

Preheat grill. Cut chicken breasts into 1 inch strips. Sprinkle seasoned salt on chicken and grill 10 minutes, turning once. Remove from grill. Chop, cover and set aside.

In a large bowl, place romaine with next 7 ingredients and toss together. In a small bowl, mix together barbecue sauce and ranch dressing. Pour over salad. Add chicken, avocado and corn. Stir and serve for a full meal deal everyone loves!

Makes 6 servings

HOW TO BOIL AN EGG:

Place eggs in a saucepan and fill with cold water. Add 1/2 teaspoon salt. Bring to a full, rolling boil. Turn off heat and cover pan 10 minutes. Drain, run under cold water 1 minute, then refrigerate. For easier peeling, use eggs that are 7 to 10 days old.

EGG SALAD WRAPS

1/3 cup mayonnaise *(page 77)*

1 tablespoon prepared mustard

3/4 teaspoon salt

1/4 teaspoon pepper

1/4 teaspoon turmeric

8 hard boiled eggs, peeled and diced

1/4 cup chopped onion

8 romaine lettuce leaves, washed

Paprika, optional

In a medium bowl, stir together mayonnaise, mustard, and spices. Add eggs and onion. Stir with fork, mashing to desired consistency. Spread egg mixture evenly on romaine leaves. Sprinkle with paprika, if desired. Fold into sandwich wrap.

Makes 4 servings

FAJITA LETTUCE WRAPS

1/4 cup plus 2 tablespoons Italian dressing, divided *(page 150)*

1/2 teaspoon ground cumin

1/2 teaspoon salt

2 boneless, skinless chicken breasts, cut into strips

2 red bell peppers, sliced

1 medium onion, sliced

1 cup shredded raw cheddar cheese

8 iceberg lettuce leaves, washed

Mix 1/4 cup Italian dressing, cumin and salt in a medium bowl. Add chicken, toss lightly. Cover and refrigerate 30 minutes to marinate. Put remaining Italian dressing in a large skillet. Sauté peppers and onions over medium heat 6 to 8 minutes until crisp-tender. Remove vegetables from skillet and cover to keep warm.

Add chicken with marinade to skillet. Cook 8 to 10 minutes, stirring frequently, until chicken is done. Return vegetables to skillet and cook an additional 2 to 3 minutes until heated through. Spoon fajita mixture evenly onto lettuce leaves. Sprinkle with cheese and roll up.

Makes 4 servings

EATING PURE

Are you confused about what oils to use and the health benefits of these oils? Don't feel alone. There is so much information bombarding us, and the information continues to evolve. What is deemed beneficial by one health study might be considered unhealthy in another study. We choose to use olive oil in many of our recipes as it is a time proven healthy oil used for centuries.

When purchasing olive oil, look for "unrefined (or unfiltered) extra virgin cold-pressed" olive oil to ensure that the properties have not been destroyed in processing. If it's not labeled as such, it has been processed. Use olive oil in salads or drizzled over prepared food. Never pan fry olive oil on high heat as this can alter the chemical structure of the oil making it an unhealthy oil to consume. Check out some other quality cold-pressed oils, such as avocado, sesame, walnut or macadamia nut oil. These oils can also be used as dressing on salads or served over prepared food. Enjoy the health benefits provided by these great oils.

ONIONS

DIG INTO THIS!

Fresh green onions are slender with a mild flavor. All parts are edible and these immature onions are a tasty treat in the spring.

Eat parsley to get rid of onion breath.

Chilling onions 30 minutes before cutting, and leaving root end intact when cutting, may help reduce tears.

Use low or medium heat when sautéing onions as high heat will make them bitter.

Onions are an excellent source of vitamins C and B6, iron and potassium.

Onions have many health benefits. They are anti-inflammatory, act as antihistamines and are antioxidants.

HOW DOES YOUR GARDEN GROW...?

* Days to maturity: 80 to 100.

* Onions grow best next to beets, cabbage, carrots, lettuce, peppers, strawberries, spinach or tomatoes.

* It's best not to plant next to asparagus, beans or peas.

* Onions prefer fertile, loose, well-drained soil like sandy loam with lots of organic matter.

* Purchase onion seedlings and sets from your local nursery.

* When purchasing onion sets, look for small bulbs about the size of a dime.

* Plant 1/2 inch deep for seedling transplants and 1 inch deep for onion sets.

* Plants should be spaced 3 to 4 inches apart.

* Shallow cultivation early will prevent damaging roots.

* Mulch to maintain soil moisture and control weeds.

* Water regularly each week.

* Harvest onions when most of the tops fall over.

* Gently pull from ground and leave them to cure in a warm, sunny, dry area for at least a week.

* When onion tops and skins are dry and crinkly, clip the tops about 1 inch from the bulbs and store in a cool, dry place (not the refrigerator). However, Walla Walla onions are a sweet, mild-flavored onion which should be used within a few weeks of harvest as they don't store well.

* Store chopped or sliced onions in a sealed container in your refrigerator up to 7 days.

Grow it. Preserve it. Prepare it.

FREEZING ONIONS

If you find yourself throwing away unused portions of onions, try freezing them instead!

1. There is no need to blanch onions. Simply wash, peel and chop.

2. Pack into freezer bags and label. Place bags flat on cookie sheets and freeze. When frozen, re-stack bags to take up less room in freezer.

Freezing onions this way makes it easier to quickly break off sections as needed. Frozen onions can be tossed into your ground meat mixture, soup, or casserole with little or no thawing and will keep 3 to 6 months.

HELPFUL HINTS

One medium onion yields approximately 1 cup of chopped onions.

1 teaspoon onion powder equals 2 teaspoons dried minced onion.

DEHYDRATING ONIONS

1. Slice tops off onions. Cut in half from top to bottom and peel. Place flat side down and slice into half rings. Discard bottom of onion. Place on dehydrator trays and process according to manufacturer's instructions.

2. For roasted dehydrated onions: Preheat oven to 375° F. Place onions on baking sheet and roast several hours, checking every half hour (you will see steam coming off the onions). When onions are brown, remove from oven and place on dehydrator trays. Process according to manufacturer's instructions.

3. When the onions are dry, place in food processor and pulse briefly until onions are chopped with some powder at the bottom.

4. Pour chopped onions and powder into a strainer placed over a bowl. Gently shake to separate powder and minced onions. Store in separate mason jars. *(Refer to dehydrating, page 25.)*

EASY ONION DIP AND DRIED ONION SEASONING

DRIED ONION SEASONING

2/3 cup dried minced onion *(page 156)*
2 teaspoons dried parsley
2 teaspoons onion powder *(page 156)*
1 teaspoon turmeric
2 teaspoons seasoned salt *(page 125)*

Mix all ingredients together in a small bowl and store in an airtight container.

Use this seasoning in hamburger, sprinkle on roasts or add a dash to your favorite soup.

EASY ONION DIP

1 cup sour cream
2 tablespoons dried onion seasoning

Mix all ingredients together in a small bowl and refrigerate one hour before serving.

Makes 1 cup

Enjoy this on your favorite cracker, topped on a baked potato or with raw veggies.

In our homes, onions are a staple like salt and pepper. From scrambled eggs to topping off a steak, they add a delightful taste to every meal.

FRENCH ONION DIP

1/4 cup butter
3 cups diced onions
1-1/2 cups sour cream
1/3 cup mayonnaise *(page 77)*
1/4 teaspoon garlic powder
1/4 teaspoon pepper
1 teaspoon salt

In a large skillet, sauté onions in butter over medium-low heat 20 minutes until caramelized. Remove from heat. Cool. In a medium bowl, mix together remaining ingredients.

Add cooled onions and refrigerate. Stir before serving. Serve with your favorite veggies.

Makes 3 cups

CARAMELIZED ONIONS

1 medium onion
3 tablespoons butter
1/8 teaspoon salt
1/8 teaspoon pepper

Slice top off onion. Cut in half from top to bottom and peel. Place flat side down and slice into half rings. Discard bottom of onion. Place butter in a large skillet and melt over medium heat. Add onions and stir until coated. Add salt and pepper. Continue cooking and stirring constantly until color turns darker.

Add a very small amount of water if necessary to "deglaze" onions that are sticking to the bottom of pan. The water will evaporate almost immediately while loosening the slices. Continue this process of cooking and deglazing until the onions reach a rich brown color. These are great over burgers and steak.

VARIATION:
Add sautéed mushrooms to caramelized onions.

HOMEMADE CHICKEN STOCK AND BROTH

1 whole chicken, fresh or frozen
1 onion, quartered
3 cloves garlic
2 stalks celery
2 carrots
1 tablespoon salt
1 teaspoon pepper
2 tablespoons apple cider vinegar

Place all ingredients in a large slow cooker and fill with water. Cook on high 8 to 12 hours. With a slotted spoon, remove onion, garlic, celery and carrots. Remove chicken and place in a 9 x 13 pan to cool. Pour stock through a strainer into glass containers, leaving 2 inches head space. Refrigerate until cool. Label and freeze.

Once chicken is cool enough to handle, take the skin and meat off the bones (save skin and bones to make broth). Place the chicken into glass storage containers. Label and refrigerate or freeze.

WANT MORE FOR YOUR MONEY?
Make a second batch by taking the skin and bones from cooked chicken and place in slow cooker with all new ingredients listed above. Fill with water and cook on low 12 to 24 hours. Remove vegetables, bones and skin. Let broth cool before pouring through strainer into containers.

VARIATION USING BEEF:
Following the recipe above, use beef soup bones instead of chicken.

Stock and broth can be stored up to 5 days in refrigerator or frozen for several months.

CHICKEN SOUP

4 cups chicken broth *(page 158)*
2 cups sliced celery
1 cup chopped onion
2 cups sliced carrots
2 cups chopped cooked chicken
1-1/2 teaspoons salt
1/2 teaspoon pepper
1/4 teaspoon garlic powder
1 teaspoon dried parsley
1/2 teaspoon poultry seasoning, optional *(page 127)*

Place broth, celery, onions and carrots in a large sauce pan. Bring to a boil over high heat. Reduce heat, cover and simmer 20 to 30 minutes until vegetables are tender. Add chicken and seasonings. Continue cooking until chicken is heated through.

Makes 4 servings

VARIATION:
For a heartier soup, add 1/4 cup uncooked basmati rice with broth.

FRENCH ONION SOUP

1/2 cup butter
4 to 5 medium onions, sliced
3 cloves garlic, minced
2 bay leaves
1 teaspoon dried thyme
2 teaspoons salt
3/4 teaspoon pepper
6 cups beef broth *(page 158)*
1 cup shredded raw cheddar cheese

Melt butter in a large pot over medium heat. Add onions, garlic, bay leaves, thyme, salt and pepper. Cook 25 minutes until onions are soft and caramelized. Discard bay leaves. Add beef broth and bring to a boil. Reduce heat and simmer 10 minutes. Garnish with cheese.

Makes 6 servings

EATING PURE

Both of us remember butchering chickens when we were growing up. It was usually a long, cold day in the fall and everyone had a job. Some of our children have experienced raising their own grass-fed chickens, loading them up and hauling them to the local butcher who processed them. Nowadays, we like to hop in the car with our coolers, drive to a local producer, and package them ourselves straight from the ice water tank on butchering day.

Some people say they can't afford to buy free-ranged organic chickens. When you consider a 5 pound chicken will provide at least 20 cups of stock and broth and about 8 cups of shredded chicken, you are getting a bargain for good quality meat, free from harmful antibiotics or hormones!

Chicken stock and broth is very gentle on the stomach and has been known for centuries to aid digestion. The gelatinous soft tissue around the bones and the bone marrow is what provides the most healing benefits. Therefore, it's essential that you use the bones and joints when making broth. You can also make delicious broth from good quality beef and turkey bones. Broth is inexpensive to make and is great to have on hand in the freezer at all times. You will certainly appreciate it the next time you need to make a quick batch of healing soup when someone's sick.

DEVILED EGGS

RECIPES

DEVILED EGGS

12 eggs, hard boiled (*page 152*)
1/2 cup mayonnaise (*page 77*)
1 teaspoon prepared mustard
1/4 teaspoon paprika
1/4 teaspoon onion powder
1/8 teaspoon garlic powder
1/2 teaspoon salt
1/8 teaspoon pepper
1/8 teaspoon cayenne pepper, optional
Chopped chives, optional

Peel eggs and cut in half lengthwise. Scoop out yolks. Place yolks in a medium bowl and mash with fork until fine. Mix in remaining ingredients and stir. Spoon mixture into a quart size storage bag. Snip off corner of bag. Pipe mixture into egg white halves. Sprinkle with chives.

Makes 8 servings

SPICY SCRAMBLED EGGS

1/4 cup butter
1/2 cup chopped onions
1 cup chopped green, red or yellow pepper
6 eggs
3 cloves garlic, minced
1/2 cup shredded raw cheddar cheese
1/2 teaspoon salt
1 tablespoon Italian seasoning (*page 125*)
2 teaspoons turmeric

In a large skillet, sauté onions and pepper in butter over medium-low heat 8 to 10 minutes. In a medium bowl, whisk together eggs, garlic, cheese, salt and Italian seasoning. Cook 5 to 8 minutes, stirring constantly. Stir in turmeric before serving.

Makes 4 servings

We use large eggs in all our recipes to obtain the best flavor, height and texture.

PINEAPPLE CHICKEN KABOBS

6 to 8 wooden skewers
2 boneless, skinless chicken breasts, cut in 1 inch pieces
2 medium onions, peeled, halved and quartered
1 red bell pepper, cut in 1-1/2 inch chunks
1 green bell pepper, cut in 1-1/2 inch chunks
1-1/2 cups pineapple chunks
1/4 cup sesame oil
2 tablespoons seasoned salt (*page 125*)

Soak skewers in water while you cut up the chicken and vegetables. Alternately thread chicken, onion, peppers and pineapple on skewers. Place oil in a shallow pan and roll skewers in it to evenly coat. Sprinkle with seasoned salt. It's best if they can marinate at least 1 to 2 hours before grilling.

Makes 6 to 8 skewers

Storage containers are another thing to consider. We prefer glass for various reasons—they don't absorb the flavor from what is stored in them, food stays fresher, most can go directly from the freezer to the oven, and they last longer making them more economical in the long run. Large glass jars are a favorite for storing anything from nuts and seeds to broth.

PARSNIPS

DIG INTO THIS!

Parsnips are a good source of fiber.

Parsnips are rich in potassium and B vitamins.

Parsnips are in season from October to April.

Some people refer to parsnips as the pale cousin of the carrot.

Parsnips were actually used in Europe as a sweetener before sugar.

It's best to choose parsnips which are 1 to 2 inches in diameter.

Larger parsnips can have a woody center. This can be cut out and discarded before cooking.

HOW DOES YOUR GARDEN GROW...?

* Days to maturity: 110 to 120.
* Parsnips grow best next to bush beans, garlic, onions, peas, peppers, potatoes or radishes.
* It's best not to plant next to carrots or celery.
* Parsnips need a long growing season of 16 weeks.
* Loosen soil in early spring to a depth of 12 to 15 inches. Mix in a 2 to 4 inch layer of compost.
* Plant seeds 1/2 inch deep with rows 4 to 6 inches apart.
* Seeds begin to grow in 12 to 14 days.
* When parsnips are 5 inches high, thin them to 3 to 4 inches apart.
* Water moderately if rainfall is less than 1 inch per week during the summer.
* For sweeter parsnips, harvest after a few frosts.
* If left in the ground for winter, cover with a thick layer of mulch and harvest immediately after ground thaws in spring.
* Store parsnips in refrigerator several weeks.

Mulch is a protective covering usually made up of organic matter like leaves, grass clippings, straw, hay, pine needles or bark chips. Mulch can be used to help control weeds, conserve soil moisture, moderate soil temperature, add nutrient content to soil and help with pH levels. Always think about the quality of the mulch you are using in your garden. You do not want to spray your lawn with weed killers and then use your grass clippings in your garden.

Composting helps nourish both the plants and soil in your garden. We keep a small compost bucket under our kitchen sink for tossing in our fruit and vegetable peels, coffee grounds, potato skins and eggshells. We empty the bucket frequently into our garden compost bin located near the garden. Instead of discarding your vegetable peels, put them to good use!

Grow it. Preserve it. Prepare it.

FREEZING PARSNIPS

1. Select parsnips that are firm and have a smooth skin. Remove tops, wash and peel.

2. Slice and blanch 3 minutes in boiling water. Drain, immerse in cold water, and drain again. Cool completely.

3. Pack into freezer containers. Seal, label and freeze.
   (Refer to freezing, page 26)

HELPFUL HINTS

Four large parsnips equals approximately 1 pound.

ROASTED PARSNIPS

SAUTÉED PARSNIPS

2 tablespoons sesame oil
4 large parsnips, peeled and sliced
6 large carrots, peeled and sliced
1-1/2 teaspoons salt
1/4 teaspoon pepper
2 tablespoons butter
1 teaspoon dried rosemary, optional
1-1/2 tablespoons honey

In a large skillet, sauté parsnips and carrots in oil over medium-high heat 12 to 15 minutes. Add remaining ingredients. Stir to coat evenly. Continue cooking 5 minutes until heated through and glazed.

Makes 4 to 6 servings

BAKED PARSNIPS

6 medium parsnips, peeled
2 tablespoons butter, melted
1 teaspoon salt
1/4 teaspoon pepper
1/3 cup chicken broth *(page 158)*
2 tablespoons butter, softened
2 teaspoons finely chopped parsley
2 teaspoons minced chives
1 clove garlic, minced

Preheat oven to 400° F. Cut parsnips into 2-1/2 inch long strips the width of a pencil. In a 9 x 13 glass pan, toss the parsnips with melted butter, salt and pepper. Add the broth and cover with foil.

Bake 45 minutes, stirring occasionally, until tender. Remove foil and bake 5 minutes until broth is evaporated. Combine softened butter, parsley, chives and garlic. Stir into parsnips and serve.

Makes 4 servings

ROASTED PARSNIPS

8 medium parsnips, peeled
6 to 8 medium carrots, unpeeled
1/4 cup butter, melted
1 tablespoon salt
1/2 teaspoon pepper
2 tablespoons minced fresh dill, optional

Preheat oven to 400° F. Slice parsnips and carrots in 1/4 to 1/2 inch thick slices. Place on a rimmed baking sheet. In a small bowl, combine butter, salt and pepper. Pour over vegetables and toss well. Roast 30 to 40 minutes, stirring occasionally, until tender. Sprinkle with dill and serve.

Makes 6 servings

VEGETABLE SOUP

1/4 cup butter
2 medium onions, chopped
2 cloves garlic, minced
2 stalks celery, sliced
2 medium carrots, sliced
2 small parsnips, peeled and sliced
6 cups beef broth *(page 158)*
1/4 head cabbage, shredded
2 large potatoes, cubed
2 teaspoons salt
3/4 teaspoon pepper
2 tablespoons dried parsley
2 cups tomato juice *(page 254)*

In a large pot, sauté onions, garlic, celery, carrots and parsnips in butter over medium-high heat 15 minutes. Add remaining ingredients. Bring to a boil. Reduce heat, cover and simmer 30 minutes.

Makes 6 servings

PEAS

DIG INTO THIS!

Edible pea pods such as snow peas and sugar snap are good for stir-fries.

Garden peas, also referred to as English peas, need to be shelled and are good for fresh eating.

The smaller the peas, the sweeter they taste.

Half of the sugar content of peas will turn to starch within 6 hours if kept at room temperature after harvest.

Peas should be frozen within a few hours of picking to lock in nutrients.

Garden peas contain healthy amounts of fiber and are rich in B vitamins along with many great minerals.

Sugar snap peas are loaded with the antioxidant vitamin C.

HOW DOES YOUR GARDEN GROW...?

✳ Days to maturity: 49 to 62.

✳ Peas grow best next to carrots, corn, cucumbers, radishes, spinach, strawberries or peppers.

✳ It's best not to plant next to onions or potatoes.

✳ Pea varieties include bush and climbing.

✳ Plant seeds 1 inch deep, 1 inch apart in rows 2 feet apart.

✳ A trellis may be used to support plants. Secure plants to trellis with twine.

✳ Seeds will begin to grow in 14 days.

✳ Water peas 1/2 inch every week until they start to bloom, then water 1 inch a week until the pods fill out.

✳ Peas supply their own nitrogen, so not much additional fertilizer is needed. Too much nitrogen produces lush foliage but few peas.

✳ For best flavor and texture, harvest garden peas when pods are filled out, but not bulging around peas.

✳ Harvest snow peas when the pods reach mature length and before peas are fully developed. Pick often.

✳ Harvest sugar snap peas at their peak when both the pods and the peas are plump.

✳ Eat or freeze peas within a few hours of picking for maximum nutrients.

✳ Store unwashed peas—all varieties—in an unsealed bag in refrigerator up to 5 days.

Grow it. Preserve it. Prepare it.

FREEZING PEAS

GARDEN PEAS

1. Remove peas from their pods, a process known as shelling.

2. Once shelled, blanch 2 minutes in boiling water. Drain. Immerse in cold water. Drain and pack into freezer bags or containers. Seal, label and freeze. *(Refer to freezing, page 26)*

SNOW OR SUGAR SNAP PEAS:

1. Wash pods and trim stem end, removing string.

2. Blanch pea pods 5 minutes in boiling water. Drain. Immerse in cold water. Drain and pack into freezer bags or containers.

3. Seal, label and freeze. *(Refer to freezing, page 26)*

Frozen peas can be added straight from the freezer to any recipe—no preparation needed.

HELPFUL HINTS

There are about 14 sugar or snap pea pods in a cup. One pound of shelled peas equals 1-1/2 cups.

MARINATED PEA SALAD

STEAMED PEAS

3 cups garden peas or pea pods
1 tablespoon butter
1/2 teaspoon salt
1/8 teaspoon pepper

Steam shelled peas or pea pods in a covered pan 5 to 10 minutes until tender (*refer to steaming, page 27*). Transfer to a bowl. Top with butter and sprinkle with salt and pepper.

Makes 4 servings

MARINATED PEA SALAD

2 cups frozen peas
2 cups frozen green beans
1/4 cup chopped onion
4 stalks celery, chopped
1/2 red bell pepper, chopped
1/2 yellow bell pepper, chopped
1-1/2 teaspoons salt

DRESSING:
1/3 cup honey
1/2 cup apple cider vinegar
1/4 cup olive oil
1/2 teaspoon Dijon mustard
1/2 teaspoon paprika
1/8 teaspoon pepper

Steam peas and green beans in a covered pan 3 minutes (*refer to steaming, page 27*). Cool. In a large bowl, combine peas, beans, onions, celery, peppers and salt. Cover and refrigerate 1 hour. Drain off excess liquid. In a small bowl, whisk together dressing ingredients and pour over salad. Toss and refrigerate several hours.

Makes 6 servings

LAYERED SALAD

1 head crisp lettuce, washed and chopped
1 cup celery, chopped
2 carrots, chopped
1-1/4 cups frozen peas, thawed
1 medium onion, chopped
8 slices bacon, cooked crisp and crumbled
2 tablespoons honey
2 cups mayonnaise (*page 77*)
2 cups shredded raw cheddar cheese

Layer first 6 ingredients in a 9 x 13 glass pan in order listed. In a small bowl, combine honey and mayonnaise. Spread over top of salad and sprinkle cheese over all. Cover and refrigerate at least one hour before serving.

Makes 8 servings

OVERNIGHT PEA SALAD

2 cups frozen peas
1 teaspoon butter
1/3 cup slivered almonds
6 slices bacon, fried and crumbled
1/2 cup chopped green onions
1/2 cup cubed raw cheddar cheese
1/2 cup mayonnaise (*page 77*)
2 tablespoons apple cider vinegar
1/4 teaspoon pepper

Steam peas in a covered pan 2 minutes (*refer to steaming, page 27*). Place in a large bowl. Cool. In a small skillet, toast almonds in butter over medium heat, stirring constantly until brown. Combine with peas. Stir in bacon, onions and cheese. In a small bowl, whisk together mayonnaise, vinegar and pepper. Pour over salad. Toss to coat evenly. Cover and refrigerate overnight.

Makes 8 servings

Where is the unprocessed food located in grocery stores? Around the outside edges—this helps make your shopping go quickly. Produce, meat and dairy can all be found on the perimeter of grocery stores.

ITALIAN CHICKEN STIR-FRY

2 tablespoons butter
3 cloves garlic, minced
1 large onion, sliced
2 boneless, skinless chicken breasts, cut into thin strips
1 small zucchini, sliced
1 yellow bell pepper, cut into thin strips
1 red bell pepper, cut into thin strips
1 cup frozen garden peas
1 tomato, diced
1 teaspoon Italian seasoning *(page 125)*
1-1/2 teaspoons salt
1/2 cup grated Parmesan cheese

In a large skillet, sauté garlic and onion in butter 3 minutes over medium-high heat. Add chicken and continue cooking 8 minutes. Reduce heat to medium. Add zucchini, peppers, peas, tomatoes, Italian seasoning and salt. Cook 10 minutes until tender. Sprinkle with Parmesan cheese. Can be served with brown rice.

Makes 4 to 6 servings

CASHEW CHICKEN STIR-FRY

2 tablespoons butter
4 cloves garlic, minced
1 large onion, sliced
4 boneless, skinless chicken breasts, cut into 1 inch pieces
1 tablespoon seasoned salt *(page 125)*
2 tablespoons coconut aminos
1 red bell pepper, thinly sliced
1 chili pepper, thinly sliced
2 cups frozen pea pods
1 tablespoon ground cumin
1/3 cup maple syrup
2 tablespoons parsley
1 cup raw cashews

In a large skillet, sauté garlic and onion in butter 3 minutes over medium-high heat. Add chicken and continue cooking 5 minutes. Sprinkle with salt. Stir and add coconut aminos, peppers and peas. Cook an additional 5 minutes. Stir in remaining ingredients and cook until heated through. Can be served over brown rice.

Makes 4 to 6 servings

PEPPERS

DIG INTO THIS!

Green bell peppers are simply red, orange and yellow peppers that have not ripened fully.

The sugar content increases as peppers mature, making colored peppers sweeter than green peppers.

A "suntanned" pepper is a green pepper with colored spots just starting to ripen and is good to eat.

Red and yellow bell peppers are loaded with vitamin C.

Anaheim or poblanos are a couple of the most common chili peppers.

Jalapeño is a popular moderately hot pepper. Some of the hottest peppers are cayenne, serrano and habanero.

HOW DOES YOUR GARDEN GROW...?

❋ Days to maturity from transplant: Green 50 to 65, red, yellow and orange 70 to 85.

❋ Peppers grow best next to carrots, onions, parsnips, peas or tomatoes.

❋ It's best not to plant next to kohlrabi.

❋ Purchase plants from your local nursery or start pepper seedlings indoors 6 to 8 weeks before last frost. Sow seeds 1/4 inch deep in seed starter mix and water. Place in sunny window.

❋ Seeds will begin to grow in 6 to 8 days.

❋ Harden off seedlings.

❋ Peppers can also be grown in pots on your patio or balcony. They need sun and a lot of heat.

❋ Transplant seedlings when soil temperature is 70° F to 85° F.

❋ Plant 1 foot apart in rows 24 to 36 inches apart. Leaves of mature plants should barely touch each other.

❋ Water at least 1 inch each week until fruit sets and then less as it matures.

❋ Harvest peppers when they reach desired size and color. Peppers left on plant longer will turn from green to colored.

❋ Peppers can be stored in refrigerator 7 to 10 days (hot peppers in a paper bag).

"Harden off" your seedlings before planting outdoors to help them adjust to a variety of temperatures, direct sunlight and wind. This is accomplished by putting them outside in a sheltered spot for a short time the first day, then increased time the next day, and so on for about a week before planting in garden.

Grow it. Preserve it. Prepare it.

FREEZING PEPPERS

Peppers become soft when frozen and thawed. Use them in cooked dishes where texture is not important. They do not require blanching.

1. Select shiny, bright colored peppers with firm skin and no wrinkles.

2. Wash, core and seed. Slice or dice peppers and pack into freezer bags. Seal, label and freeze.

HELPFUL HINTS

One pound equals 2 cups chopped peppers or 2 bell peppers, 5 to 8 small chilies or about 20 jalapeño peppers.

DEHYDRATING PEPPERS

SWEET PEPPERS:

1. Wash and remove core, seeds and membranes. Cut into 3/8 inch discs.

2. Place on dehydrator trays and dehydrate according to manufacturer's instructions.

HOT PEPPERS:

1. Cut large peppers in half with seeds and stems removed. Small peppers can be split to speed drying. Wash and wipe peppers clean with damp cloth.

2. Arrange in thin layer on dehydrator trays and dehydrate according to manufacturer's instructions. Peppers can also be tied together and hung to dry until pods are shriveled, dark, red and crisp.

3. Grind dried peppers and use them as seasoning. *(Refer to dehydrating, page 25)*

It's best to wear gloves to protect your hands from burning when cutting hot peppers and removing seeds. Be careful not to touch your eyes or mouth.

JALAPEÑO POPPERS

RECIPES

HOT PEPPER SAUCE

12 ripe red jalapeño peppers, washed and stemmed

3 cloves garlic, minced

3/4 cup chopped onions

1 teaspoon salt

2 cups water

1 cup apple cider vinegar

Combine all ingredients except vinegar in a small saucepan. Cook 20 to 30 minutes until tender. Puree with an immersion blender or cool and process in a blender or a food processor 15 seconds until smooth. Stir in vinegar. Refrigerate. Let age at least 2 weeks before using. Serve on tacos, fajitas or enchiladas.

Makes 3 cups

JALAPEÑO POPPERS

10 fresh green or red jalapeño peppers

1 cup shredded raw cheddar cheese

2/3 cup yogurt *(page 236)*

1/4 teaspoon salt

1/2 teaspoon ground cumin

1/4 cup grated Parmesan cheese

Preheat oven to 350° F. Wash and cut peppers in half lengthwise. Remove seeds and membranes. Leave tops intact to form a bowl. Place in a 9 x 13 glass pan. In a small bowl, stir together cheddar cheese, yogurt, salt and cumin. Spoon equally into peppers. Sprinkle with Parmesan cheese. Bake 45 minutes until peppers are tender and light brown.

Makes 6 to 8 servings

ROASTED PEPPERS

8 bell peppers (any color), washed

Sesame oil or olive oil

Salt

Heat oven to 450° F. Place peppers on a rimmed baking sheet covered with foil. Roast 50 to 60 minutes. Turn peppers every 15 minutes to roast all sides. They will become brown, darkened and collapsed when done.

Gather up foil from corners of pan and tightly wrap peppers. Cool 15 minutes. Remove skin, seeds and stems. Drizzle with oil and salt as desired.

TO ROAST ON A GRILL:

Heat grill to medium-high and place grates 4 inches from heat. Place peppers directly on grill.

Roast 15 to 20 minutes, turning as each side blackens. Wrap in foil. Cool 15 minutes. Remove skin, seeds and stems. Drizzle with oil and salt as desired.

Makes 6 to 8 servings

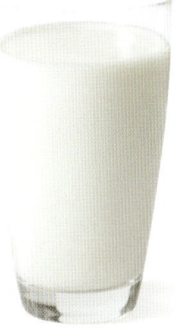

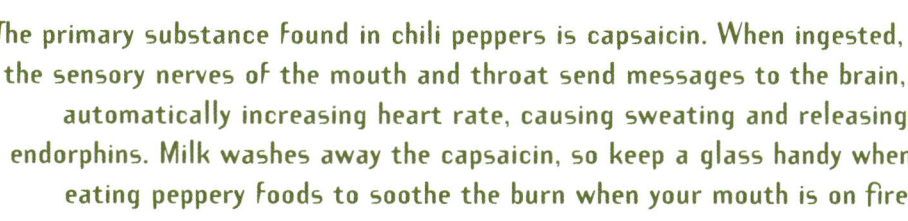

The primary substance found in chili peppers is capsaicin. When ingested, the sensory nerves of the mouth and throat send messages to the brain, automatically increasing heart rate, causing sweating and releasing endorphins. Milk washes away the capsaicin, so keep a glass handy when eating peppery foods to soothe the burn when your mouth is on fire!

CANNING PEPPERS

PICKLED JALAPEÑO PEPPERS

6 pounds jalapeño peppers

6 cups apple cider vinegar

1-1/2 cups water

2 tablespoons salt

1 Wash peppers and slice into 1 inch pieces. Pack tightly into hot jars, leaving 1/2 inch space at top.

2 Combine vinegar, water and salt. Heat to boiling. Cover and simmer 5 minutes. Pour boiling brine over peppers to 1/2 inch from top of jar. Remove air bubbles. Wipe jar rims. Put on lids.

3 Process in boiling water canner 10 minutes. *(Refer to canning, page 24)*

Makes 7 pints

STUFFED PEPP

STUFFED PEPPERS

4 large green or red bell peppers
2 pounds ground beef
1 large onion, chopped
6 cloves garlic, minced
2 teaspoons salt
1 teaspoon pepper
2 teaspoons ground cumin
2 teaspoons dried oregano
2 teaspoons dried parsley
2 cups shredded raw cheddar cheese
4 cups seasoned tomato sauce, divided *(page 256)*
1/3 cup grated Parmesan cheese

Preheat oven to 350° F. Wash and cut tops off peppers. Remove seeds and membranes. In a large skillet over medium-high heat, brown beef with onion, garlic, salt, pepper, cumin, oregano and parsley. Remove from heat. Stir in 2 cups tomato sauce. Stir in cheddar cheese. Place 1 cup tomato sauce in bottom of a 9 x 13 inch glass baking dish. Spoon ground beef mixture into each pepper. Place in baking dish and drizzle with remaining tomato sauce. Cover and bake 50 minutes. Sprinkle Parmesan cheese on top of each pepper. Bake 10 minutes uncovered.

Makes 4 to 6 servings

FIESTA LIME CHICKEN

4 boneless, skinless chicken breasts
1/4 cup lime juice
1/4 cup sesame oil
3 cloves garlic, minced
1 large onion, sliced
1 red bell pepper, sliced
1 green bell pepper, sliced
1 cup sliced mushrooms
3 tablespoons butter
2 teaspoons seasoned salt *(page 125)*
1 teaspoon lime juice

Cut chicken breasts in half. In a small bowl, combine 1/4 cup lime juice, sesame oil, and garlic. Pour over chicken and marinate in refrigerator 2 hours. In a large skillet, sauté onions, peppers and mushrooms in butter over medium-high heat until lightly browned. Remove from pan. In same skillet, sauté chicken, sprinkled with seasoned salt, 10 minutes until done. Top with sautéed vegetables and heat through. Sprinkle lime juice over all.

This recipe can also be used for kabobs!

Cut chicken in bite size pieces and marinate 2 hours. Place chicken and vegetables (cut into chunks, instead of sliced) on skewers. Sprinkle with seasoned salt. Grill 7 minutes on each side over medium heat. Skewers can also be placed in oven on a baking sheet. Bake 15 minutes at 400° F.

Makes 4 to 6 servings

EATING PURE

Peppers (including paprika), tomatoes, potatoes, and eggplant are some of the common "nightshade" vegetables. While all of these vegetables have beneficial properties, they may trigger inflammation in sensitive individuals. Some indications that you might be sensitive to nightshade vegetables include muscle pain, joint stiffness, insomnia, middle back pain, weather sensitivity, heart burn and gall bladder problems. It's amazing what one can learn when you dig in and start to research nightshades! If you suspect you may be sensitive to nightshade vegetables, avoid having them with every meal. We have learned the key to optimal health seems to be eating a wide variety of vegetables, keeping in mind the motto "everything in moderation."

PEPPER SALAD

1 green bell pepper, thinly sliced
1 red bell pepper, thinly sliced
1 yellow bell pepper, thinly sliced
2 cucumbers, peeled and cut in thin sticks
1/2 small onion, chopped
2 tablespoons olive oil
2 tablespoons lemon juice
1 clove garlic, minced
1/4 cup fresh chopped dill
1-1/2 teaspoons salt
1/2 teaspoon pepper

Place peppers, cucumbers and onions in a large bowl. In a small bowl, mix together remaining ingredients. Pour over vegetables and stir. Refrigerate overnight to blend flavors.

Makes 6 servings

Peppercorns are not members of the nightshade family. Fresh ground pepper is best. Once peppercorns have been ground, the flavorful essential oils begin to evaporate, allowing a mold to grow, producing the same toxin that occurs with peanuts. Freshly ground pepper aids in digestion while pre-ground pepper does not.

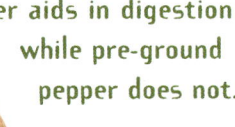

POTATOES

DIG INTO THIS!

Potatoes are extremely rich in potassium and are a great source of fiber when eaten with the skin.

Select potatoes that are well-formed, smooth and firm with no discoloration, cracks or soft spots.

It's best to buy organic potatoes that have not been genetically modified.

Know your source as to where potatoes are grown. Check to see where potatoes are listed on the dirty dozen list found on the Environmental Working Group website.

Potatoes have a high glycemic index, raising blood sugar more quickly than other vegetables. Red-skinned "new potatoes" are the least starchy variety of potatoes.

HOW DOES YOUR GARDEN GROW...?

* Days to maturity: 90 to 120.
* Potatoes grow best next to bush beans, cabbage, corn, parsnips or peas.
* It's best not to plant next to cucumbers, pumpkins, raspberries, rutabaga, squash, tomatoes or turnips.
* Cut seed potatoes into 1-1/2 inch pieces with at least 2 "sprout eyes" just beginning to sprout per piece.
* Plant 3 to 4 inches deep, 12 inches apart.
* To control potato beetles, hand pick beetles off plants.
* Enrich the soil with compost, not manure, to avoid potato scabbing, which is common in high pH soils.
* Plants will begin emerging from soil 14 to 28 days from planting.
* When plants are a few inches tall, apply 1 inch of compost, topped with a layer of clean straw to cover about 1/2 to 2/3 of plant. Continue adding straw as plants grow to keep mulch 6 inches thick.
* Keep plants well watered once they start flowering.
* "New" potatoes can be harvested a couple months after planting. The entire plant can be pulled from ground or 1 or 2 new potatoes from each plant can be harvested, leaving the rest of the plant undisturbed.
* When foliage dies back, the full size potatoes are ready for harvest. Gently loosen soil with garden fork and feel around for potatoes under the soil. Brush soil off potatoes, but do not wash them.
* Store potatoes at about 40° F. Do not store with apples.

Grow it. Preserve it. Prepare it.

FREEZING POTATOES

HASH BROWNS

2-1/2 to 5 pounds red potatoes
1/2 teaspoon salt

1. Place washed and unpeeled potatoes with salt in a large pot. Cover with water and bring to a boil over high heat.

2. Turn down to medium heat and boil 7 to 10 minutes until soft enough to poke with a knife (just par boiled). Be careful not to overcook.

3. Drain. Cool. Line rimmed baking sheet with parchment paper. Add potatoes to food processor and shred. Press shredded potatoes firmly into pan.

4. Cut in squares. Freeze. When frozen, transfer to freezer bags with parchment paper between squares.

To cook, place partially thawed squares on buttered griddle and fry on medium-high heat until browned on both sides.

BASIC POTATO VARIETIES

Red-skinned "New Potatoes"
These are best roasted and used in potato salads.

Russets
This variety makes great mashed potatoes, baked potatoes and french fries.

DEHYDRATING POTATOES

1. Gently scrub and wash red potatoes. Slice into 1/8 inch thick rounds.

2. Blanch 4 minutes in boiling water. While blanching, fill sink with ice water. *(Refer to freezing, page 26)*

3. Drain. Immerse in ice water 15 minutes. Drain again and blot dry.

4. Arrange in single layer on dehydrator trays. Dehydrate according to manufacturer's instructions.

Potatoes will be leathery or brittle when fully dried. These are great for scalloped potatoes or soup.

Yellow fleshed—
This type works well for au gratin potatoes, boiling and pan frying.

White potatoes—
The most versatile variety. Use for salads, boiled, steamed or oven fries.

Blue/purple potatoes—
These are excellent roasted.

POTATO WEDGES

BAKED POTATOES

Preheat oven to 400° F. Wash and scrub potatoes. Pat dry. Rub butter on outside of potato. Place on a rimmed baking sheet. Poke holes in potato with a fork. Sprinkle with salt. Bake 1 hour or until tender. Slice into it, fluff it up and add butter.

Optional toppings: chili, broccoli, cheese, bacon, sour cream, etc.

MASHED POTATOES

5 medium potatoes
1-1/2 teaspoons salt, divided
1/4 cup heavy cream
1/4 cup butter
1/8 teaspoon pepper

Wash, peel and quarter potatoes lengthwise. Put in a medium saucepan. Add 1 teaspoon salt and cover with water. Bring to a boil. Cover, reduce heat and simmer 20 to 30 minutes until tender. Drain. Put hot potatoes into a bowl. Add cream and butter. Use mixer to mash potatoes. Beat until desired consistency. Add remaining salt and pepper.

Makes 4 to 5 servings

Freeze leftover mashed potatoes to use later to thicken creamy soups and stews.

HELPFUL HINTS
3 medium potatoes equals 1 pound. One pound potatoes equals 3-1/2 cups chopped or 2 to 3 cups mashed.

POTATO WEDGES

4 large potatoes
1/4 cup butter, melted
1-1/2 teaspoons salt
1/2 teaspoon garlic powder
1 teaspoon paprika
1/2 teaspoon pepper
1/3 cup grated Parmesan cheese
Dried parsley, optional

Preheat oven to 425° F. Wash and cut potatoes into wedges. Place potatoes in a bowl of ice water. Let stand 30 minutes. Drain and pat dry. Place salt, garlic powder, paprika and pepper in a large mixing bowl. Add potatoes and butter. Toss until coated. Place potatoes on a buttered rimmed baking sheet.

Bake 45 to 60 minutes until brown and crispy. Top with cheese and parsley. Serve.

Makes 4 to 6 servings

EASY POTATOES

8 medium potatoes
2 tablespoons butter, melted
1/3 cup finely chopped onion
1 teaspoon salt
1/2 teaspoon pepper
2 cups heavy cream

Preheat oven to 350° F. Place butter in a 9 x 13 glass baking dish. Boil potatoes in a large saucepan 10 minutes. Drain. Place in refrigerator until cold. Peel and shred potatoes into a large bowl. Add onion, salt and pepper. Stir and place in baking dish. Pour cream over all. Bake uncovered 1 to 1-1/2 hours.

Makes 6 to 8 servings

CHEESY POTATOES

1/2 cup heavy cream

1-1/2 cups sour cream

2 cups shredded raw cheddar cheese

1/4 cup butter, melted

1 cup chicken broth *(page 158)*

2 tablespoons dried onion seasoning *(page 157)* **or 1 tablespoon onion powder** *(page 156)*

1 teaspoon salt

1/2 teaspoon seasoned salt *(page 125)*

1/4 teaspoon pepper

2 pounds hash brown potatoes, thawed

Preheat oven to 350° F. In a large bowl, stir together all ingredients. Pour into 9 x 13 glass pan. Bake uncovered 1 hour 15 minutes.

Makes 8 servings

POTATO SOUP

5 pounds red or yellow potatoes

1 small onion, chopped

4 cloves garlic, minced

1-1/2 teaspoons salt

1/2 teaspoon pepper

8 cups chicken broth *(page 158)*

1 cup shredded raw cheddar cheese

1 cup sour cream

Peel and dice potatoes. Place in a 6 quart slow cooker. Add onion and garlic. Sprinkle in salt and pepper and pour in broth. Cover and cook 4 hours on high or until potatoes are tender.

Blend with an immersion blender. Add sour cream and cheddar cheese. Continue cooking 30 minutes until sour cream and cheddar cheese are melted.

Makes 8 servings

RECIPES

HASH BROWN EGG BAKE

6 cups frozen hash browns
1 pound ground pork
1 small onion, chopped
6 eggs
1/2 cup milk
1/4 teaspoon garlic powder
1 teaspoon salt
1/2 teaspoon pepper
1-1/2 cups shredded raw cheddar cheese, divided

Preheat oven to 350° F. Grease a 9 x 13 glass pan. Place hash browns in pan. Brown pork and onion in a skillet over medium-high heat. Drain.

Whisk together eggs, milk, garlic powder, salt and pepper. Pour over potatoes. Layer 3/4 cup cheese, browned pork and top with remaining cheese. Bake 1 hour. Let stand 5 minutes to set up before serving.

Makes 6 servings

ROASTED POTATOES

2 pounds new potatoes, washed
1/4 cup butter, melted
1 teaspoon salt
1/2 teaspoon pepper

Preheat oven to 400° F. Cut potatoes in half or quarters and place in a large bowl. Toss with remaining ingredients. Place on a rimmed baking sheet and bake 1 hour, turning once.

Makes 6 servings

VARIATION:
When limited for time, add 2 teaspoons dried onion seasoning *(page 157)* and place in a 9 x 13 glass pan. Cover and bake 30 to 45 minutes.

SCALLOPED POTATOES AND HAM

6 medium potatoes, peeled and sliced
3 tablespoons butter
1/3 cup finely chopped onion
2-1/2 cups heavy cream
1 cup frozen mashed potatoes, thawed
1/2 cup shredded raw cheddar cheese
1 teaspoon salt
1/4 teaspoon pepper
2 cups diced cooked ham

Preheat oven to 350° F. Place potatoes in a buttered 9 x 13 glass pan. In a large sauce pan, sauté onion in butter over medium-high heat 2 minutes.

Stir in cream, mashed potatoes, cheese, salt and pepper. Cook until mashed potatoes are blended and cheese is melted. Add ham and pour over potatoes. Bake, covered 60 to 90 minutes.

Makes 6 servings

VARIATION:
Place 4 cups dehydrated potatoes in a 9 x 13 glass pan. In a medium sauce pan, bring 2 cups chicken broth to a boil over medium-high heat. Pour over potatoes and let sit 5 minutes. Continue with recipe as written.

FRENCH FRIES

6 white potatoes, washed and peeled
1 tablespoon sesame oil
1-1/2 teaspoons salt, divided

Preheat oven to 400° F. Lightly grease a rimmed baking sheet with sesame oil. Cut potatoes into pencil-size fries. Place in a large bowl and cover with ice water. Let sit 30 minutes. Drain. Dry thoroughly in a clean dish towel. Toss potatoes with oil and 1 teaspoon salt. Roast 45 to 60 minutes until golden brown. Remove from oven, sprinkle with remaining salt and let sit 5 minutes before serving.

Makes 4 servings

PUMPKINS

DIG INTO THIS!

The United States produces more than 1 billion pounds of pumpkins each year.

Pumpkins are a fruit and are 90% water.

Roast pumpkin seeds for a snack that's super nutritious and high in fiber.

You can interchange pumpkin and squash in any recipe as pumpkins are a variety of winter squash– with the exception of jack-o-lantern pumpkins.

Scratch a child's name in a small, soft pumpkin and it will grow with the pumpkin and be a fun surprise for your child.

Pumpkins are loaded with antioxidant vitamins Beta-Carotene and vitamin E.

A heavy ice cream scoop works great to scoop out pumpkin seeds and scrape inside clean.

HOW DOES YOUR GARDEN GROW...?

* Days to maturity from direct seed: 95 to 120. Days to maturity from transplant: 80 to 105.

* Pumpkins grow best next to corn, celery, radishes and onions.

* It's best not to plant next to potatoes.

* Till area and work in lots of compost or well-rotted manure.

* Plant when soil temperature reaches 70° F.

* Plant seeds 1/2 to 1 inch deep, 12 to 18 inches apart.

* Seeds can be planted in hills. Space hills 24 inches apart with 3 seeds per hill, thinning later to 1 plant per hill.

* Started plants can also be purchased from your local nursery.

* Plant on edge of garden so vines trail away from the garden.

* Seeds will begin to grow in 6 to 10 days.

* Water heavily.

* Harvest when stems are dry and shriveled and skin is hard.

* Cut pumpkin stems from vine and let them sit in sun for a few days to harden skins.

* Store in cool, moderately dry area. Stemless pumpkins don't store well.

Ever wonder what the difference is between a Jack-O-Lantern pumpkin and a pie pumpkin? Jack-O-Lantern pumpkins are bred for carving. They have a thick rind and fibrous flesh with hollow cavities. Pie pumpkins are smaller in shape and have a very thin skin; the flesh is finer-grained and much sweeter, making it a great choice for cooking.

Grow it. Preserve it. Prepare it.

FREEZING PUMPKIN

1 Preheat oven to 350° F. Wash pumpkin and cut in half. Scoop out seeds and scrape inside clean. Save the seeds for roasting.

Place pumpkin, cut side up, on a rimmed baking sheet with 1/2 to 1 cup water. Cover and bake 1 to 2 hours until soft.

2 Scoop out the cooked pumpkin and puree with an immersion blender or regular blender.

3 Pack into freezer bags or containers (measure out by cups needed in favorite recipes). Seal, label and freeze.

Use pureed pumpkin in many recipes including pies and muffins.

HELPFUL HINTS

5 pounds fresh pumpkin equals 4-1/2 cups cooked, mashed pumpkin.

PUMPKIN MUFFINS

PUMPKIN CHAI TEA LATTE

CHAI SPICE

2 tablespoons ground cinnamon
2 teaspoons ground cloves
1 teaspoon ground cardamom
1 teaspoon ground coriander
2 teaspoons ground ginger
1/2 teaspoon pepper
1/8 teaspoon salt

Combine all ingredients in a small bowl and store in airtight container. Use 1/4 teaspoon in a cup of black tea. If desired, add a little cream and honey for a delicious treat. This is a fun spice mix to substitute in muffins, coffee cakes or pancakes.

PUMPKIN CHAI TEA LATTE

3 black tea bags
1 cup hot water
1/4 cup pumpkin (or 2 frozen pumpkin cubes)
2 cups milk
2 teaspoons vanilla
3 tablespoons maple syrup
1/2 teaspoon chai spice
Whipped cream (page 37)
Cinnamon to top

In hot water, steep tea 6 minutes. In a blender, puree pumpkin with tea. In a small saucepan, add milk, vanilla, maple syrup and chai spice. Heat until almost boiling. Combine with tea. Pour into 2 cups. Top with whipped cream and cinnamon.

Makes 2 servings

ROASTING PUMPKIN SEEDS

Place seeds in a colander and run water over them while separating seeds from stringy membranes. Place seeds in a bowl and cover with water. Stir in 1 tablespoon salt. Soak 12 hours.

Preheat oven to 400° F. Drain seeds, rinse and spread in single layer on a rimmed baking sheet. Roast 15 to 25 minutes until lightly browned. Cool before eating. Use in granola (page 62) or enjoy with various seasonings.

PUMPKIN PIE SPICE

2 tablespoons ground cinnamon
2 teaspoons ground nutmeg
2 teaspoons ground ginger
1 teaspoon ground cloves

Combine all ingredients in a small bowl and store in airtight container.

PUMPKIN SMOOTHIE

1 cup yogurt (page 236)
1 ripe banana, sliced
3 tablespoons maple syrup
1 teaspoon vanilla
3/4 teaspoon pumpkin pie spice
1/2 cup pumpkin or 4 frozen pumpkin puree cubes

Place all ingredients in a blender in order listed. Blend until smooth.

Makes 2 servings

Freeze pureed pumpkin in ice cube trays and toss pumpkin cubes in smoothies and lattes for added nutrition. One frozen pumpkin cube equals 2 tablespoons.

RECITPES

CARROTS WITH PUMPKIN SEEDS

6 carrots, sliced
1 tablespoon fresh chopped parsley
1 tablespoon fresh chopped mint
2 tablespoons chopped pumpkin seeds
2 tablespoons lemon juice
1 tablespoon olive oil
1/2 teaspoon salt
1/8 teaspoon pepper

Steam carrots in a covered pan 8 to 10 minutes (*refer to steaming, page 27*). In a medium bowl, mix remaining ingredients and toss with carrots.

Makes 6 servings

PUMPKIN PIE CUSTARD

4 eggs, beaten
2 cups pumpkin puree
2/3 cup heavy cream or coconut milk
1/2 teaspoon salt
2 teaspoons vanilla
2-1/2 teaspoons pumpkin pie spice
(*page 189*)
2/3 cup maple syrup

Preheat oven to 350° F. Butter 6 ramekin or custard cups. In a medium mixing bowl, beat eggs until frothy. Mix in pumpkin, cream and syrup. Add spices and mix well.

Pour evenly into ramekins. Bake 40 minutes or until knife comes out clean. Cool and refrigerate. Top with whipped cream (*page 37*). Sprinkle with nutmeg.

This can also be put into a pie shell to make a delicious pumpkin pie!

Makes 6 servings

PUMPKIN MUFFINS

4 eggs
1 cup pumpkin puree
1/2 cup maple syrup
1/4 cup coconut oil
2 teaspoons vanilla
1 cup rolled oats, ground
1/4 cup coconut flour
1-1/2 teaspoons chai spice *(page 189)*
3/4 teaspoon baking soda
1/4 teaspoon salt
1/2 cup dark chocolate chips, optional

Preheat oven to 350° F. Line muffin tin with paper liners. In a large bowl, beat eggs until frothy. Add pumpkin, maple syrup, coconut oil and vanilla. Mix until smooth.

Grind oats in a blender, bullet or coffee grinder. Add oats and remaining dry ingredients. Stir in chocolate chips and pour into muffin liners. Bake 20 to 25 minutes.

Makes 12 muffins

PUMPKIN COFFEE CAKE

2 eggs
1 cup pumpkin puree, fresh or frozen
2 teaspoons vanilla
2 tablespoons coconut oil or butter, melted
1/2 cup coconut sugar
1/3 cup coconut flour
1 teaspoon baking soda
1-1/2 teaspoons pumpkin pie spice *(page 189)*
1/4 teaspoon salt

TOPPING:
1 cup chopped pecans
1/4 cup coconut sugar
1/4 cup butter
1 teaspoon ground cinnamon

Preheat oven to 350° F. Grease an 8 x 8 glass baking pan. In a large mixing bowl, beat eggs until frothy. Mix in pumpkin, vanilla, oil and sugar. Add dry ingredients. Mix to blend well. Let batter sit 3 minutes while mixing together topping. Pour batter into pan and top with pecan mixture. Bake 25 to 35 minutes until toothpick inserted comes out clean.

Makes 9 servings

EATING PURE

Many of us know that nuts and seeds are very nutritious—providing vital minerals, amino acids and fats. However, we were unaware that they contain enzyme inhibitors, making them hard to digest for some people. Because of this, it's best to buy raw, unprocessed nuts and seeds and soak them (shelled) in salt water about 12 hours. After draining and rinsing, these can be eaten wet or also ground to use in baking right away. To store for later use, dry them in your oven or dehydrator. We like to soak, drain and dehydrate 5 to 7 pounds of various nuts and seeds at a time and store in glass jars for quick access for smoothies, trail mix, granola and baking.

MEATLOAF

1-1/2 pounds ground beef
2 eggs, beaten
1/4 cup pumpkin
or 2 frozen pumpkin cubes, thawed
1/4 cup chopped onion
1 teaspoon salt
1/4 teaspoon pepper
1/2 teaspoon dried sage
1/4 teaspoon ground nutmeg

GLAZE:

1/3 cup ketchup *(page 255)*
1/4 teaspoon ground nutmeg
1/3 cup maple syrup
1 teaspoon dry mustard

Preheat oven to 350° F. In a large bowl, mix meatloaf ingredients. Place in a glass loaf pan.

In a small bowl, mix together glaze ingredients and pour over meatloaf. Bake uncovered 1 hour.

Makes 4 to 6 servings

VARIATION:

For a kid-friendly version of meatloaf, form meat mixture into 2 inch balls and place in a 9 x 9 glass pan. Bake uncovered 30 minutes. Pour glaze over meatballs and continue baking an additional 15 minutes.

PUMPKIN DESSERT

1-1/2 cups shredded coconut
1 tablespoon maple syrup
1 tablespoon butter

In a large skillet, brown coconut in syrup and butter over medium heat, stirring constantly. Press into 9 x 9 glass pan, reserving 1/3 cup for topping.

1/2 cup cold water
1 tablespoon unflavored gelatin
1 cup pumpkin puree
2 cups heavy cream
3/4 cup maple syrup
2 tablespoons vanilla
2 teaspoons pumpkin pie spice *(page 189)*

In a small bowl, sprinkle gelatin over water. Let stand 5 minutes to dissolve. Stir in pumpkin.

In a medium bowl, whip cream with mixer until soft peaks form. Mix in maple syrup, vanilla and pumpkin pie spice. Gently fold pumpkin gelatin mixture into whipped cream. Spread on coconut crust and sprinkle with reserved topping.

Makes 9 servings

PUMPKIN BARS

4 eggs
1/4 cup coconut oil
3/4 cup maple syrup
1-1/2 cups pumpkin puree
1 tablespoon vanilla
1 cup rolled oats, ground
1/3 cup coconut flour
2 teaspoons pumpkin pie spice *(page 189)*
1 teaspoon baking soda
1/2 teaspoon salt

Preheat oven to 350° F. In a large bowl, beat eggs until frothy. Mix in oil, syrup, pumpkin and vanilla. Add dry ingredients. Stir just until blended. Pour into buttered 9 x 13 glass pan. Bake 22 to 25 minutes. Cool. Frost with Cream Cheese Frosting.

Makes 24 servings

CREAM CHEESE FROSTING

1-1/2 cups heavy cream
1 (8 ounce) cream cheese, room temperature
3/4 cup maple syrup
1-1/2 teaspoons vanilla

In a large bowl, beat cream with a mixer until soft peaks form. In a medium bowl, ombine cream cheese, syrup and vanilla. Beat until smooth. Gently fold mixture into whipped cream. Refrigerate before spreading on cooled bars.

Frosts a 9 x 13 pan

Seasonal cooking can help you save money as you eat a variety
of vegetables by taking advantage of what's in season in your area.
Fall brings the delicious tastes and aromas of apple, pumpkin and cinnamon spice treats.
Thanksgiving wouldn't have been the same without my aunt's pumpkin dessert in the line-up of pies
on the buffet table. We've recreated two of our favorite pumpkin treats using pure ingredients.
We hope you enjoy them as much as we do!

RADISHES

DIG INTO THIS!

Radishes are one of the first vegetables to enjoy in early spring.

Radishes belong to the Brassica family, sometimes referred to as a cruciferous vegetable.

The original radish was black and also grows in red, pink and white.

Radishes have antifungal, antibacterial, and detoxifying properties.

Radishes are a natural diuretic that help remove excess fluids by increasing urination, therefore helping purify kidney and urinary systems.

To save space, plant radish and carrot seeds together. Pick radishes, leaving room for carrots to continue to grow.

HOW DOES YOUR GARDEN GROW...?

* Days to maturity: 21 to 30.
* Radishes grow best next to beans, beets, carrots, parsnips, peas or spinach.
* Radishes prefer cool, moist soil with lots of organic matter.
* Leaves worked into soil the previous fall make for a good seed bed.
* Plant seeds in early spring, 1/2 inch deep, 2 inches apart.
* Radishes can be planted successively all season long for continuous harvest.
* Seeds will begin to grow in 4 to 12 days.
* Water moderately to keep the soil from drying out.
* Harvest as soon as they mature for the best flavor and texture. If left in ground too long, they will develop a bitter taste and pithy texture.
* Store radishes in refrigerator 1 to 2 weeks.

The idea of companion planting is to place family plants near each other. Good plant companions work to support each other. Under our "How does your garden grow" section you will find plants that grow best next to each other. By taking some time to plan out your garden you can improve the use of space, provide protection from heat and wind, reduce weeds and garden pests, and best of all, increase yields.

Remember to take into consideration the height of each plant, the amount of sun or shade the plant will receive, the herbs that might help with pest control and the maturity dates of each plant.

Grow it. Preserve it. Prepare it.

RADISH FAN GARNISH

Wash radishes. Cut off tops and bottoms. Lay radish on its side and cut parallel 1/8 inch thick slices about three-fourths of the way through radish. Be careful not to cut all the way through.

Place in ice water. Chill in refrigerator several hours until radish fans out. Drain well and use as garnish.

RADISH ROSE GARNISH

Wash radishes. Cut off tops and bottoms. Cut a thin vertical slice down one side of radish about three-fourths of the way through radish.

Continue rotating radish and cut three or four additional slices (spaced evenly around radish) down the sides, being careful not to cut all the way through.

For larger radishes, you may want to make a second series of cuts about 1/8 inch away from the first set.

Place in ice water in refrigerator until radish opens slightly. Drain well and use as garnish.

RECIPES

RADISH SALSA

1 cup finely chopped radishes
1/4 cup finely chopped cilantro
1/4 cup finely chopped onion
1/2 jalapeño pepper, finely chopped
1 tablespoon olive oil
1 tablespoon lime juice
1/2 teaspoon ground cumin
1/2 teaspoon salt
1/8 teaspoon pepper

In a medium bowl, mix all ingredients thoroughly and refrigerate at least 1 hour before serving (best marinated overnight). Serve on grilled chicken, wraps, burritos, enchiladas, etc.

Makes 1 cup

RADISH SALAD

2 cups sliced radishes
1 cup sliced green onions
1 cup sliced cucumber
1/3 cup olive oil
2 tablespoons apple cider vinegar
1 teaspoon salt
1/4 teaspoon pepper
1 clove garlic, minced
2 teaspoons chopped fresh dill

Place radishes, onions and cucumbers in a medium bowl. Whisk the remaining ingredients together in a small bowl. Pour over salad. Toss well. Cover and refrigerate at least 1 hour before serving.

Makes 6 servings

HELPFUL HINTS

One bunch of radishes equals approximately 12 radishes or 1 cup sliced.

TUNA SALAD WRAPS

10 to 12 ounces canned fresh water tuna
1/3 cup mayonnaise *(page 77)*
1/2 teaspoon salt
1/4 teaspoon pepper
1/2 cup finely chopped celery
2 green onions, thinly sliced
8 large lettuce leaves (romaine, iceberg, or butter)
1/2 cup chopped radishes

Wash and dry lettuce leaves. Drain tuna. In a medium bowl, stir together mayonnaise, salt and pepper. Add tuna, celery and onions. Place in lettuce leaves and garnish with radishes.

Makes 8 wraps

SHRIMP LUNCHEON SALAD

SALAD:
1 small cucumber, peeled and chopped
8 large radishes, sliced
1/2 red onion, chopped
1/2 cup fresh chopped cilantro
1/4 cup lime juice
2 tablespoons olive oil
1/2 teaspoon salt
1/4 teaspoon pepper

GRILLED SHRIMP:
1 pound large shrimp, peeled and deveined
1 tablespoon sesame oil
1/8 teaspoon cayenne pepper
1/2 teaspoon salt

In a large bowl, combine salad ingredients. Set aside. Preheat oil in a large skillet over medium-high heat. Add shrimp and sprinkle with cayenne pepper and salt. Cook 2 to 3 minutes per side. Serve alongside salad for a delicious lunch.

Makes 2 to 4 servings

RASPBERRIES

DIG INTO THIS!

An average raspberry has 100 to 120 seeds.

Select berries that are firm and dark in color.

Raspberries do not ripen after picking.

Refrigerate fresh picked berries and wash right before using.

Raspberries have a hollow core in the middle while blackberries do not.

Raspberries come in several colors—red, yellow, black and purple.

Raspberries are anti-inflammatory, high in fiber, and low in calories.

Raspberries are an excellent source of vitamin C and potassium.

Berries are a low glycemic index fruit.

HOW DOES YOUR GARDEN GROW...?

* Raspberries are a perennial which comes up every year. The root can live for up to 10 years.

* Raspberry types include summer bearing and everbearing.

* Do not plant raspberries where eggplant, tomatoes, potatoes or peppers have grown in the past 4 years.

* Planting garlic near your raspberries helps keep insects away.

* Purchase bare root plants from your local nursery.

* Plant raspberries in well-drained soil in area with good air circulation.

* Plant 18 to 24 inches between plants with at least 6 feet between rows.

* Water 1 to 1-1/2 inches per week.

* Mulch with organic material that is free of weed seeds (wood chips, shavings, leaves) to discourage weed growth and keep soil evenly moist.

* Apply a 10-10-10 fertilizer in early spring.

* Prune canes annually according to your variety.

* Raspberries are ready to harvest when they come off the bush easily with gentle pulling.

* Pick berries in early morning when they are cool. Then refrigerate.

* Store raspberries in the refrigerator up to 3 days. If storing more than 3 days, wash in solution of 3 parts water to 1 part vinegar to prevent mold.

Have you ever found little black bugs in your raspberries? Place raspberries in a sink of cold water with 2 teaspoons salt. Swish gently and the black bugs will float to the top of the water.

Grow it. Preserve it. Prepare it.

FREEZING RASPBERRIES

1. Select well colored berries that are fully ripe. Remove any immature, moldy or discolored berries.

2. Place in a colander and submerge 2 to 3 times in a sink full of cold water. Drain well.

3. Pack into freezer bags (measure out by cups needed in favorite recipes) or freezer containers. Seal, label and freeze.

ALTERNATIVE METHOD:

1. Place washed and thoroughly dried berries in a single layer on a rimmed baking sheet.

2. Place in freezer until berries are solid. Remove and transfer into freezer containers. Seal, label and return to freezer.

HELPFUL HINTS

1 pint of raspberries equals 2 cups. A 10 ounce bag of frozen raspberries equals 1-1/4 cups. 1 pound of raspberries equals 2 cups.

RASPBERRY FREEZER JAM

4 cups mashed raspberries
2 tablespoons lemon juice
3/4 cup honey, warmed
3/4 cup water
3 teaspoons Pomona's Universal Pectin powder
4 teaspoons calcium water from Pomona's Universal Pectin powder

1. Rinse berries and remove any that are spoiled or blemished. Mash berries.

2. Place warm honey in a large bowl. Stir in mashed berries and lemon juice.

3. Bring water to a boil in a small saucepan. Whisk in pectin powder 1 to 2 minutes until dissolved.

4. Pour hot pectin water over berries and stir until mixed well. Stir in calcium water. Read Pomona's Universal Pectin instructions for further information.

5. After ladling hot jam into jars, let sit on counter to cool. Store in freezer up to 1 year.

Makes 7 small jelly jars

CANNING RASPBERRIES

RASPBERRY JAM

12 cups raspberries, fresh or frozen
3 cups honey
2 apples, unpeeled and grated
1 tablespoon lemon juice

1. Rinse berries and remove any that are spoiled or blemished.

2. Combine all ingredients in a large pot. Bring to a boil on medium-high heat.

3. Reduce to medium heat and simmer 45 to 50 minutes, stirring frequently until it reaches desired consistency. The longer it cooks, the thicker it gets.

4. Ladle into sterilized jars. Let sit on counter overnight. Jam can be refrigerated 3 to 4 weeks.

Makes 4 pints

CANNING OPTION: After ladling hot jam into jars, process in hot water bath 10 minutes. *(Refer to canning, page 24)*

FREEZING OPTION: After ladling hot jam into jars, let sit on counter to cool. Store in freezer up to 1 year.

RASPBERRY SMOOTHIE

1/3 cup apple juice or cider
1 teaspoon vanilla
1/4 cup honey
1 cup yogurt *(page 236)*
1 cup frozen raspberries
2 cups ice

Place all ingredients in a blender in order listed and blend until smooth.

Makes 2 servings

RASPBERRY CRANBERRY SALAD

3 cups cranberries, fresh or frozen
1-1/4 cups raspberries, fresh or frozen
1 orange, peeled and cut in quarters
1/3 cup honey

Place all ingredients in a food processor or blender and mix until desired consistency. Delicious eaten alone or served with chicken, turkey or pork.

Makes 4 servings

BANANA MUFFINS

2 eggs
3 ripe bananas, mashed
1 tablespoon honey
1 tablespoon vanilla
1 teaspoon baking soda
1/2 teaspoon salt
1/3 cup coconut flour
1/4 cup dark chocolate chips

Preheat oven to 350° F. In a large bowl, beat eggs with a mixer until frothy. Mix in next 5 ingredients. Stir in coconut flour and chocolate chips. Put liners in muffin pan and pour batter into each liner. Bake 20 minutes or until toothpick inserted into center comes out clean. Remove muffins from pan and place on cooling rack.

Makes 10 servings

SWEETENED CONDENSED MILK

1-1/2 cups heavy cream
1/4 cup honey
1 tablespoon butter
1 teaspoon vanilla

In a small saucepan, heat cream and honey on medium-low heat. When cream begins to steam, reduce heat to low.

Continue cooking, stirring occasionally, until it's reduced to half—approximately 2 hours. Add butter and vanilla. Use as a substitute for condensed milk.

CHOCOLATE SYRUP

1-1/4 cups honey
1 cup cocoa powder
1 cup water
1/4 teaspoon salt
1 tablespoon vanilla
1/8 teaspoon ground cinnamon
1/3 cup dark chocolate chips
1/4 cup butter

In a medium saucepan, bring honey, cocoa, water, salt, vanilla and cinnamon to a boil over medium-high heat. Cook 3 minutes, stirring constantly. Remove from heat.

Stir in chips and butter. Continue stirring until smooth and creamy. Store in refrigerator.

Makes 3 cups

If your honey granulates, don't think it is bad and throw it away. Simply place the jar in a pan of warm water to dissolve the crystals.

BELGIAN WAFFLES
AND RASPBERRY SYRUP

RECIPES

RASPBERRY SYRUP

2 cups raspberries, fresh or frozen
1/2 cup honey
1/3 cup water

Place all ingredients in a saucepan and simmer on medium-low heat 10 minutes until berries are completely soft. Stir occasionally. Cool and strain seeds out (if desired) using a fine mesh strainer or cheesecloth. Store in refrigerator 2 weeks or freeze in ice cube trays for later use.

Serve on waffles, pancakes or ice cream.

Makes 2-1/2 cups

BELGIAN WAFFLES

4 eggs
3 tablespoons maple syrup
2 tablespoons coconut oil, melted
1/4 cup coconut milk
1 teaspoon vanilla
1/4 cup coconut flour
1/2 teaspoon baking soda
1/4 teaspoon salt
1/2 teaspoon ground cinnamon

Preheat waffle maker. In a large bowl, beat eggs with mixer until frothy. Add syrup, oil, milk and vanilla. Mix well. Add dry ingredients. Mix until thoroughly blended. Let sit 5 minutes.

Pour batter into waffle maker and cook 1 to 2 minutes. These are delicious served with raspberry, strawberry or rhubarb syrup or with jam! For a special touch, drizzle chocolate syrup on top.

Makes 2 to 4 waffles

This recipe can also be made into pancakes!

RASPBERRY GELATIN

3 cups frozen raspberries
3 cups cold water, divided
3 tablespoons unflavored gelatin
1/2 cup honey
2 cups raspberries, fresh or frozen

Place 3 cups raspberries and 2 cups water in a medium saucepan. Boil 5 minutes, stirring occasionally.

While cooking raspberries, sprinkle gelatin over remaining 1 cup cold water and let sit 3 minutes. Pour cooked mixture through a fine sieve or cheesecloth to remove seeds. Place strained juice back into saucepan. Add honey and gelatin mixture. Cook over medium-high heat 2 to 3 minutes until gelatin is dissolved. Refrigerate 1 to 2 hours until set around edges. Add in remaining raspberries. Chill until fully set.

Makes 6 servings

VARIATION:
To make a kid-friendly treat, simply add 1 more tablespoon of unflavored gelatin to recipe and pour into a 9 x 13 glass pan. Refrigerate. Cut into bite-size pieces.

RASPBERRY VINAIGRETTE

2 tablespoons lemon juice
1/4 cup olive oil
1/2 cup fresh or frozen raspberries
1 tablespoon honey
1/4 teaspoon pepper
1/4 teaspoon salt

Blend all ingredients in a blender or food processor until smooth. Great with salads, grilled chicken or used as a marinade.

Makes 1 cup

RASPBERRY DELIGHT

CRUST:
1 cup almond flour
3 tablespoons coconut flour
3/4 cup chopped walnuts
1/4 cup butter
3 tablespoons honey
1 teaspoon salt

Preheat oven to 350° F. In a large bowl, mix all ingredients together and press into bottom of a 9 x 9 glass pan or a spring form pan lined with parchment. Bake 15 minutes. Cool.

FILLING:
1/2 cup cold water
1 tablespoon unflavored gelatin
1/2 cup honey
2 cups sour cream
1 tablespoon vanilla

In a medium saucepan, sprinkle gelatin over cold water and let sit 3 minutes. Add honey and heat 2 to 3 minutes to dissolve gelatin. Remove from heat and stir in remaining ingredients. Refrigerate 20 minutes until partially set. Pour mixture on top of cooled crust. Refrigerate until set.

TOPPING:
1/2 cup cold water
1 tablespoon unflavored gelatin
1 cup frozen raspberries, thawed
3 tablespoons honey
1 teaspoon lemon juice
1/3 cup fresh raspberries

In a medium saucepan, sprinkle gelatin over cold water and let sit 3 minutes. Add thawed raspberries, honey and lemon juice. Bring to a boil over medium-high heat. Reduce heat and simmer 2 to 3 minutes, stirring occasionally until gelatin is dissolved. Chill until half set. Stir in fresh raspberries. Spoon over cooled filling. Refrigerate 2 hours until set.

Makes 8 to 9 servings

RECIPES

RASPBERRY LEMON PIE

Prepared Crust *(page 62)*
1/2 cup cold water
1 tablespoon unflavored gelatin
2 cups fresh raspberries
1/4 cup honey
3/4 cup heavy cream
1/2 cup sweetened condensed milk *(page 201)*
1/4 cup lemon juice
Fresh raspberries, optional garnish

In a medium saucepan, sprinkle gelatin over cold water. Let sit 3 minutes. Add raspberries and honey. Heat 3 minutes over medium-high heat until gelatin is dissolved. Chill. In a large bowl, whip cream with a mixer until soft peaks form. Add sweetened condensed milk and lemon juice. Whip together until smooth. Pour 1/2 of mixture on crust. Spoon chilled raspberry mixture over whipped cream. Top with remaining cream. Garnish with berries. Chill.

Makes 8 servings

CHOCOLATE RASPBERRY TORTE

1/2 cup coconut oil
1 cup dark chocolate chips
1/2 cup honey
2 teaspoons vanilla
4 eggs
1/4 cup cocoa powder
1/2 teaspoon salt
1/2 cup ground walnuts
1 tablespoon coconut flour

GLAZE:
1/4 cup dark chocolate chips
1 teaspoon coconut oil
Raspberry syrup *(page 203)*

Preheat oven to 350° F. Line the bottom of a round cake pan with parchment paper and lightly butter paper. Place oil, chocolate chips and honey in a small pan. Stir constantly over medium-low heat until chips are melted. Remove from heat and stir in vanilla. While mixture is cooling, beat eggs with mixer in a medium bowl until frothy. Add melted chocolate mixture and rest of ingredients. Mix well. Spread in pan and bake 30 to 35 minutes. Cool completely in pan. Run a knife around edge of pan to loosen. Remove from pan. For glaze, melt chips and oil over low heat. Drizzle glaze on torte and serve with raspberry syrup.

Makes 10 servings

EATING PURE

Throughout our recipes we use raw honey, pure maple syrup, coconut sugar and date sugar as sweeteners. Raw honey is our favorite! Honey is a healthy natural sweetener, but not just any old honey. You will need to read the label to insure you are purchasing raw, unprocessed honey. Much of the honey today has been heavily processed with heat that destroys some of the natural enzymes, vitamins and minerals. The color and taste of raw honey varies greatly based on the location of the beehives and the nectar they consume. We love the taste of raw wild flower and sweet clover honey and have based all the recipes in this book from those varieties. Use half the amount of honey when substituting for sugar: 1/2 cup honey equals 1 cup sugar.

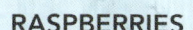

Another great sweetener is maple syrup. Pure maple syrup is a healthy natural food with beneficial nutrients including trace minerals. Use half the amount of maple sugar when substituting for sugar: 1/2 cup maple syrup equals 1 cup sugar.

We use coconut and date sugar in a few of our recipes. Coconut sugar is a minimally processed sweetener with a low glycemic index. Date sugar is unprocessed finely chopped dry dates. Both sugars contain vitamins and minerals making them a healthy choice. Use equal amounts of coconut sugar or date sugar when substituting for sugar: 1/2 cup coconut sugar equals 1/2 cup sugar, 1/2 cup date sugar equals 1/2 cup sugar.

Add raw honey, pure maple syrup, coconut sugar or date sugar to your shopping list to enjoy their many health benefits.

RHUBARB

DIG INTO THIS!

One of the first signs of spring is the appearance of rhubarb.

Rhubarb leaves are poisonous and not to be ingested.

Red colored stalks contain more vitamin A than green varieties.

Fresh rhubarb stalks are readily available from April until August.

Rhubarb is listed right up there with salmon and spinach for high calcium content.

Rhubarb is very high in vitamin K, which helps support healthy bone growth.

The high fiber content of rhubarb aids digestion and regularity.

HOW DOES YOUR GARDEN GROW...?

* Rhubarb is a perennial, which means it comes up every year.

* Rhubarb is easy to grow and lives 10 to 20 years once established.

* Purchase crowns from your local nursery.

* Plant in early spring.

* Choose a site that is well-drained, rich in organic matter.

* Plant crowns 1 to 2 inches below soil surface with buds up and spaced 3 feet apart.

* Water well and keep soil moist throughout growing season.

* Do not harvest any stalks during the first growing season. Harvest a few stems the second year and all you want on the third year.

* Harvest when stalks are 12 to 18 inches long. Grab the base of the stalk and twist as you pull up. Leave at least 2 stalks per plant to ensure continued production.

* Store unwashed rhubarb stalks in plastic bags in refrigerator 2 to 3 weeks.

When selecting garden seeds, there are many options available. We prefer to purchase heirloom (historic) varieties. High Mowing Seeds, a non-GMO certified organic seed company, is one of our favorite resources.

If purchasing through a catalog, you will want to make your seed selection 2 to 3 months prior to planting to get the seeds of your choice. Seed catalogs show growing zones to help you purchase seeds that grow well in your region.

When purchasing from your local nursery, read the labels on plants and seed packets to ensure they grow well in your area.

Grow it. Preserve it. Prepare it.

FREEZING RHUBARB

1. Choose firm, tender stalks.

2. Wash, trim and cut into 1 to 2 inch lengths.

3. Pack into freezer bags (measure out by cups needed in favorite recipes) or freezer containers. Seal, label and freeze.

Traditional jams and jellies contain a lot of sugar. We choose to use honey as our sweetener. Because of this, you get a healthier product but the shelf life is limited.

Jams and jellies made with honey and pectin should be consumed within 1 week from freezer to refrigerator to prevent molding.

HELPFUL HINTS

1 pound of rhubarb equals 3 to 4 cups chopped.

RHUBARB STRAWBERRY FREEZER JAM

2 cups crushed strawberries
2 cups finely chopped rhubarb
1 cup honey
2 tablespoons lemon juice
3/4 cup water
3 teaspoons Pomona's Universal Pectin powder
4 teaspoons calcium water from Pomona's Universal Pectin powder

1. Rinse berries and remove any that are spoiled or blemished. Stem, crush and measure 2 cups strawberries. Place berries in bowl.

2. Place honey in a large saucepan. Add finely chopped rhubarb and cook 5 minutes over medium-high heat. Pour rhubarb over berries and add lemon juice. Stir.

3. Bring water to a boil in a small saucepan. Whisk in pectin powder 1 to 2 minutes until dissolved. Pour hot pectin water over berry and rhubarb mixture. Stir until mixed well. Stir in calcium water. Read Pomona's Universal Pectin instructions for further information. Let sit 5 minutes and ladle into sterilized jars. Immediately store in freezer, up to 1 year.

Makes 5 to 6 jelly jars

RHUBARB STRAWBERRY FREEZER JAM

RECIPES

RHUBARB STRAWBERRY SMOOTHIE

1 cup milk
1 cup yogurt *(page 236)*
2 tablespoons honey
1 teaspoon vanilla
1-1/2 cups strawberries, fresh or frozen
1-1/2 cups rhubarb, fresh or frozen
1/2 cup ice

Place all ingredients in a blender in order listed and blend until smooth.

Makes 2 servings

RHUBARB STRAWBERRY POPSICLES

3 cups fresh rhubarb, cut into 1/2 inch pieces
1/3 cup honey
3/4 cup water
3 cups strawberries, stemmed and quartered

Place all ingredients in a saucepan and heat over medium-high heat until boiling. Reduce heat and simmer 10 minutes until tender. Cool. Puree until smooth with an immersion blender or regular blender. Pour into popsicle molds and freeze until solid.

Makes 8 popsicles

RHUBARB SAUCE

3 cups chopped rhubarb, fresh or frozen
1 cup maple syrup
1/4 cup water
1/2 teaspoon vanilla

In a medium saucepan, simmer rhubarb, maple syrup and water over medium-low heat 30 minutes until thick. Remove from heat and stir in vanilla. Serve hot or cold on pancakes, waffles or ice cream.

Makes 3 cups

OATMEAL PANCAKES

2 eggs
1-1/4 cups coconut milk
2 tablespoons maple syrup
2 teaspoons vanilla
1 teaspoon cinnamon
1/4 teaspoon salt
3/4 teaspoon baking soda
2 cups rolled oats, ground

Preheat pancake griddle. In a large bowl, beat eggs with a mixer until frothy. Add remaining ingredients and mix well. Pour batter onto greased, preheated griddle. Cook pancakes 2 to 3 minutes until bubbly and lightly browned. Flip. Continue cooking until done.

Makes 12 to 14 (4 inch) pancakes

PANCAKES

6 eggs
2 ripe bananas, broken into thirds
1/4 cup almond or peanut butter
1 teaspoon cinnamon
1/4 teaspoon salt

Preheat pancake griddle. Beat eggs until frothy in a blender or in a large bowl with a mixer. Add remaining ingredients. Blend well. Pour batter onto greased, preheated griddle. Cook pancakes until lightly browned. Flip. Continue cooking until done.

QUICK SNACK OPTION:

These pancakes freeze well and are great kid snacks to have on hand. Cool pancakes completely on cooling rack. Layer in freezer bags with parchment paper between pancakes. Eat cold straight from the freezer or pop in toaster and eat with your favorite topping!

Makes 12 to 14 (4 inch) pancakes

RHUBARB CRISP

4 cups chopped, fresh rhubarb
1 cup honey, warmed
1 teaspoon ground cinnamon
1 tablespoon plus 2 teaspoons unflavored gelatin
1/2 cup cold water

TOPPING:
1/3 cup butter, softened
1-1/2 cups rolled oats
1 teaspoon ground cinnamon
1/4 cup coconut flour

Preheat oven to 350° F. In a large bowl, combine rhubarb, honey and cinnamon. Place gelatin in water and let sit 3 minutes. Stir into rhubarb mixture. Pour into a greased 8 x 8 glass pan.

In a medium bowl, combine topping ingredients and spoon over rhubarb. Bake 45 minutes until bubbly and golden brown. Cool 1 hour before serving.

Makes 9 servings

VARIATION:
When peaches are in season, reduce honey to 2/3 cup and substitute fresh peaches for rhubarb to enjoy a delicious peach crisp!

RHUBARB STRAWBERRY MUFFINS

1/4 cup butter or coconut oil
1/3 cup honey
4 eggs
2 teaspoons vanilla
1/2 cup coconut flour
3/4 teaspoon baking soda
1/2 teaspoon salt
1 teaspoon ground cinnamon
1/4 teaspoon ground ginger
1/2 cup finely chopped rhubarb, fresh or frozen
1/2 cup finely chopped strawberries, fresh or frozen
1/3 cup chopped walnuts or pecans, optional

Preheat oven to 350° F. In a small saucepan, melt butter and honey. In a large bowl, beat eggs with a mixer until frothy. Add melted butter, honey and vanilla. Stir in flour, soda, salt, cinnamon and ginger. Mix together until well combined. Gently fold in rhubarb and berries. Put liners in muffin pan and pour batter into each liner. Top with nuts. Bake 20 to 25 minutes or until toothpick inserted into center comes out clean. Remove muffins from pan and place on cooling rack.

Makes 10 muffins

EATING PURE

Making our own food at home with real whole food has helped us more than any special diet. We have tried going gluten-free on and off over the years. We'd feel better for a while, but then would start feeling like it wasn't making any difference. Now we realize it may have been because the gluten-free food we were eating was still processed, made with sugar, and full of preservatives for longer shelf life. When purchasing prepackaged, gluten-free products and mixes, beware, they may contain many hidden ingredients.

If you suspect you might be sensitive to gluten, there is much information available on the subject with the increasing number of people reacting to gluten these days. We have included some delicious gluten-free recipes using alternative flours and sweeteners.

RHUBARB STRAWBERRY DESSERT

CRUST:

1/3 cup butter	**1/2 teaspoon salt**
1/4 cup honey	**1-1/2 cups almond flour**
1 teaspoon vanilla	**3 tablespoons coconut flour**

Preheat oven to 350° F. In a medium bowl, mix all ingredients together and pat into a buttered 9 x 13 glass pan. Bake 15 to 20 minutes until golden brown. Cool.

FILLING:

6 cups chopped rhubarb	**6 egg yolks, whisked**
1-1/4 cups honey	**1 cup heavy cream**
1/2 teaspoon salt	**1 tablespoon lemon juice**
2 tablespoons gelatin	**3 cups quartered strawberries**

Stir fresh rhubarb, honey and salt together in a large sauce pan. Sprinkle gelatin over all and stir to combine. Cook over medium-high heat until it comes to a boil. Reduce heat and continue cooking at a low boil, stirring constantly, about 20 minutes. Add 1 to 2 cups of boiling mixture slowly to the whisked egg yolks to temper. Stir. Slowly mix tempered eggs back into the boiling rhubarb. Continue cooking and stirring an additional 5 minutes. Remove from heat. Cool 5 minutes and stir in cream and lemon juice. Wash, stem and quarter strawberries. When mixture has thickened and is lukewarm, stir in strawberries. Pour over crust and chill 6 hours.

MERINGUE:

1/2 cup honey	**1/2 teaspoon lemon juice**
6 egg whites	**1/8 teaspoon salt**

In a small pan, heat honey until boiling. In a large bowl, beat egg whites 3 to 4 minutes until soft peaks form. While beating, slowly pour boiling honey in a steady stream down the side of mixing bowl. Add lemon juice and salt. Continue beating 8 to 10 minutes until meringue is doubled in volume. Spread on chilled dessert, making sure all edges are sealed. Place under broiler 20 to 30 seconds to brown top of meringue. Meringue burns quickly, so keep your eye on it!

Makes 15 servings

Placing a pan in a clean sink filled with 2 to 3 inches of cold water helps to cool down a hot mixture quickly.

RUTABAGA

DIG INTO THIS!

Rutabagas are a cross between a turnip and a wild cabbage.

Vitamin C, potassium, and fiber are provided in this Brassica vegetable.

Rutabagas have a firm yellow flesh and peppery cabbage flavor that sweetens as it cooks.

Rutabagas are a good replacement for potatoes.

Peel raw rutabagas and slice, cube or grate for a crunchy snack with dips or added to salads.

Rutabagas purchased at a grocery store will have a protective wax coating on them. Peel rutabagas before using.

HOW DOES YOUR GARDEN GROW...?

❈ Days to maturity: 90 to 95.

❈ Rutabaga grows best next to onions or peas.

❈ It's best not to plant next to potatoes.

❈ Work compost into soil before planting.

❈ Plant seeds 1/2 inch deep in early spring.

❈ Seeds will begin to grow in 3 to 5 days.

❈ Thin plants when they are 3 to 4 inches tall so they are spaced 8 inches apart.

❈ Water at least 1 inch a week for good root development.

❈ Fertilize with compost tea throughout growing season. *(Refer to page 93)*

❈ Rutabagas are sweetened by a little frost. Harvest when they are 6 to 8 inches in diameter. Pull or carefully dig plants and cut the tops an inch from top of root.

❈ Store in a plastic bag in refrigerator several weeks.

Fertilize or not to fertilize? The key is to start with good soil that has plenty of organic matter and is rich in nutrients for growing plants. If the soil is depleted, you will have an unhealthy plant. Plants need to be supplied with the right amount of nutrients and moisture to maintain steady growth. If in doubt, fertilize.

Fish emulsion and compost tea are well balanced fertilizers. These fertilizers can provide quick nutrients to a starved plant. When using store bought fertilizers, follow the manufacturer's directions.

Grow it.   Preserve it.   Prepare it.

FREEZING RUTABAGA

1. Select young, medium sized rutabagas. Cut off tops, wash and peel.

2. Cut into cubes and blanch 3 minutes.

3. Drain, immerse in cold water, and cool completely.

4. Drain again and pack into freezer containers. Seal, label and freeze. *(Refer to freezing, page 26)*

FREEZING MASHED RUTABAGA:

1. Cook peeled and cubed rutabagas in boiling water 30 to 40 minutes until tender.

2. Drain, mash, cool and pack into freezer containers. Seal, label and freeze.

HELPFUL HINTS

1 pound of rutabagas diced and cooked equals 2-1/2 cups.

RECIPES

RUTABAGA STEW

1 large onion, chopped
2 carrots, sliced
2 large potatoes, peeled and cubed
1 small rutabaga, peeled and cubed
1 cup shredded cabbage
1 cup cut green beans, fresh or frozen
1 pound beef stew meat
1 bay leaf
2 cloves garlic, minced
3 cups beef broth *(page 158)*
1 tablespoon maple syrup
1 teaspoon salt
1/2 teaspoon pepper
1/2 teaspoon basil

Place all ingredients in a slow cooker. Stir to combine. Cover and cook on low 8 to 9 hours until beef is tender. Stir and serve.

Makes 6 servings

To thicken this stew, throw in some leftover frozen mashed potatoes or mashed rutabaga.

The best beef is from cattle that have been grass-fed and also grass-finished. Cattle that have been raised on a chemical-free pasture have a better ratio of omega-3 to omega-6 healthy animal fat.

Speaking of omega-3 fats, this brings to mind fish—which is best, wild caught or farm raised? Once again, the research shows much debate. We prefer to buy wild-caught fish whenever possible.

RECIPES

RUTABAGA SOUP

4-1/2 cups rutabaga, peeled and coarsely chopped
3 tablespoons butter
1 medium onion, chopped
2 celery stalks, chopped
1-1/2 teaspoons salt
4 cups chicken broth *(page 158)*
2 cups heavy cream
2-1/2 teaspoons smoked paprika
1 teaspoon pepper

Melt butter in a large pot over medium heat. Add onion, celery and salt. Sauté 5 minutes. Add rutabaga and broth. Bring to a boil. Cover, reduce heat and simmer 30 to 40 minutes until tender. Add cream, paprika and pepper. Puree with an immersion blender and serve.

Makes 6 to 8 servings

ROASTED RUTABAGA

1 large rutabaga
1 tablespoon butter, melted
1 teaspoon salt
1/4 teaspoon pepper
1/2 teaspoon apple cider vinegar
1 tablespoon chopped fresh parsley

Preheat oven to 400° F. Wash and peel rutabaga. Cut into 1/2 inch cubes. In a large bowl, toss with butter, salt and pepper. Place on a rimmed baking sheet and roast 30 to 40 minutes until golden brown and tender. Remove from oven and toss with vinegar and parsley.

Makes 2 to 4 servings

RUTABAGA COUNTRY FRIES

1 large rutabaga
1 tablespoon butter, melted
1/4 teaspoon garlic granules
1 teaspoon smoked paprika
1-1/2 teaspoons salt
1/2 teaspoon pepper

Preheat oven to 400° F. Wash and peel rutabaga. Cut into 1/2 inch cubes. Place all ingredients in a large bowl. Toss to coat evenly. Arrange in single layer on a rimmed baking sheet. Bake 40 to 50 minutes until brown.

Makes 2 servings

MASHED RUTABAGA AND POTATOES

1 large rutabaga
1-1/2 teaspoons salt, divided
6 large potatoes
1/4 cup heavy cream
1/3 cup butter
1/4 teaspoon pepper

Wash, peel and cut rutabaga into 1 inch chunks. Place in a large pot and cover with water. Add 1 teaspoon salt. Bring to a boil. Cover, reduce heat and simmer 45 minutes. Add potatoes (washed, peeled and cut into 1 inch chunks). Simmer another 20 minutes until tender. Drain. Add butter and cream. Whip until smooth. Season with remaining salt and pepper.

Makes 4 servings

**Rutabaga is an uncommon vegetable we encourage you to try.
Both the stew and soup were delightful surprises to those we served during our taste testing days!**

SPINACH

DIG INTO THIS!

Spinach is best eaten fresh as it loses nutritional properties with each passing day.

Always wash your spinach even if it's been prewashed. Spinach has been recalled for E. coli and Salmonella. Both are poisonous bacteria.

Spinach leaves are a mild diuretic and laxative.

Spinach is high in antioxidant vitamins, Beta-Carotene, vitamin E and is rich in calcium.

A quick and easy way to dry spinach is with a salad spinner.

Refer to the "Dirty Dozen" list when purchasing spinach.

HOW DOES YOUR GARDEN GROW...?

❋ Days to maturity: 35 to 40.

❋ Spinach grows best next to cabbage, lettuce, onions, peas, radishes and strawberries.

❋ It's best not to plant next to potatoes.

❋ Spinach grows best in cool weather.

❋ Plant 1/2 inch deep in early spring in rows 12 to 18 inches apart.

❋ For a longer harvest, plant a series of plantings 7 to 10 days apart. Stop planting when warm weather sets in and resume again in late summer for a fall harvest.

❋ Spinach seeds will begin to grow in 7 to 14 days.

❋ Harvest spinach as soon as the leaves are big enough to use. Cut leaves an inch above soil level for continuous regrowth. Spinach can also be hand picked.

❋ Spinach is best eaten fresh. Store unwashed in a plastic bag in refrigerator. Wash when ready to use.

In gardening, succession planting is used to increase the availability of a vegetable during a growing season and to maximize the use of space. There are a few ways to accomplish this. One way of succession planting is to harvest a quick growing vegetable, such as spinach, and then plant another vegetable in the same space.

Another way of succession planting is to plant the same vegetable at timed intervals rather than all at once. Spinach and lettuce are great examples of using this method. By planting seeds over a period of several weeks, you can ensure a continuous harvest from spring until fall.

Grow it. Preserve it. Prepare it.

FREEZING SPINACH

1. Pick spinach early in the morning when it is at its freshest. Remove any weeds, or brown, damaged leaves.

2. Rinse several times to remove dirt. Blanch 2 minutes. Drain, immerse in cold water, and cool completely.

3. Drain again and dry in salad spinner or lay on paper towels and pat dry.

4. Pack into freezer bags or containers. Seal, label and **freeze.** *(Refer to freezing, page 26)*

Frozen spinach can be used in smoothies, soups or casseroles.

HELPFUL HINTS

2 handfuls of spinach equals 2 cups, and 1 pound equals 10 to 12 cups of torn spinach leaves.

SPINACH DIP AND SNACK CRACKERS

SPINACH SMOOTHIE

1/2 cup yogurt *(page 236)*
1 handful spinach
1 ripe banana, sliced
1 cup fresh or frozen blueberries
1 cup ice

Place all ingredients in a blender in order listed and blend until smooth.

Makes 1 serving

SNACK CRACKERS

3 cups almond flour
2 teaspoons salt
1 cup sesame seeds
1 cup sunflower seeds
2 eggs
2 tablespoons water
1 tablespoon sesame oil

Preheat oven to 350° F. In a large bowl, stir together all ingredients with a fork. Divide dough into 2 balls. Flatten each ball into a large patty. Place between two layers of parchment paper cut to the size of your baking sheet. Roll into a thin layer. Remove top sheet of paper. Using a pizza cutter, cut into 2 inch squares. Slide crackers and parchment paper on baking sheets. Bake 15 minutes. Flip crackers over with a spatula. Continue baking 10 to 15 minutes until brown and crispy.

Makes 12 servings

SPINACH DIP

2 tablespoons butter
1/2 cup shredded carrots
1/2 cup finely minced onion
4 cloves garlic, minced
1-1/2 teaspoons salt
1/2 teaspoon pepper
20 ounces (approximately 14 cups) baby spinach, washed
1 cup sour cream
1/2 cup mayonnaise *(page 77)*
1/2 teaspoon lemon juice
1 teaspoon seasoned salt *(page 125)*

In a large skillet, sauté carrots, onions, garlic, salt and pepper in butter over medium heat 6 minutes until tender. Transfer to a bowl and set aside. Return skillet to heat and add half of spinach. Cover and steam 4 minutes until wilted. Remove from skillet and place in colander. Drain. Using a large spoon, press down on spinach to remove liquid. Place spinach on a triple layer of paper towels and pat off excess moisture. Repeat process with remaining spinach.

Place spinach and sautéed vegetables in a food processor. Pulse a few times to chop. In a medium bowl, whisk together sour cream, mayonnaise, lemon juice and seasoned salt. Combine with spinach mixture. Stir. Cover and refrigerate dip 2 hours to meld flavors. Serve with your favorite crackers, vegetables, quesadillas or paninis.

Makes 4 cups

EATING PURE

Growing up, one of our favorite breakfasts was fried eggs with bacon. We still love the smell of eggs frying in butter with lots of salt and pepper. Little did we know then that eggs are an easy-to-digest protein. Eat them daily! It's best to buy free-range organic eggs from a source you trust.

SPINACH STRAWBERRY SALAD

1/4 cup honey
1/3 cup olive oil
1/4 cup apple cider vinegar
1/4 teaspoon paprika
1 tablespoon minced onion
7 cups fresh spinach, rinsed and dried
5 cups whole strawberries, cleaned, hulled and sliced
1/4 cup slivered almonds
3 tablespoons sesame seeds

Place honey, oil, vinegar, paprika and onion in a blender. Blend until smooth. Cover and chill 1 hour. In a large bowl, combine spinach, strawberries and almonds.

Just before serving, toss well with dressing and sesame seeds.

Makes 4 servings

SPINACH SALAD AND STEAK

6 cups fresh spinach, rinsed and dried
1/3 cup dried cranberries
1/3 cup walnut halves
1 tomato, chopped
1/2 medium red onion, sliced
Salt and pepper to taste
Cranberry or raspberry vinaigrette
(*page 150*)
4 steaks, grilled

In a large bowl, combine all salad ingredients. Sprinkle with salt and pepper. Drizzle with your favorite vinaigrette. Serve with grilled steak.

Makes 4 servings

STEAMED SPINACH

7 cups fresh spinach
1 tablespoon olive oil
1 tablespoon lemon juice
1/4 teaspoon salt
1/8 teaspoon pepper

Steam spinach in a covered pan 2 minutes until wilted (*refer to steaming, page 27*). Transfer spinach to a serving bowl and toss with remaining ingredients.

Makes 4 servings

CURRIED CHICKEN AND SPINACH

2 tablespoons butter
1 medium onion, thinly sliced
5 cloves garlic, minced
1/2 teaspoon ground ginger
1 teaspoon turmeric
1-1/2 teaspoons curry powder
3 boneless, skinless chicken breasts, cut in 1 inch pieces
1/3 cup chicken broth (*page 158*)
1/4 cup coconut milk
1 red bell pepper, chopped
1/2 teaspoon salt
1/4 teaspoon pepper
8 cups fresh spinach, rinsed and drained

In a large skillet, sauté onion in butter over medium-high heat 5 minutes. Add garlic, ginger, turmeric and curry. Stir and sauté another minute. Add chicken, broth and coconut milk. Simmer 5 minutes. Add peppers, salt and pepper and cook another 5 to 7 minutes until chicken is done. While chicken is cooking, steam spinach 2 minutes. Drain. Place spinach on plates and top with chicken.

Makes 4 servings

SAUTÉED SPINACH

4 large handfuls baby spinach
3 tablespoons sesame oil
2 cloves garlic, minced
1 teaspoon salt
1/2 teaspoon pepper
1 tablespoon butter
1/2 lemon

Rinse spinach well and spin or shake dry to remove excess water. In a large skillet, sauté garlic in oil on medium heat 1 minute. Add spinach, salt and pepper. Cover and cook 2 minutes. Uncover, and cook an additional minute until wilted. Place in a serving bowl and top with butter and a squeeze of lemon.

Makes 4 servings

CRUSTLESS QUICHE

2 tablespoons butter
1 cup chopped onion
1 (10 ounce) package frozen spinach, thawed and drained or 7 cups fresh spinach
6 eggs, beaten
2 cloves garlic, minced
2 cups shredded raw cheddar cheese
3/4 teaspoon salt
1/8 teaspoon pepper

Preheat oven to 350° F. Butter a 9 inch pie pan. Sauté onions in butter in a large skillet over medium-high heat until tender. Stir in spinach and cook until excess moisture is evaporated. In a large bowl, combine remaining ingredients. Add spinach mixture and stir. Pour into prepared pan. Bake 25 to 30 minutes until eggs have set and are lightly brown. Let cool 5 minutes before serving.

Makes 6 servings

When cooked, spinach reduces in volume by about three-quarters.

DIG INTO THIS!

Summer squash is yellow or green (zucchini).

Summer squash have soft, edible skin packed with nutrients, so eat the entire squash.

Yellow or green summer squash can be interchanged in recipes.

Choose summer squash 5 to 7 inches long with firm, bright, glossy exteriors.

Winter squash includes acorn, buttercup, butternut, delicata, hubbard, spaghetti and pumpkin.

Winter squash have a hard shell or skin.

Different varieties of winter squash can be interchanged in recipes as they have similar texture and flavor, with the exception of spaghetti squash.

HOW DOES YOUR GARDEN GROW...?

* Summer squash days to maturity from direct seed: 45 to 50. From transplant: 30 to 45.
* Winter squash days to maturity from direct seed: 85 to 100. From transplant: 70 to 90.
* Squash grows best next to celery, corn, onions and radishes.
* It's best not to plant next to potatoes, melons, or cucumbers.
* Work lots of compost or well-rotted manure into site.
* Plant seeds in hills 1/2 to 1 inch deep in mid-spring when soil is good and warm.
* Space hills 18 inches apart with 3 seeds to a hill, later thinning to 1 seed per hill.
* Started plants can also be purchased from your local nursery.
* Plant on edge of garden so vines trail away from garden.

* Seeds will begin to grow in 6 to 10 days.
* Planting the herb catnip near squash may help repel squash bugs and aphids.
* Water heavily.
* Harvest summer squash daily when they are 5 to 7 inches long.
* Store summer squash in refrigerator up to 2 weeks.
* Harvest winter squash prior to frost when stems are dry and shriveled and skin is hard. (Butternut squash is sensitive to frost.)
* Cut winter squash stems from vine and let them sit in sun for a few days to harden skins unless frost is predicted.
* Store in cool, moderately dry area up to 3 months.

Grow it. Preserve it. Prepare it.

FREEZING SQUASH

SLICED SUMMER SQUASH:

1. Wash and slice in rounds 1/4 inch thick. Blanch 3 minutes.

2. Drain, immerse in cold water, and cool completely.

3. Drain again and pack into freezer bags or containers. Seal, label and freeze. *(Refer to freezing, page 26)*

MASHED WINTER SQUASH:

1. Preheat oven to 375° F. Wash, cut in half and remove pulp and seeds.

2. Place cut side up on a rimmed baking sheet. Cover and bake until tender (baking time will depend on size of squash).

3. Remove from oven and cool. Scoop out squash and pack into freezer bags or containers (measure out by cups needed in favorite recipes). Seal, label and freeze.

GRATED SUMMER SQUASH:

1. Wash and grate.

2. Pack into freezer bags or containers (measure out by cups needed in favorite recipes).

3. Seal, label and freeze.

CUBED BUTTERNUT WINTER SQUASH:

1. Wash, cut off stem and slice in half. Remove pulp and seeds. Peel off skin with a peeler or knife. Cut into 1 inch cubes.

2. Blanch 3 minutes. Drain, immerse in cold water, and cool completely. Drain again.

3. Pack into freezer bags or containers. Seal, label and freeze. *(Refer to freezing, page 26)*

Use an ice cream scoop for quick, easy removal of pulp and seeds from squash.

CITRUS SQUASH SOUP

BAKED WINTER SQUASH

1 winter squash
1/2 cup maple syrup, divided
1/2 cup soft butter, divided
Salt and pepper

Preheat oven to 375° F. Wash, cut in half and remove pulp and seeds. Place cut sides up on a rimmed baking sheet. Place 1/4 cup of syrup and butter in each squash half. Cover and bake until tender. (May take longer if baking with other foods, or at a lower temperature.) Remove from oven and let sit 10 minutes. Remove juice and flesh from skin and place in a serving bowl. Stir and sprinkle with salt and pepper before serving.

Makes 4 to 6 servings

CURRIED LENTIL SQUASH SOUP

2 tablespoons butter
1 cup chopped onion
4 cloves garlic, chopped
3 cups butternut squash, peeled and cut in 1/2 inch cubes, or 2 cups frozen puree, thawed
1/2 teaspoon ground ginger
1 teaspoon turmeric
1-1/2 teaspoons curry powder
1 teaspoon salt
1/2 teaspoon pepper
3 cups chicken broth (page 158)
3/4 cup coconut milk
1-1/2 cups prepared lentils (page 121)

In a large saucepan, sauté onion and garlic in butter over medium heat 5 minutes. Add raw squash with remaining ingredients except milk and lentils. Bring to a boil over high heat. Reduce heat to medium, cover and cook 20 minutes until squash is tender. Puree until smooth with an immersion blender. Add milk and lentils. Simmer 5 minutes.

Makes 4 servings

CITRUS SQUASH SOUP

3 cups chicken broth (page 158)
3 cups fresh or frozen butternut squash, peeled and cut in 1 inch pieces
2 tablespoons butter
3 tablespoons lime juice
3/4 teaspoon salt
1/4 teaspoon pepper

In a large saucepan, cook broth and squash over medium-high heat 20 minutes. Add remaining ingredients. Blend with an immersion blender until smooth.

Makes 2 to 4 servings

SQUASH SOUP

8 cups butternut squash
2 onions, quartered
1 apple, peeled, cored and quartered
1/4 cup butter
2 tablespoons maple syrup
6 cups chicken broth (page 158)
1/4 teaspoon ground nutmeg
1/4 teaspoon cayenne pepper
1-1/2 teaspoons salt
1/2 teaspoon pepper
1/2 cup heavy cream

Preheat oven to 425° F. Wash, peel and cut squash in 2 inch pieces. Place in a 9 x 13 glass pan with onions and apples. Heat butter and maple syrup on medium-low heat until melted. Drizzle over vegetables. Bake 45 minutes until browned and tender. Place in a large soup pot and combine with broth and spices. Cook over medium-high heat 20 minutes. Puree with an immersion blender until smooth. Stir in cream.

Makes 8 servings

Add more protein to Squash Soup by adding shredded, cooked chicken. These soups make a great freezer meal to share with others!

ROASTED DELICATA

2 delicata squash
2 tablespoons melted butter, divided
1/2 teaspoon salt
1/4 teaspoon pepper
1/2 teaspoon dried thyme
1/4 cup dried cranberries
2 tablespoons pumpkin seeds *(page 189)*
1 teaspoon lemon juice

Preheat oven to 425° F. Wash squash. Cut in half lengthwise and scoop out pulp and seeds. Brush insides of each piece with butter. Sprinkle with a little salt and pepper.

Place cut sides down in a 9 x 13 buttered glass pan. Bake 20 minutes. Turn squash over in pan. In a small bowl, combine rest of butter with remaining ingredients. Divide evenly into squash and bake an additional 20 minutes. Eat skins and all like a baked potato. This is delicious!

Makes 4 servings

SIMPLE DELICATA

2 delicata squash
3 tablespoons butter
1 teaspoon salt
1/8 teaspoon pepper

Preheat oven to 350° F. Wash squash. Cut in half lengthwise and scoop out pulp and seeds. Cut into 1 inch cubes. Place all ingredients in a 9 x 13 glass baking dish. Bake 30 minutes, stirring once.

Makes 4 servings

RECIPES

SQUASH FRIES

1 butternut or 2 delicata squash
1/2 tablespoon sesame oil
2 teaspoons salt, divided

Preheat oven to 425° F. Wash squash. For butternut, peel and remove pulp and seeds. Slice into pencil size fries. (If using delicata, keep skin on and slice in half lengthwise. Remove pulp and seeds. Cut in 1/4 inch crescent slices.) In a large bowl, toss with oil and 1 teaspoon salt. Place a cooling rack on a rimmed baking sheet. Lay fries in a single layer on rack and bake 15 minutes. Flip fries and bake an additional 15 minutes. Turn off oven. Leave fries in oven 10 more minutes for further crisping. Sprinkle with remaining salt before serving.

Makes 4 servings

SAUTÉED SUMMER SQUASH

2 yellow or green summer squash
3 tablespoons butter
1/2 red bell pepper, chopped
1/2 medium onion, sliced
1/2 teaspoon salt
1/8 teaspoon pepper
1 tablespoon chopped fresh parsley leaves

Wash and slice squash in 1/4 inch rounds. In a large skillet, melt butter over medium heat. Sauté squash, pepper and onion 12 to 15 minutes until tender. Add salt, pepper and parsley.

Makes 4 servings

This recipe can easily be turned into a quick main dish by tossing grilled chicken into the summer squash. For different variations try adding: spaghetti sauce, cheese, tomatoes, etc.

STUFFED ACORN SQUASH

2 acorn squash, cut in half lengthwise with seeds and pulp removed
4 tablespoons butter, divided
4 tablespoons maple syrup, divided

FILLING:
1 pound ground pork
1 cup chopped onion
1 cup chopped celery
2 cups water
1/2 cup brown rice
1/2 teaspoon dried thyme
1 teaspoon salt
1/4 teaspoon pepper

Preheat oven to 450° F. Place squash, cut side up on a rimmed baking sheet. Place 1 tablespoon butter and 1 tablespoon maple syrup in center of each squash. Cover with foil and roast 25 minutes.

In a large skillet, brown pork with onion and celery over medium-high heat. In a medium pan, bring water to a boil and add rice. Reduce heat, cover and cook 20 minutes. Combine pork mixture and rice. Add salt and pepper. Divide evenly and spoon into squash. Cover and bake 30 minutes until squash is tender.

Makes 4 servings

HELPFUL HINTS
One pound squash equals 1 large acorn squash or 1-1/2 cups mashed squash.

BROWN BREAD AND RASPBERRY FREEZER JAM

RECIPES

BROWN BREAD

1/2 cup warm water, 112-115° F
1 teaspoon honey
1 tablespoon yeast
1 cup cold milk
1/3 cup honey
1/4 cup butter, softened
1 cup unbleached white flour
2-1/2 cups whole wheat flour
1 cup rolled oats soaked in 1/2 cup boiling water
1 teaspoon salt

Mix 1/2 cup warm water with 1 teaspoon honey. Add yeast and let sit 5 minutes *(this is called proofing your yeast)*.

In a large bowl, place milk, honey, butter, yeast, 1 cup white flour and 1 cup wheat flour. Mix by hand or with dough hook on your mixer. Let batter rest 20 minutes. Mix in oatmeal, remaining flour and salt. Knead 6 to 9 minutes. Place dough in a large buttered bowl covered with a damp cloth. Bread rises best when the air temperature is 70° F. Allow dough to rise approximately 1 hour or until doubled in size.

Punch dough down and let rise again. Once the dough has risen twice, place on floured work surface, gently flatten dough and form into 2 loaves. Place loaves in buttered loaf pans. Cover with damp cloth and let rise until doubled in size (approximately 1 hour).

Preheat oven to 400° F. Bake 10 minutes and turn oven temperature down to 330° F. Bake 30 minutes or until golden brown. Remove from pans, place on cooling rack and brush tops with melted butter.

Makes 2 loaves

For those of you who like bread, we have included this recipe using certified organic flour. You may be unaware that some of the best breads on the market may contain residue from harmful chemicals applied to wheat at harvest.

SQUASH COOKIES

1/2 cup coconut flour
1/2 teaspoon baking soda
1 teaspoon pumpkin pie spice *(page 189)*
1/4 cup coconut oil
1/4 cup butter
1/4 cup honey
1/4 cup water
1 teaspoon vanilla
1/2 cup frozen mashed winter squash, thawed

Preheat oven to 350° F. In a large bowl, place dry ingredients. Stir. Heat oil, butter and honey until melted. Add water, vanilla and squash. Mix wet ingredients with dry ingredients. Stir to blend well. Drop by teaspoonfuls onto baking sheets lined with parchment paper. Bake 15 minutes.

Makes 20 cookies

These squash cookies were a great little sweet treat for our grandson when he couldn't eat eggs. We loved them, too! They're especially good when eaten straight from the freezer.

STRAWBERRIES

DIG INTO THIS!

Strawberries are the only fruits with seeds on the outside—about 200 per strawberry!

Choose berries that have a sweet aroma, shiny skin and fresh green leaves.

For best flavor, serve strawberries at room temperature.

Leave stems and leaves on when washing strawberries to prevent water soaking into them and diminishing flavor.

Strawberries are packed with vitamin C, and are a rich source of minerals including copper, iron and iodine.

HOW DOES YOUR GARDEN GROW...?

* Strawberries grow best next to beans, lettuce, onions, peas and spinach.

* It's best not to plant next to cabbage or broccoli.

* Purchase started plants at your local nursery.

* Transplant in mid spring.

* Set plants 12 to 16 inches apart and allow 28 inches between rows.

* Plant upper crown slightly above or level with ground, set roots downward.

* Water moderately. Drip irrigation is recommended to keep moisture away from fruit to prevent fruit rot.

* Fertilize with liquid fish and seaweed fertilizer.

* To protect berries from birds, purchase netting from local nursery and cover when berries start to ripen.

* Harvest when berries are completely red and pull off plant easily.

* Strawberries are a perennial and can be overwintered. In the northern region, mulch with clean straw after the strawberries go dormant (20° F range for a few days). Apply loose straw 3 to 6 inches deep. Gently rake straw off in spring when temperature begins to warm.

* The average strawberry bed will produce berries for 3 to 5 years.

* Store unwashed berries in refrigerator 7 to 10 days.

Strawberries can also be grown in narrow planter boxes or containers.

Grow it. Preserve it. Prepare it.

FREEZING STRAWBERRIES

WHOLE:

1. Wash strawberries, remove any damaged berries or leaves. Drain and pat dry.

2. Remove stems (hull) and place in single layer on a rimmed baking sheet. Freeze 4 to 6 hours until firm.

3. Transfer to freezer bags (measure out by cups needed in favorite recipes) or containers.

4. Seal, label and replace in freezer. Use within 6 months.

CRUSHED:

1. Wash strawberries, remove any damaged berries or leaves. Drain and pat dry.

2. Remove stems (hull) and crush.

3. Place in freezer containers. Seal, label and freeze. Use within 6 months.

HELPFUL HINTS

1-1/2 pounds strawberries equals 4 cups. 2 cups equal about 24 medium strawberries.

STRAWBERRY FREEZER JAM

4 cups crushed strawberries
2 tablespoons lemon juice
3/4 cup honey, warmed
3/4 cup water
3 teaspoons Pomona's Universal Pectin powder
4 teaspoons calcium water from Pomona's Universal Pectin powder

1. Rinse, hull and crush berries (remove any that are spoiled or blemished).

2. Place warm honey in a large bowl. Stir in crushed berries and lemon juice.

3. Bring water to a boil in a small saucepan. Whisk in pectin powder 1 to 2 minutes until dissolved.

4. Pour hot pectin water over berries and stir until mixed well. Stir in calcium water. Read Pomona's Universal Pectin instructions for further information.

5. Let sit 5 minutes and ladle into sterilized jars. Immediately store in freezer, up to 1 year.

Makes 7 small jelly jars

CANNING STRAWBERRIES

STRAWBERRY JAM

4 quarts fresh strawberries
3-1/2 cups honey
2 green apples, washed, cored and grated with skins on
1-1/2 tablespoons lemon juice

1. Wash, hull and cut strawberries in half.

2. Place all ingredients in a large stockpot. Heat on high, stirring constantly, until mixture boils.

3. Reduce heat and simmer 20 minutes until berries are soft.

4. Puree with an immersion blender. Simmer about an hour (the longer it simmers, the thicker it becomes) until desired thickness.

5. Ladle hot jam into sterilized jars. You can either allow them to cool to room temperature and then place in freezer, or process 10 minutes in hot water bath. *(Refer to canning, page 24)*

Makes 4 to 5 pints

STRAWBERRY HERB LEMONADE

3/4 cup fresh mint, chopped
1/3 cup fresh basil, chopped
4 cups hot water
1/2 cup plus 2 tablespoons honey
6 lemons, squeezed
2 cups strawberries, washed, hulled and chopped into 1/2 inch pieces

Place mint and basil in a pitcher and crush with wooden spoon. Add hot water. Stir in honey until dissolved. Add fresh squeezed lemon juice. Chill 3 hours. Add chopped strawberries and infuse in refrigerator another 3 hours or overnight.

Makes 8 servings

PEANUT BUTTER AND CHOCOLATE CRISPIE BARS

3/4 cup honey
1 cup brown rice syrup
1 cup peanut butter
6 cups brown rice crispies
1 cup dark chocolate chips
1 tablespoon peanut butter

In a large pan, melt honey, syrup and 1 cup peanut butter over medium-high heat. Slow boil 3 minutes, stirring constantly. Add rice crispies. Pat into a buttered 9 x 13 glass pan. In a small saucepan, melt chocolate chips and 1 tablespoon peanut butter over low heat, stirring constantly. Spread on bars.

Makes 24 bars

STRAWBERRY SAUCE

2 cups strawberries, fresh or frozen
1/2 cup honey
1/4 cup water

If using fresh berries, wash, hull and chop. Place ingredients in a medium saucepan and simmer on medium-low 15 minutes. Stir occasionally. Store in refrigerator 2 weeks or freeze in ice cube trays for later use.

Serve on yogurt, waffles, pancakes or ice cream.

Makes 2-1/2 cups

CHEWY OATMEAL COOKIES

3 eggs
1-1/2 cups coconut sugar
1/2 cup butter or coconut oil
1-1/2 cups almond butter or peanut butter
2 teaspoons vanilla
2 teaspoons baking soda
4-1/2 cups oatmeal
2 tablespoons coconut flour
3/4 cup dark chocolate chips

Preheat oven to 350° F. In a large bowl, beat eggs with mixer until frothy. Mix in next 4 ingredients. Add soda, oatmeal and coconut flour. Stir—dough will be stiff. Add chocolate chips. Drop by large spoonfuls onto parchment lined baking sheet. Flatten slightly. Bake 10 to 12 minutes. Remove from oven and let sit on baking sheet 5 minutes before placing on cooling rack.

Makes 2 to 3 dozen

VARIATION:

Add 1-1/2 teaspoons cinnamon, 1/2 cup chopped nuts or coconut and substitute 3/4 cup raisins or dried cranberries in place of chocolate chips for a delicious granola-type cookie.

Did you know that a lot of strawberries are sprayed with a fungicide to prevent mold prior to harvest? It's important to know your source or buy organic to be certain you have the cleanest strawberries available.

STRAWBERRY SMOOTHIE

1 cup yogurt
1/3 cup orange juice
2 tablespoons honey
1 ripe banana, sliced
2 cups frozen strawberries

Place all ingredients in a blender in order listed and blend to desired consistency. This can also be made into strawberry yogurt freezer pops.

Makes 2 servings

YOGURT

1 gallon whole milk
4 packets freeze dried yogurt starter (we use Yogourmet)
2 vanilla beans (cut in half lengthwise), optional

Place milk and vanilla beans in a large pot. Heat over medium-high heat to 180° F. Cool to 115° F. Remove vanilla beans and discard. Whisk in yogurt starter until well blended. Pour into pint jars. Place in dehydrator set at 95° F for 26 hours to remove all lactose. Store in refrigerator up to 2 weeks.

Makes 8 pints

Yogurt is our "go-to" staple. The uses are endless—with berries and granola for breakfast; a dollop on pancakes or waffles topped with fruit sauce; in smoothies, salad dressings, baked goods, toppings for desserts, etc.

STRAWBERRY SALSA

2 cups strawberries, hulled and sliced
1 small jalapeño pepper,
stemmed, seeded and finely chopped
2/3 cup diced cucumber
1/4 cup chopped onion
1-1/2 tablespoons lime juice
1 teaspoon honey
1/4 teaspoon salt
1/8 teaspoon pepper

In a medium bowl, combine berries, pepper, cucumber and onion. In a small bowl, mix lime juice, honey, salt and pepper together. Pour over strawberry mixture. Stir. Let sit at least 30 minutes before serving to meld flavors. Serve with lime chips.

Makes 2-1/2 cups

LIME CHIPS

3 cups almond flour
2 eggs
1 tablespoon cold water
1 tablespoon sesame oil
1 teaspoon lime juice
2 teaspoons salt
1/8 teaspoon pepper
1/8 teaspoon garlic granules
1 teaspoon chopped cilantro, optional

Preheat oven to 350° F. In a large bowl, mix all ingredients together. Divide dough into 2 balls. Flatten each ball into a large patty. Place between two layers of parchment paper cut to the size of your baking sheet. Roll into a thin layer. Remove top sheet of paper. Using a pizza cutter, cut into 2 inch squares. Slide chips and parchment paper onto baking sheet. Bake 15 minutes. Flip the chips over with a spatula. Continue baking 7 to 10 minutes until brown and crispy. Watch carefully; the baking time might need to be adjusted based on thickness of chips.

Makes 12 servings

STRAWBERRY GELATIN

3 cups frozen strawberries
3 cups cold water, divided
3 tablespoons unflavored gelatin
1/2 cup honey
2 cups strawberries, fresh or frozen
2 bananas

Place 3 cups strawberries and 2 cups water in a medium saucepan. Boil 5 minutes, stirring occasionally. While cooking strawberries, sprinkle gelatin over remaining 1 cup cold water and let sit 3 minutes. Pour cooked mixture through a fine sieve or cheesecloth to remove seeds. Place strained juice back into saucepan. Add honey and gelatin mixture. Cook over medium-high heat 2 to 3 minutes until gelatin is dissolved. Refrigerate 1 to 2 hours until set around edges. Fold in remaining strawberries and bananas. Chill until fully set.

Makes 6 servings

STRAWBERRY MOUSSE

1 tablespoon unflavored gelatin
1/4 cup orange juice
1-3/4 cups fresh strawberries, slightly mashed
1-1/2 teaspoons vanilla
1 cup heavy cream
3 tablespoons maple syrup
Additional fresh berries for top, optional

In a medium saucepan, sprinkle gelatin over orange juice. Let sit 1 minute to soften. Cook over low heat until dissolved completely. Remove from heat and stir in berries and vanilla. Pour into a blender and process until smooth. Refrigerate 10 minutes. In a medium bowl, beat cream with maple syrup until soft peaks form. Fold berry mixture into cream until well mixed. Spoon into individual goblets. Refrigerate 15 minutes until set. Garnish with berries before serving.

Makes 4 to 6 servings

This can also be placed in a prepared pie shell to make a delicious pie!

CHOCOLATE SYRUP

STRAWBERRY FRUIT LEATHER

4-1/2 cups strawberries, washed and hulled
1/4 cup honey
2 tablespoons lemon juice

Preheat oven to 170° F. Line 2 baking sheets with parchment paper. Blend all ingredients together in a blender until smooth. If desired, strain to remove seeds. Divide mixture evenly and spread on parchment paper. Bake 6 to 10 hours until no longer sticky, rotating pans occasionally. When done, fruit leather should peel off paper easily. Cut into desired shapes or strips. Wrap in parchment or wax paper. Store in airtight container. This recipe can be made with other fruit or berries. This can also be made in a dehydrator following manufacturer's instructions.

EASY FROZEN DESSERT

2 cups heavy cream
1 teaspoon almond flavoring
1/4 cup honey, optional
2 cups crushed fresh strawberries
1-1/2 cups slivered almonds
2 cups chocolate syrup (page 201)

In a large bowl, whip cream until soft peaks form. Add almond flavoring and honey. Fold in crushed berries and almonds. Place in a 9 x 13 glass pan. Freeze. Remove from freezer 5 minutes before serving. Drizzle syrup over each piece. Delightful!

Makes 15 servings

STRAWBERRY RHUBARB CRISP

2 cups strawberries, washed, hulled
and cut into quarters
2 cups rhubarb, chopped
2 tablespoons honey
1 tablespoon lemon juice
1 tablespoon unflavored gelatin
3/4 cup chopped nuts (pecans, walnuts, or almonds)
1 cup shredded coconut
1 cup almond flour
1 teaspoon ground cinnamon
1/2 cup coconut oil
1/4 cup honey

Preheat oven to 350° F. In a large bowl, toss together first five ingredients. Spread in a buttered 9 x 9 glass pan. Bake 20 minutes. In a small pan, heat oil and honey over medium-low heat until melted. Mix nuts, coconut, flour and cinnamon in a medium bowl. Stir in oil and honey. Sprinkle mixture over rhubarb and berries. Bake 25 minutes.

Makes 9 servings

We keep coconut oil on hand for cooking and baking because its healthy properties remain unchanged when heated. Unrefined virgin coconut oil that has not been hydrogenated and damaged in processing is best.

EATING PURE

Probiotics are beneficial bacteria found in fermented food which helps replace damaged flora. For thousands of years people fermented milk, fruit and vegetables, fish and meats. The process of fermenting food makes it more digestible and preserves it. Yogurt, kefir, sauerkraut, cheese, olives and fish are a few of these foods. We encourage you to try making some of these fermented foods and incorporating them into your daily meals.

SWEET CORN

DIG INTO THIS!

Some of the sweet corn grown today is genetically modified.

You can take great steps towards protecting your family from GMO's by eating certified organic sweet corn.

When buying sweet corn from roadside stands, ask about herbicides, pesticides or other chemicals used.

Sweet corn is high in natural sugars.

The sugar in sweet corn rapidly turns into starch, so refrigerate or eat the same day as picked.

An average ear of sweet corn equals 86 calories without butter.

There is one silk per kernel on a cob of sweet corn.

Sweet corn varieties include white, yellow and speckled.

Sweet corn contains vitamins A and B6.

HOW DOES YOUR GARDEN GROW...?

* Days to maturity: 65 to 90.
* Sweet corn grows best next to bush beans, beets, cabbage, cantaloupe, cucumbers, peas, potatoes, pumpkins and squash.
* It's best not to grow next to tomatoes.
* Sweet corn needs plenty of sun, water and fertilizer.
* Prepare the site for sweet corn in the fall by applying at least an inch of compost or rotted manure and working it into soil.
* In the spring apply more compost.
* Plant seeds 1 inch deep, 8 inches apart in rows 30 inches apart.
* Seeds will begin sprouting in approximately 4 days.
* Water moderately and then heavily after cobs set in. A drip hose works well laid between rows.
* Fertilize every 2 weeks with a complete organic fertilizer such as fish emulsion.
* Sweet corn is ripe for picking when the silk is dry and brown but still green near the husk.
* Harvest in the early morning and refrigerate in husk until cooking.

Crop rotation is generally used to nourish the soil. For instance, corn needs a lot of nitrogen and phosphorus. If corn is planted in the same spot year after year, your soil will become depleted in these two nutrients and get out of balance.

A good rule of thumb is to avoid planting the same crop in the same place each year. By following this rule of crop rotation, you will also help reduce the problems with diseases and insect's.

Grow it. Preserve it. Prepare it.

FREEZING SWEET CORN

1. Pick corn in the early morning. Husk and remove silk.

2. Blanch 5 minutes. Drain, immerse in ice water, and cool completely.

3. Cut kernels from cob. Pack into freezer bags or containers.

4. Seal, label and freeze. *(Refer to freezing, page 26)*

FROZEN CORN WITH HONEY

9 cups corn, washed and cut

3 tablespoons honey

2 teaspoons salt

2 cups water

1. Bring honey, salt and water to a boil. Add corn and simmer 3 minutes.

2. Remove from heat. Cool.

3. Pack into freezer bags or containers.

4. Seal, label and freeze.

CORN AND BLACK BEAN SALSA WITH LIME CHIPS

CORN AND BLACK BEAN SALSA

1 cup frozen corn
3 cups prepared black beans *(page 121)*
1 avocado, diced
1 orange bell pepper, chopped
3 tomatoes, chopped
1/4 cup chopped onion
1/2 cup chopped cilantro
1/3 cup lime juice
1/2 cup olive oil
2 cloves garlic, minced
1 teaspoon salt
1/8 teaspoon cayenne pepper

Place first 7 ingredients in a large bowl. In a small bowl, combine lime juice, olive oil, garlic, salt and cayenne pepper. Mix well. Stir into salsa. Cover and refrigerate 2 hours to meld flavors. Stir before serving.

Makes 5 cups

GRILLED SWEET CORN

6 ears sweet corn
Butter
Salt and pepper

Preheat grill and lightly oil grate. Keeping husks attached to cob, peel back and remove all silk. Spread butter on each cob and sprinkle with salt and pepper. Close husks. Wrap individually in foil. Grill 30 minutes, turning occasionally, until tender.

Makes 6 servings

HELPFUL HINTS
2 medium cobs of sweet corn equals 1-1/4 cups.

EATING PURE

Genetically Modified Organisms (GMO's) are becoming more widespread throughout our food chain and are highly controversial. These foods are derived from organisms where DNA has been modified in a way that does not occur naturally (genetically engineered). The list of "high-risk" GMO crops in commercial production is always changing so it's best to do your research to be an informed consumer. Check out the Non-GMO Project website for a current list of high-risk crops. You might be surprised to see foods such as canola, corn, soy, sugar beets, yellow summer squash and zucchini on the list.

Reading food labels will help you find where some of these GMO crops might be hidden. According to the Non-GMO Project website, these are a few of the common ingredients where GMO's might be hidden: Flavorings ("natural" and "artificial"), high-fructose corn syrup, xanthan gum, vitamins and yeast products.

RECIPES

BAKED CREAM CORN

5 cups sweet corn, fresh or frozen
1 red bell pepper, diced
1 chili pepper, diced
1 cup heavy cream
1 teaspoon salt
1/2 teaspoon pepper
1/3 cup butter

Preheat oven to 350° F. Husk sweet corn. Cut corn off cobs. In a large bowl, mix all ingredients and pour into a greased 9 x 13 glass baking dish. Bake uncovered 45 to 55 minutes.

Makes 6 servings

SOUTHWEST CHILI

1 medium zucchini, cubed
1-1/2 cups prepared black beans *(page 121)*
1-1/2 cups prepared navy beans *(page 121)*
1 cup whole kernel corn
4 cups chicken broth *(page 158)*
1 cup tomato sauce *(page 256)*
2 cups salsa *(page 258)*
2 cups shredded cooked chicken
2 cloves garlic, minced
2 teaspoons chili powder
2 teaspoons ground cumin
1-1/2 teaspoons salt

Place all ingredients in a slow cooker. Cook on low 4 hours. Serve with shredded cheese, sour cream, chips, etc.

Makes 6 to 8 servings

SWEET POTATOES

DIG INTO THIS!

Sweet potatoes are available in two dominant types: paler-skinned with thin, light yellow skin and pale yellow flesh which has a dry, crumbly texture similar to a white baking potato; darker-skinned (most often called "yam" in error) with thick, dark orange-reddish skin with an orange, sweet flesh and a moist texture.

Sweet potatoes are a good source of fiber when eaten with the skin left on.

Sweet potatoes contain antioxidant and anti-inflammatory components, and are loaded with vitamin C.

Select sweet potatoes with tight skin and no blemishes or bruises.

Discard bruised sweet potatoes as they deteriorate rapidly and the flavor of the entire potato is affected.

HOW DOES YOUR GARDEN GROW...?

❋ Days to maturity from transplant: 90.

❋ Sweet potatoes like to grow next to marigolds.

❋ It's best not to plant next to beets, carrots or potatoes.

❋ Sweet potatoes are grown from rooted cuttings (slips) purchased at your local nursery.

❋ Plant slips after the last danger of frost has past.

❋ Space 14 to 18 inches apart in loose, fertile soil.

❋ Too much nitrogen will diminish yield, so fertilize only if plants do not appear healthy.

❋ Harvest sweet potatoes 3 to 4 months after planting.

❋ Cold weather can damage sweet potatoes so be sure to harvest before the first frost.

❋ Cut back vines and lift roots carefully with a garden fork.

❋ Let roots set in sun for a day then move to a shady area and let sit 7 to 10 days to cure.

❋ Curing heals cuts and triggers sugar-creating enzymes.

❋ Cured sweet potatoes store well for a month in a cool, dry location.

Sweet potato vine is a beautiful addition to your flower planters!

Grow it. Preserve it. Prepare it.

FREEZING SWEET POTATOES

1. Preheat oven to 375° F.

2. Wash sweet potatoes and place on a rimmed baking sheet.

3. Bake 1 hour until tender. Remove from oven and cool.

4. Peel skin and puree pulp in a blender.

5. Pack into freezer bags or containers. Seal, label and freeze.

HELPFUL HINTS

1 pound sweet potatoes equals 4 cups grated or 1 cup cooked and pureed.

To keep your oven clean, place sweet potatoes on a rimmed baking sheet to catch the juices when baking.

TWICE BAKED SWEET POTATOES

ROASTED SWEET POTATOES

4 medium sweet potatoes
2 tablespoons sesame oil
2 tablespoons maple syrup
1 teaspoon lemon juice
1 teaspoon salt

Preheat oven to 350° F. Peel and cut potatoes into 1 inch pieces. Place potatoes in a 9 x 13 glass baking dish. In a small bowl, whisk together remaining ingredients. Pour over potatoes and toss to coat. Bake, stirring occasionally, 1 hour until tender.

Makes 4 servings

SWEET POTATO FRIES

2 medium sweet potatoes, washed
1 tablespoon sesame oil
1 teaspoon salt

Preheat oven to 400° F. Cut sweet potatoes into pencil-size fries. Soak in a large bowl of ice water 1 hour. Drain, rinse and pat dry. Toss fries with oil and 1/2 teaspoon salt. Lay fries in single layer on a rimmed baking sheet and bake 45 minutes. Sprinkle with remaining salt. Let sit on top of stove 5 minutes before serving.

Makes 4 servings

TWICE BAKED SWEET POTATOES

6 sweet potatoes, even in size
1/4 cup maple syrup
1/4 cup butter
1/2 cup sour cream
1 teaspoon salt
1/4 teaspoon pepper

Preheat oven to 375° F. Wash sweet potatoes and place on a rimmed baking sheet. Bake 1 hour until soft. Remove from oven and cool. Cut potatoes in half lengthwise. Place flesh in a medium size bowl. Combine with remaining ingredients and whip until smooth. Scoop filling evenly back into potato skins. Bake an additional 15 minutes until golden brown.

Makes 6 to 12 servings

SWEET POTATO CHIPS

2 medium sweet potatoes, washed
2 tablespoons sesame oil
1 teaspoon chili powder
1 teaspoon salt
1/8 teaspoon cumin
Ranch dressing, optional *(page 125)*

Preheat oven to 400° F. Cut sweet potatoes into 1/8 inch thick rounds. A food processor works well. Place in a large bowl and cover with ice water. Let sit 1 hour. Drain, rinse and pat dry. Toss potatoes with oil and spices. Place in a single layer on rimmed baking sheets lined with parchment paper. Roast 30 to 40 minutes, turning once, until golden brown and crisp. Chips burn easily, so keep your eye on them. Remove from oven. Let sit 5 minutes before serving. Delicious served alone or with ranch dressing.

Makes 4 to 6 servings

STUFFED SWEET POTATOES

2 sweet potatoes, washed and pricked with fork
1/2 pound ground beef
1/2 small onion, chopped
1/2 green bell pepper, chopped
1 teaspoon ground cumin
1 teaspoon smoked paprika
1/2 teaspoon salt
1/4 teaspoon pepper
1 cup kale, chopped

Preheat oven to 425° F. Place sweet potatoes on a rimmed baking sheet. Bake 40 to 45 minutes until tender. In a large skillet, brown beef with onions and bell pepper over medium-high heat. Add spices and mix well. Add kale and cook an additional 3 minutes until wilted. Remove potatoes from oven. Slice in half lengthwise. Mash sweet potato with fork, gently leaving it in skin. Spoon beef mixture evenly over mashed potato halves.

Makes 2 servings

TOMATOES

DIG INTO THIS!

Roma tomatoes are a good variety for making sauces and paste.

An heirloom tomato is an open pollinated variety whose seeds have been passed down for several generations through a family.

Tomatoes are packed with vitamins A and C as well as calcium, potassium and lycopene.

Tomatoes are botanically a fruit.

A lot of a tomato's flavor comes from the gel surrounding the seeds.

Did you know you can ripen green tomatoes indoors? Green tomatoes will ripen in approximately 2 weeks in temperatures above 65° F.

HOW DOES YOUR GARDEN GROW...?

✳ Days to maturity: 60 to 80 from transplant.

✳ Tomatoes grow best next to asparagus, bush beans, cabbage, carrots, cucumbers, lettuce, onions or peppers.

✳ It's best not to plant next to dill, pole beans or potatoes.

✳ Tomatoes produce more fruit in light, fertile soil with little nitrogen.

✳ Transplant in late spring.

✳ Purchase started plants from your nursery or start seedlings indoors 6 to 7 weeks prior to planting. Seeds begin to grow in 6 to 8 days. Place young seedlings in a sunny window.

✳ "Harden off" your seedlings before planting outdoors to help them adjust to a variety of temperatures, direct sunlight and wind *(page 173)*.

✳ Dig a hole deep enough so that only about 4 inches of the plant will be above soil. Snip off any leaves that will be buried. Gently press soil around plant until firm. Water.

✳ Space plants 15 inches apart if supported or 24 inches apart if unsupported.

✳ Support tomato plants with cages or tie the main stem loosely to a stake. Continue to tie the main stem as it grows.

✳ Mulch with straw.

✳ Water moderately during growing season—water with drip hose to reduce soil splash and damage to fruit.

✳ Fertilize with fish emulsion every 2 to 3 weeks.

✳ To encourage strong main stems, cut out all suckers. Suckers are non-flowering stems that grow in the axils between the main stem and the leaves. This pruning will help plants produce maximum yield.

✳ Tomatoes are ripe to pick when the skin yields slightly to finger pressure.

✳ The top shoulder of the tomato is the last part to change color. Most tomatoes will continue ripening indoors.

✳ Store tomatoes on the counter until ready to use.

Grow it. Preserve it. Prepare it.

FREEZING TOMATOES

1. Select ripe tomatoes, wash and dry.

2. Place whole tomatoes in freezer bag. Seal, label and freeze.

3. Remove frozen tomatoes from bag and place under running water. Skins fall off easily.

4. Chop and add to soups or casseroles. For people who do not like tomato chunks, simmer in saucepan and puree with an immersion blender before adding to your favorite recipes.

REMOVING SKINS FROM TOMATOES

1. Wash tomatoes.

2. Scald in boiling water 1 to 2 minutes until skins crack.

3. Plunge into cold water.

4. Peel, core and quarter or chop according to recipe.

DEHYDRATING TOMATOES

SUN DRIED ROSEMARY BASIL TOMATOES

15 Roma tomatoes
2 tablespoons olive oil
3/4 teaspoon garlic granules
2 teaspoons dried basil
1 tablespoon dried rosemary
1 tablespoon salt

1. Wash and core tomatoes. Cut into 1/4 inch wedges. Place in a large bowl with remaining ingredients. Toss gently to blend well.

2. Place tomatoes in single layer on dehydrator trays.

3. Dehydrate according to manufacturer's instructions. Tomatoes will be dry on outside and barely fleshy on inside. Store in airtight containers in refrigerator or freezer.

CANNING TOMATOES

1. Wash tomatoes. Remove peels per directions below left. Peel, core and quarter.

2. In sterilized jars, add 1 tablespoon bottled lemon juice to each pint jar or 2 tablespoons bottled lemon juice to each quart jar.

3. Pack tomatoes into hot jars, pressing gently on tomatoes until juice fills the spaces between tomatoes. Leave 1/2 inch head space. If desired, add 1/2 teaspoon salt to each pint jar or 1 teaspoon to each quart jar.

4. Process pints 40 minutes and quarts 45 minutes in a boiling water canner.
(Refer to canning, page 24)

Bottled lemon juice needs to be added to canned tomato products to prevent bacteria growth.

DEHYDRATED TOMATOES

CANNING TOMATOES

TOMATO JUICE

12 pounds tomatoes
7 tablespoons lemon juice,
divided

1. Wash tomatoes. Peel
(page 252), core and
quarter tomatoes.

2. Place in a large pot. Cook
over medium heat, stirring
occasionally until soft.

3. Juice in a blender or a food
processor. Strain to remove
seeds.

4. Place 1 tablespoon lemon
juice in each pint jar. Ladle
hot juice into jars leaving
1/2 inch head space. Process
pints 35 minutes, quarts 40
minutes, in a boiling water
canner. (Refer to canning,
page 24)

Makes 7 pints

One 6 ounce can of tomato
paste mixed with 1-1/2
cups of water can be
substituted for a 14.5
ounce can of tomato sauce.

SLOW COOKER TOMATO PASTE

48 large Roma tomatoes
3 red bell peppers, chopped
1 teaspoon salt
2 cloves garlic, minced
1 tablespoon lemon juice

1. Wash tomatoes. Peel
(page 252), core and cut
tomatoes in half.

2. Place tomatoes, peppers,
salt and garlic in a slow
cooker with lid askew for
steam to escape. Cook on
high 2 hours.

3. Puree with an immersion
blender. Continue cooking
on high several hours until
thick. This is best to start
at night so in the morning
when it starts becoming
thick, you can stir every
hour. Once thick, stir in
lemon juice.

4. Cool and transfer to freezer
safe containers or keep in
glass jar in refrigerator.

Makes 2 cups

TOMATO PASTE

48 large Roma tomatoes
3 red bell peppers, chopped
2 green bell peppers, chopped
3 medium onions, chopped
2 carrots, chopped
or thinly sliced
5 cloves garlic, minced
5 tablespoons lemon juice, divided

1. Wash tomatoes. Peel
(page 252), core and
quarter tomatoes.

2. Place tomatoes, peppers,
onions, carrots and garlic
in a 5 quart pan and bring
to a boil. Reduce heat and
simmer 20 minutes. Puree
with an immersion blender.
Continue simmering, uncovered, 4 to 5 hours. Stir often
to prevent sticking. Paste
is done when a spoonful of
puree stays in a mound on
spoon. Cook longer if it runs
off spoon.

3. Add 1 tablespoon bottled
lemon juice to each pint jar
or 2 tablespoons bottled
lemon juice to each quart jar.

4. Ladle paste into hot jars,
leaving 1/2 inch head space.
Process pints 35 minutes,
quarts 40 minutes, in a
boiling water canner.
(Refer to canning, page 24)

Makes 5 pints

KETCHUP

2-1/4 cups tomato paste *(page 254)*
1/2 cup apple cider vinegar
1 medium onion, finely chopped
1/8 teaspoon garlic powder
1/4 teaspoon ground cinnamon
1/4 teaspoon ground cloves
1/4 teaspoon ground allspice
1/4 teaspoon celery seeds
1/4 teaspoon red pepper flakes
1 teaspoon paprika
2 teaspoons salt
1/4 cup honey

Combine all ingredients except honey in a medium saucepan. Simmer uncovered on low heat 30 minutes, stirring occasionally. Puree with an immersion blender.

Add honey. Continue cooking until desired thickness, stirring frequently to prevent sticking. Cool and store in refrigerator.

If canning, ladle hot ketchup into sterilized jars and process 10 minutes in a hot water canner. *(Refer to canning, page 24)*

Makes 3 cups

One food that generally contains corn syrup is ketchup. Increasingly we hear more about the use of corn syrup or high fructose corn syrup in processed foods. You can avoid this controversy and its possible health risks by making your own ketchup full of rich nutrients and antioxidants.

KETCHUP

CANNING TOMATOES

TOMATO SAUCE

22 pounds tomatoes
Bottled lemon juice
Salt, optional

1. Wash tomatoes. Peel (*page 252*), core and quarter tomatoes.

2. In a large stockpot, cook over medium-high heat until sauce thickens, stirring to prevent sticking.

3. Puree with an immersion blender. Continue cooking until volume is reduced by one-half (this could take 1 to 2 hours).

4. Add 1 tablespoon bottled lemon juice to each pint jar or 2 tablespoons bottled lemon juice to each quart jar. If adding salt, add 1/2 teaspoon to each pint jar or 1 teaspoon to each quart jar. Ladle sauce into hot jars, leaving 1/2 inch head space.

5. Process pints 35 minutes, quarts 40 minutes, in a boiling water canner. (*Refer to canning, page 24*)

Makes 12 pints or 6 quarts

SEASONED TOMATO SAUCE

22 pounds tomatoes
3 cups chopped onions
6 cloves garlic, minced
1-1/2 teaspoons dried oregano
1 tablespoon
Italian seasoning (*page 125*)
1-1/2 teaspoons pepper
2 teaspoons honey
2 tablespoons salt
Bottled lemon juice

1. Wash tomatoes. Peel (*page 252*), core and quarter tomatoes.

2. Place all ingredients (except lemon juice) into a large pot. Bring to a boil, reduce heat and simmer 20 minutes, stirring occasionally. Puree with an immersion blender. Continue cooking until volume is reduced by one-half (this could take 1 to 2 hours).

3. Add 1 tablespoon bottled lemon juice to each pint jar or 2 tablespoons bottled lemon juice to each quart jar. Ladle sauce into hot jars, leaving 1/2 inch head space.

4. Process pints 35 minutes, quarts 40 minutes, in a boiling water canner. (*Refer to canning, page 24*)

Makes 12 pints or 6 quarts

BASIL-GARLIC TOMATO SAUCE

20 pounds tomatoes
1 cup onion, chopped
12 cloves garlic, minced
1 tablespoon sesame oil
1/2 cup finely minced, fresh basil
2 tablespoons salt
1/2 tablespoon honey
Bottled lemon juice

1. Wash tomatoes, peel (*page 252*), core and quarter tomatoes.

2. In a large pot, sauté onion and garlic in sesame oil until transparent. Add tomatoes, basil, salt and honey. Simmer 20 minutes, stirring occasionally.

3. Puree with an immersion blender. Continue simmering (approximately 1 hour) until volume is reduced by half, stirring occasionally.

4. Add 1 tablespoon bottled lemon juice to each pint jar or 2 tablespoons bottled lemon juice to each quart jar. Ladle sauce into hot jars, leaving 1/2 inch head space.

5. Process pints 35 minutes, quarts 40 minutes, in a boiling water canner. (*Refer to canning, page 24*)

Makes 8 pints or 4 quarts

RECIPES

TACO SAUCE

2 cups tomato sauce *(page 256)*
2/3 cup water
2 tablespoons apple cider vinegar
1/2 teaspoon honey
1/2 teaspoon chili powder
1 tablespoon ground cumin
1-1/2 teaspoons onion powder
1 teaspoon garlic granules
3/4 teaspoon paprika
1/2 teaspoon cayenne pepper
1/2 teaspoon salt

Place all ingredients in a saucepan and bring to a boil. Reduce heat and low boil 15 to 20 minutes uncovered, stirring occasionally. Cool and refrigerate or freeze.

Makes 3 cups

PIZZA SAUCE

2 cups tomato sauce *(page 256)*
3/4 cup tomato paste *(page 254)*
2 teaspoons ground oregano
1 teaspoon salt
1/2 teaspoon garlic powder
1/2 teaspoon onion powder
1 teaspoon paprika
1-1/2 teaspoons dried basil
1 tablespoon honey

Place all ingredients in a saucepan and bring to a boil. Reduce heat and simmer uncovered 45 to 60 minutes, stirring occasionally. Cool and refrigerate or freeze.

Makes 3 cups

BARBECUE SAUCE

1 cup tomato sauce *(page 256)*
1 cup honey
3/4 cup maple syrup
1/8 teaspoon ground cinnamon
1 teaspoon paprika
1/8 teaspoon ground ginger
1/4 teaspoon cayenne pepper
1/8 teaspoon pepper
1-1/2 teaspoons salt
1/2 teaspoon chili powder
1 clove garlic, minced
1 tablespoon prepared mustard
2 tablespoons apple cider vinegar
3/4 teaspoon liquid smoke, optional

Place all ingredients in a saucepan and bring to a boil. Reduce heat and low boil uncovered 30 minutes, stirring occasionally. Cool and store in refrigerator.

Makes 2-1/2 cups

SPAGHETTI SAUCE

1/4 cup butter
1-1/2 large onions, chopped
5 cloves garlic, minced
6 cups tomato sauce *(page 256)*
1 bay leaf
1-1/2 teaspoons dried basil
1-1/2 teaspoons dried oregano
2 teaspoons honey
1-1/2 teaspoons salt
1/2 teaspoon pepper
1/4 teaspoon red pepper flakes

In a large saucepan, sauté onion and garlic in butter until tender. Add remaining ingredients. Cover and simmer 1 hour, stirring occasionally. Remove bay leaf. Cool and refrigerate or freeze.

Makes 4 cups

CANNING TOMATOES

TRADITIONAL SALSA

9 cups chopped tomatoes, peeled *(page 252)*

6 whole jalapeños, chopped with seeds

2 cups chopped onion

1 tablespoon plus 2 teaspoons salt

8 cloves garlic, minced

1/4 cup plus 2 tablespoons apple cider vinegar

2-1/4 cups tomato paste *(page 254)*

1/2 tablespoon honey

1 Place all ingredients in a 5 quart pan. Bring to a boil over medium-high heat. Reduce heat and simmer 15 minutes.

2 For smooth salsa, puree with an immersion blender and cook an additional 15 minutes. For chunky salsa, cook 30 minutes.

3 Ladle into hot jars, leaving 1/2 inch head space. Process pints 35 minutes, quarts 40 minutes, in a boiling water canner. *(Refer to canning, page 24)*

Makes 8 pints

HELPFUL HINTS

1 large tomato is about 8 ounces and equals approximately 1 cup of chopped tomato. 1 pound tomatoes equals about 2 cups chopped. 30 small cherry tomatoes equals about 2 cups chopped tomatoes.

SWEET PEPPER SALSA

10 cups chopped tomatoes, peeled *(page 252)*

3/4 cup chopped jalapeño peppers

8 cloves garlic, minced

4 cups chopped onion

2 cups chopped green bell peppers

2 teaspoons ground cumin

1 teaspoon chopped fresh cilantro, optional

1 tablespoon plus 2 teaspoons salt

1 teaspoon chili powder

1/2 teaspoon pepper

1-1/2 cups tomato paste *(page 254)*

1-1/4 cups apple cider vinegar

1 Remove seeds from jalapeño peppers for a milder sauce. Be sure to wear gloves when working with jalapeños. Removing 1/2 of the seeds will give a medium flavor.

2 Place tomatoes, jalapeños, garlic, onion and green peppers in a 5 quart pan.

3 Bring to a boil over medium-high heat. Add spices, tomato paste and vinegar. Reduce heat and simmer 15 minutes.

4 For smooth salsa, puree with an immersion blender and cook an additional 15 minutes. For chunky salsa, cook 30 minutes.

5 Ladle into hot jars, leaving 1/2 inch head space. Process pints 35 minutes, quarts 40 minutes, in a boiling water canner. *(Refer to canning, page 24)*

Makes 9 pints

FRESH SALSA

4 cups chopped tomatoes
3/4 cup chopped onion
1 clove garlic, minced
1 jalapeño pepper, chopped
(seeded or not depending on desired heat)
1/4 cup chopped fresh cilantro
1-1/2 teaspoons salt
1/4 teaspoon pepper
2 tablespoons lime juice

In a medium bowl, combine all ingredients. Mix well and serve on tacos, enchiladas, burgers, etc.

Makes 4-1/2 cups

TOMATO LENTIL DISH

1 pound ground beef
1 cup chopped onion
4 cloves garlic, minced
1 teaspoon turmeric
1 teaspoon salt
1/4 teaspoon pepper
1 cup tomato sauce *(page 256)*
4 cups prepared lentils *(page 121)*
1 cup frozen spinach, thawed

In a large skillet, brown beef with onion and garlic over medium-high heat. Add rest of ingredients except spinach. Cover and simmer 3 to 5 minutes. Add spinach and continue simmering an additional 3 minutes.

Makes 4 servings

SUPREME PIZZA STIR-FRY

1 pound ground pork or beef
1 tablespoon Italian seasoning *(page 125)*
1 medium onion, chopped
1 clove garlic, minced
1 medium zucchini, sliced
1 red bell pepper, chopped
6 button mushrooms, sliced
1/2 cup black or green olives, sliced
1 cup pizza sauce *(page 257)*
1 teaspoon salt
1-1/2 cups shredded raw cheddar cheese

In a large skillet, brown meat with Italian seasoning, onion and garlic over medium-high heat 5 minutes. Add zucchini, pepper, and mushrooms. Cook an additional 5 minutes. Stir in olives, pizza sauce and salt. Continue cooking until heated through. Stir in cheese.

VARIATION:

On a large preheated skillet or griddle, sprinkle 1/3 cup raw shredded cheddar cheese and 1/3 cup grated Parmesan cheese. Cook until melted. Remove from heat and let sit 5 minutes to set. Top with prepared pizza stir-fry.

Makes 4 servings

Do you ever wonder why you can make the same salsa recipe year after year with the taste varying slightly? Salsa temperature varies depending on the hotness of the peppers in each batch. The hotness of the pepper is determined by the growing conditions each season.

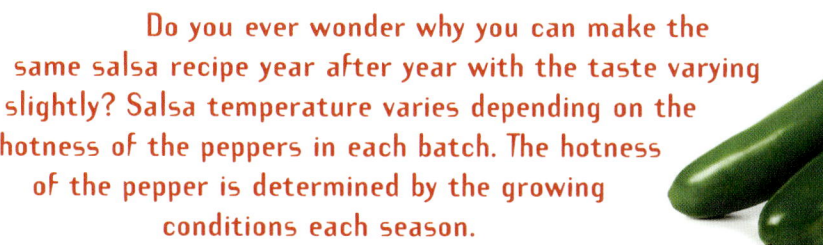

CREAMY TOMATO SOUP

2 cups seasoned tomato sauce *(page 256)*
1/4 teaspoon baking soda
2 cups chicken broth *(page 158)*
2 cups heavy cream

Scald tomato sauce in a medium saucepan over medium-high heat. In a separate large saucepan, scald broth and cream.

To keep soup from curdling, stir baking soda into hot tomato sauce. Stir well as it foams up. Remove both pans from heat. Pour tomato sauce into hot broth/cream mixture and serve.

(Mom used to say, "Pour the red in the white and you'll never be blue!")

Makes 4 servings

For a quick snack, slice a tomato, drizzle with olive oil and sprinkle with a little fresh basil, salt and pepper. Simple and yummy!

RECIPES

BLT SALAD

1 head romaine lettuce,
rinsed and shredded
6 slices bacon, chopped
2 cups cherry tomatoes, sliced
1 avocado, cubed
1/2 cup mayonnaise *(page 77)*
1/2 teaspoon salt
1/4 teaspoon pepper

In a large skillet, cook bacon over medium heat until crisp. Drain, cool and crumble. Set bacon aside.

Place lettuce, tomatoes, avocado and bacon in a large bowl. In a small bowl, combine mayonnaise, salt and pepper. Stir dressing into salad and toss to coat. Serve immediately.

Makes 4 servings

GRANDMA'S BAKED BEANS

3 cups dried navy beans, soaked overnight in 6 cups water and 2 tablespoons lemon juice
2 teaspoons dry mustard
1 cup maple syrup
1 cup ketchup *(page 255)*
1 medium onion, chopped
2 tablespoons apple cider vinegar
1 teaspoon salt
1/8 teaspoon pepper
1/2 cup water

Drain and rinse beans. Place in a 5 quart pot and cover with water. Bring to a boil over medium-high heat. Spoon off and discard thick foam as it cooks. Cover, reduce heat and low boil 45 minutes. Drain and place in a slow cooker with remaining ingredients. Cook on high 7 to 8 hours.

Makes 8 to 12 servings

HAMBURGER BEAN HOTDISH

1 pound ground beef
1/2 pound bacon, chopped
1 large onion, chopped
2 cups prepared navy beans *(page 121)*
2 cups prepared lima beans *(page 121)*
1 cup ketchup *(page 255)*
1/3 cup maple syrup
2 teaspoons dry mustard
1 teaspoon salt
1/2 teaspoon pepper

Preheat oven to 350° F. Brown beef, bacon and onion together in a skillet over medium-high heat. Stir in remaining ingredients. Place in a 2 quart glass casserole and bake covered, 30 to 45 minutes.

Makes 4 to 6 servings

Make a double recipe to reheat and enjoy the next day!

TRADITIONAL CHILI

1 pound ground beef
1 medium onion, chopped
1 cup prepared black beans *(page 121)*
1 cup prepared navy beans *(page 121)*
1 cup prepared kidney beans *(page 121)*
4 cups tomato sauce *(page 256)*
1 cup salsa *(page 258)*
2 teaspoons chili powder
1 teaspoon salt
1/4 teaspoon pepper
1/2 teaspoon ground cumin

Brown beef and onion together in a skillet over medium-high heat. Place all ingredients in a 5 quart pot. Cover and simmer 1 hour.

Makes 4 to 6 servings

RECIPES

ENCHILADA SAUCE

2 tablespoons butter
4 cloves garlic, minced
2 cups tomato sauce *(page 256)*
3 cups chicken broth *(page 158)*
1 teaspoon onion powder
1 teaspoon dried oregano
2 teaspoons chili powder
1/4 teaspoon pepper
1/2 teaspoon salt
1/2 teaspoon ground cumin
2 teaspoons dried parsley
Green chilies, optional

In a medium saucepan, sauté garlic in butter 1 to 2 minutes. Add remaining ingredients. Bring to a boil. Reduce heat and simmer uncovered 45 minutes, stirring occasionally.

Makes 3 to 3-1/2 cups

ENCHILADA DISH

1 tablespoon butter
1 green or red bell pepper, sliced
1 medium onion, sliced
2 cups shredded cooked chicken
1 teaspoon salt
1/4 teaspoon pepper
1-3/4 cup enchilada sauce, divided
4 brown rice tortillas
1/3 cup sour cream, divided
1-1/2 cups shredded raw cheddar cheese, divided

Preheat oven to 350° F. In a medium skillet, sauté pepper and onion in butter over medium-high heat 5 minutes. Add chicken, salt, pepper and 1/2 cup enchilada sauce. Stir and simmer 3 to 5 minutes until heated through. Place 1/2 cup enchilada sauce in a 9 x 9 glass pan. Evenly divide meat mixture, sour cream and 3/4 cup cheese and fill tortillas. Place filled tortillas on top of sauce and pour remaining enchilada sauce over tortillas. Sprinkle with remaining cheese. Cover and bake 30 minutes. Uncover and bake an additional 15 minutes.

Makes 4 servings

CHICKEN QUESADILLAS

1 tablespoon butter
1 medium onion, sliced
1 red bell pepper, sliced
1 small jalapeño pepper, chopped
2 cups chopped cooked chicken
1-1/4 teaspoons salt
1/2 teaspoon paprika
1 teaspoon ground cumin
1 cup shredded raw cheddar cheese, divided
1/2 cup salsa, optional *(page 258)*
1/2 cup sour cream, optional
Lettuce, optional
4 (8-inch) brown rice tortillas

Preheat oven to 400° F. In a large skillet sauté onions and peppers in butter over medium-high heat 5 minutes. Add chicken and spices. Stir and simmer 5 minutes until heated through. Butter 1 side of each tortilla. Place 2 tortillas buttered side down on rimmed baking sheet. Spoon half of mixture evenly over each tortilla. Sprinkle 1/2 cup cheese on each tortilla. Top with remaining 2 tortillas butter side up. Bake 10 minutes until tortillas are lightly browned. Cut quesadillas into wedges. Spoon salsa and sour cream over each quesadilla. Garnish with lettuce.

Makes 4 servings

BEEF FAJITAS

1 pound round steak
1 medium onion, sliced
1 red bell pepper, sliced
3 cloves garlic, minced
1/2 teaspoon chili powder
1/2 teaspoon ground cumin
1/2 teaspoon salt
1/4 teaspoon pepper
2/3 cup salsa *(page 258)*

Place all ingredients in a slow cooker. Cook on high 4 to 5 hours. Shred beef and stir. Serve in lettuce wraps, tortillas or over chopped salad greens with sour cream and shredded raw cheddar cheese.

Makes 4 servings

TURNIPS

DIG INTO THIS!

Select turnips that are about 3 inches in diameter for best flavor and texture.

Salad turnips taste like radishes and are great eaten raw or on salads.

Baby turnip greens are delicious sautéed.

Fresh turnips will have firm white flesh and will not be spongy in the middle.

When baking a pot roast with carrots, potatoes and onions, try substituting turnips in place of potatoes for a less starchy alternative.

Turnips are a great source of minerals, antioxidants and fiber.

Turnip greens are an excellent source of vitamin K.

HOW DOES YOUR GARDEN GROW...?

* Days to maturity: 38 to 50.
* Turnips grow best next to onions and peas.
* It's best not to plant next to potatoes.
* Turnips like cool weather and need loose soil with lots of organic matter.
* Plant seeds in early spring when soil begins to warm up.
* Plant 1/4 to 1/2 inch deep, 4 inches apart. Plant salad turnips 1 to 2 inches apart.
* Seeds will start to grow in 2 to 5 days.
* Water moderately.
* Begin harvesting turnip greens when the plants are young.
* Harvest salad turnips when they are 1 inch in diameter.
* Mature turnip roots should be harvested when they are about 3 inches in diameter.
* Turnips are best eaten fresh, but can be stored a few weeks in refrigerator.

Part of having a successful garden is to eliminate the competition from weeds. This starts as soon as Spring arrives and plants begin to grow. These weeds steal nutrients and moisture, leaving you with a stunted plant and a poor crop.

There are different ways to control weeds. The key is to ensure no light is reaching the soil. One option is to place your plants close together so weeds are less likely to thrive. Or you can put on your gloves, reach for your hoe and destroy the root system of the weed. You can also put down a thick layer of organic mulch or purchase a piece of dark plastic used for mulching. No matter what weed control method you choose, keep in mind the great harvest that is ahead.

Grow it. Preserve it. Prepare it.

FREEZING TURNIPS

1. Wash, peel and rinse turnips.

2. Slice or dice.

3. Blanch 3 minutes in boiling water. Drain and immerse in cold water until completely cool.

4. Drain and pack into freezer bags or containers. Seal, label and freeze. *(Refer to freezing, page 26)*

HELPFUL HINTS
One pound of turnips equals 2-1/2 cups chopped.

POT ROAST

RECIPES

CREAMY TURNIP AU GRATIN SOUP

5 tablespoons butter, melted
4 cloves garlic, minced
4 turnips, peeled and cut into 1/2 inch cubes
2 cups chicken broth (*page 158*)
3/4 teaspoon salt
2 cups shredded raw cheddar cheese
1 cup heavy cream
1/2 teaspoon pepper

In a large saucepan, sauté garlic in butter over medium-high heat 1 minute. Add turnips, broth and salt. Bring to a boil. Reduce to medium heat and low boil, uncovered, 25 to 30 minutes until tender. Remove from heat. Partially puree with an immersion blender leaving some chunks. Stir in cheese, cream and pepper.

Makes 4 servings

SAUTÉED TURNIPS

2 turnips, peeled and thinly sliced
1 tablespoon butter
1 tablespoon sesame oil
1/2 teaspoon salt
1/4 teaspoon pepper

In a large skillet, sauté turnips in butter and oil over medium-high heat 5 minutes. Flip turnips over and continue sautéing an additional 3 to 5 minutes until brown. Sprinkle with salt and pepper.

Makes 2 servings

POT ROAST

3 pounds beef roast, thawed
6 small turnips, peeled
6 carrots
1 onion, quartered
1 bay leaf
1 teaspoon salt
1/4 teaspoon pepper

Preheat oven to 350° F. Place roast and vegetables in a covered casserole. Add 2 inches of water, bay leaf, salt and pepper. Bake 2 to 3 hours until vegetables are tender and meat is done. This can also be cooked 6 to 8 hours on high in a slow cooker.

Makes 4 to 6 servings

BREAKFAST EGG AND TURNIP BAKE

2 turnips, peeled and diced
2 small potatoes, peeled and diced
3/4 teaspoon salt, divided
2 tablespoons chopped onion
3 eggs, beaten
1/8 teaspoon pepper
1 tablespoon butter, divided
1 cup shredded raw cheddar cheese
4 slices bacon, cooked and crumbled

Preheat oven to 425° F. Place 1/2 tablespoon butter in an 8 x 8 glass pan. Melt in oven 1 minute and remove from oven. Place turnips, potatoes and 1/2 teaspoon salt in a large saucepan. Cover with water and cook 15 minutes until tender. Drain. Place in a large bowl with remaining 1/4 teaspoon salt, onion, eggs, pepper and 1/2 tablespoon butter. Blend together with a mixer. Pour into prepared pan. Bake 30 minutes. Sprinkle with cheese and top with bacon. Place under broiler 5 minutes until cheese is melted and browned.

Makes 6 servings

ROASTED ROOT VEGETABLES

2 turnips
2 carrots
1 rutabaga
1 sweet potato
1 onion
2 tablespoons sesame oil
2 teaspoons salt
1/4 teaspoon pepper
1/4 teaspoon dried rosemary
1/4 teaspoon dried thyme
1/4 cup maple syrup
2 tablespoons butter

Preheat oven to 400° F. Wash, peel and cut all vegetables into 1/2 inch slices or 3/4 inch chunks. In a large bowl, toss vegetables with oil and spices to coat well. Place in single layer on a rimmed baking sheet. Roast 40 minutes until golden brown, stirring once. In a small pan, heat maple syrup and butter on low heat. Drizzle over vegetables and bake another 5 minutes.

Makes 6 to 8 servings

WATERMELON

DIG INTO THIS!

Seedless watermelons are hybrids and not necessarily genetically modified.

Watermelon is about 90 percent water.

Watermelons are ripe when you hear a low pitched thump when you tap on rind.

For a fun serving container, hollow out melons and fill with your favorite melon salad.

Watermelon is an excellent source of the antioxidant lycopene, which may help with inflammation.

Lycopene also gives watermelon the deep rich color.

Watermelon is a healthy source of vitamins A, C and B6.

HOW DOES YOUR GARDEN GROW...?

✳ Days to maturity from direct seed: 70 to 85. Days to maturity from transplant: 60 to 75.

✳ Grow melons away from cucumbers and winter squash as their flavor will be bitter if blossoms are pollinated by these plants.

✳ Melons love heat and the soil temperature should be 70° F to 90° F when planting.

✳ Plant 1/2 inch deep, 16 inches apart.

✳ Seeds can be planted in hills. Space hills 24 inches apart with 3 seeds per hill, thinning later to 1 plant per hill.

✳ Watermelon seeds will begin to grow in 3 to 5 days.

✳ Started plants can also be purchased from your local nursery.

✳ Melons are particular about pH. Use a complete organic fertilizer—fish emulsion or kelp. Until flowers appear, use a fertilizer with more nitrogen than phosphorus or potassium. After vines flower, until melons reach maturity, use a fertilizer with more phosphorus and potassium than nitrogen.

✳ Water evenly, but not too much throughout season. Check soil moisture frequently—should not be too dry or too wet.

✳ Heavy watering during harvest period will cause watermelon to be less sweet.

✳ For larger melons, remove some of the blossoms so the plant can feed fewer fruit, thus producing larger melons.

✳ Watermelons are ripe when the tendril nearest to the melon turns from green to brown and the underside of the melon is yellow.

Grow it. Preserve it. Prepare it.

WATERMELON LEMONADE SLUSHIE

10 cups cubed watermelon
1/3 cup honey
3-1/2 cups water, divided
3/4 cup lemon juice

Place watermelon in single layer on a rimmed baking sheet. Freeze overnight. In a saucepan, warm 1/2 cup water and honey. Remove from heat. Stir in 3 cups cold water and lemon juice. Refrigerate. To make 2 slushies, remove 2-1/2 cups of watermelon from freezer and let sit 15 to 20 minutes to partially thaw. Place 1 cup lemonade mix in a blender along with 2-1/2 cups watermelon. Blend to desired consistency.

Makes 8 servings

STRAWBERRY MELON SALAD

1 cup yogurt *(page 236)*
1 tablespoon honey
2 teaspoons lemon juice
2 cups watermelon balls or chunks
1 cup cantaloupe balls or chunks
1 cup halved fresh strawberries
1 cup fresh blueberries
1 cup fresh raspberries

Wash berries. Place fruit in a large bowl. In a small bowl, whisk together yogurt, honey and lemon juice until smooth. Before serving, pour dressing over fruit and gently toss to coat.

Makes 4 servings

MELON FRUIT SALAD

1 watermelon
1 honeydew melon
1 cantaloupe
1 fresh pineapple
2 cups fresh strawberries
2 cups fresh blueberries
2 cups fresh raspberries
2 tablespoons lemon juice

Wash and slice watermelon one third of the way from top to create your bowl (You may have to slice a small portion off bottom so it lays flat.)

Ball or chunk melons. Chunk pineapple. Wash berries. Combine all ingredients in a very large bowl. Drizzle lemon juice over fruit and toss lightly to coat. Chill. Place into watermelon bowl before serving.

Makes 20 to 30 servings

Meat and fruit are foods which are more difficult to digest. It's best to eat fruit for snacks between meals. Honey aids in digestion making the Strawberry Melon Salad a great dessert!

ZUCCHINI

DIG INTO THIS!

Zucchini is actually green summer squash.

Summer squash have soft, edible skin packed with nutrients so eat skin and all.

Zucchini is high in potassium, a nutrient which helps blood pressure levels.

Zucchini is rich in B-complex vitamins as well as minerals like zinc and magnesium.

Yellow or green summer squash can be interchanged in recipes.

Biggest is NOT best. Small to medium size zucchini (4 to 7 inches) are most flavorful.

You might be surprised to know that most zucchini is genetically modified. You can learn more by checking the Non-GMO Project website.

HOW DOES YOUR GARDEN GROW...?

❊ Days to maturity from direct seed: 45 to 50. Days to maturity from transplant: 30 to 45.

❊ Zucchini grows best next to celery, corn, onions or radishes.

❊ It's best not to plant next to potatoes.

❊ Work lots of compost or well-rotted manure into site.

❊ Plant seeds in hills 1/2 to 1 inch deep in mid spring when soil is good and warm.

❊ Space hills 18 inches apart with 3 seeds to a hill, later thinning to 1 seed per hill.

❊ Seeds will begin to grow 6 to 10 days after planting.

❊ Started plants can also be purchased from your local nursery.

❊ Water heavily.

❊ For a great zucchini harvest, pick young and often. Harvest daily when they are 4 to 7 inches long.

❊ Zucchini plants will continue producing if harvested often.

❊ Store zucchini in refrigerator up to 2 weeks.

Did you know most summer squash grow in bush form unlike the vines of winter squash?

Grow it. Preserve it. Prepare it.

FREEZING ZUCCHINI

DEHYDRATING ZUCCHINI

SLICED:

1. Select firm zucchini with bright, glossy skin. Wash and slice 1/2 inch thick. Blanch 3 minutes in boiling water.

2. Drain, immerse in cold water, and cool completely.

3. Drain again and pack into freezer bags (measure out by cups needed in favorite recipes) or containers. Seal, label and freeze. *(Refer to freezing, page 26)*

Frozen sliced zucchini is great to toss into soups and casseroles straight from the freezer!

SHREDDED:

1. Shredded zucchini does not require blanching. Select firm zucchini with bright, glossy skin. Wash and shred in a food processor or grate.

2. Pack into freezer bags or containers (measure out by cups needed in favorite recipes). Seal, label and freeze.

Frozen shredded zucchini should be thawed and drained before using in recipes.

1. Choose 4 to 6 inch zucchini. Wash and slice into 1/4 inch rounds.

2. Place in single layer on dehydrator trays. Dehydrate according to manufacturer's instructions.

3. Toss in soups, casseroles or stir-fries.

HELPFUL HINTS

1 pound zucchini equals approximately 2 cups shredded. 1 pound zucchini is approximately 3 medium zucchini.

ITALIAN ZUCCHINI BOATS

RECIPES

SAUTÉED ZUCCHINI

3 tablespoons butter
1 clove garlic, minced
1/4 teaspoon red pepper flakes
4 medium zucchini
1-1/2 teaspoons salt
1/4 teaspoon pepper

Wash zucchini and cut into 1/4 inch slices. In a large skillet, sauté garlic and red pepper flakes in butter 1 minute over medium-high heat.

Add zucchini. Cover and cook 5 minutes. Remove cover and stir. Continue cooking and stirring until crisp-tender. Sprinkle with salt and pepper.

Makes 4 servings

CREAMY CHICKEN ALFREDO SOUP

1/4 cup butter
1/2 cup chopped onion
4 cloves garlic, minced
2 cups heavy cream
3/4 cup grated Parmesan cheese
1/2 cup shredded raw cheddar cheese
1/2 cup sour cream
2 teaspoons Italian seasoning *(page 125)*
1 teaspoon salt
1/2 teaspoon pepper
2 cups chopped cooked chicken
2 large zucchini, spiralized

In a large saucepan, sauté onion and garlic in butter over medium heat until translucent. Add cream, cheese, sour cream and seasonings. Stir while heating until scalding. Add chicken and zucchini noodles. Reduce heat and cook, covered, 10 to 12 minutes until zucchini is tender.

Makes 4 servings

ITALIAN ZUCCHINI BOATS

1 tablespoon butter
4 medium zucchini
1 pound ground beef or pork
1 small onion, chopped
1/2 cup sliced mushrooms
1-1/2 cups spaghetti sauce *(page 257)*
1 tablespoon Italian seasoning *(page 125)*
1 teaspoon salt
1/4 teaspoon pepper
1-1/2 cups shredded raw cheddar cheese
1/3 cup grated Parmesan cheese

Preheat oven to 350° F. Place butter in a 9 x 13 glass pan and melt in oven 1 to 2 minutes. Remove from oven. Wash and cut zucchini in half lengthwise. Scoop out pulp leaving 1/4 inch on sides of shell. Finely chop pulp. Place zucchini shells in a buttered pan. In a large skillet, cook meat, zucchini pulp, onion, and mushrooms over medium-high heat until meat is no longer pink. Stir in spaghetti sauce, Italian seasoning, salt, pepper and 3/4 cup cheddar cheese. Spoon into zucchini shells. Sprinkle with remaining cheddar and top with Parmesan. Bake uncovered 30 to 40 minutes until zucchini is tender and cheese is browned.

Makes 4 servings

When cooking, it's important to use the right equipment. Non-stick or Teflon pans have a coating that is possibly linked to health problems. To limit your exposure to chemicals, it's best to use stainless steel, cast iron or ceramic cookware.

QUICK STOVE TOP ZUCCHINI MEAL

2 tablespoons butter

2 cloves garlic, minced

2 boneless, skinless chicken breasts, cut into 1 inch pieces

1 teaspoon salt, divided

1/4 teaspoon pepper

2 small onions, sliced

1 yellow summer squash, sliced

1 medium zucchini, sliced

1 red bell pepper, sliced

In a large skillet, sauté garlic in butter over medium-high heat 2 minutes. Add chicken, 1/2 teaspoon salt and pepper. Cook 5 minutes. Add rest of salt and remaining ingredients. Cook 5 to 7 minutes until tender.

Makes 4 servings

ZUCCHINI FUDGE BROWNIES

1-1/2 cups grated zucchini

1 cup almond butter or peanut butter

1/2 cup honey

2 teaspoons vanilla

1 teaspoon baking soda

1/2 cup cocoa powder

1/4 teaspoon salt

1/2 cup dark chocolate chips

Preheat oven to 350° F. Generously grease bottom and sides of an 8 x 8 glass pan. In a large bowl, stir together all ingredients. Pour batter into pan and bake 35 to 40 minutes. Remove from oven and cool. Cover and put into refrigerator to harden before cutting and serving—this is key. Store in refrigerator.

Makes 16 servings

ZUCCHINI MUFFINS

3 eggs

1/2 cup coconut sugar

2 tablespoons coconut oil

1 teaspoon vanilla

1/3 cup coconut flour

3/4 teaspoon baking soda

1/2 teaspoon salt

2 teaspoons ground cinnamon

1 cup shredded zucchini, fresh or frozen

1/2 cup walnuts, optional

Preheat oven to 350° F. Line muffin tin with paper liners. If using frozen zucchini, thaw and drain.

In a large bowl, beat eggs with mixer until frothy. Mix in sugar, oil and vanilla. Add dry ingredients and mix well. Stir in zucchini and walnuts. Fill muffin liners and bake 20 to 25 minutes until toothpick inserted in center comes out clean.

Makes 9 muffins

When faced with a health challenge, you may need to substitute ingredients in recipes. We like salt, and if you are watching your sodium intake, you may need to cut back on the salt.

Good dairy substitutes are coconut milk or blended cashews that have been soaked in broth. Applesauce is a great egg substitute for baked goods.

You don't have to sacrifice great taste. Focus on the foods you can eat, not on what you have to eliminate. We've done it and you can, too!

INDEX

INDEX

INDEX

INDEX

INDEX

INDEX

HELPFUL RESOURCES

Listed are a few resources we have referenced within this book to help you grow, preserve and prepare healthy, delicious foods.

The Vegetable Gardener's Bible
Edward C. Smith

Ball Blue Book Guide to Preserving

Don't forget to check out the Farm Girl Fresh Blog at farmgirlfresh.com

We are dedicated to your journey toward growing, preserving and preparing simple, fresh, real whole foods. Visit us often for new recipes, cooking tips, the latest information and insights on how cooking and eating pure—and delicious—foods can impact your health and well being!

We hope you find
the information in this book to
be practical, motivating, encouraging
and inspirational. Make a commitment
today to *Eating Pure in a Processed Foods
World*® and make this your goal for life.

This book is about a lifestyle change, not a diet. Start by taking baby
steps toward this goal and don't get discouraged when a morsel of unhealthy
food hits your lips or when the garden is overtaken with some invading weed. Don't despair.
You can do it! Get back up, dust yourself off and continue pursuing your new way of life.

Our desire for you and your family is to live a successful life that is healthy—physically, emotionally
and spiritually. We leave you with this challenge: go, equip and bless the next generation.

NOTES

NOTES

NOTES